FROM OUTRAGE TO ACTION

The Politics of Grass-Roots Dissent

LAURA R. WOLIVER

UNIVERSITY OF ILLINOIS PRESS
Urbana and Chicago

An earlier version of chapter 3 appeared as "Feminism at the Grassroots: The Recall of Judge Archie Simonson" in *Frontiers: A Journal of Women's Studies* 11, nos. 2–3 (1990). An earlier version of chapter 4 appeared as "A Measure of Justice: Police Conduct and Black Civil Rights, the Coalition for Justice for Ernest Lacy" in *Western Political Quarterly* 43 (June 1990): 415–36.

This book is printed on acid-free paper.

Library of Congress Cataloging-in-Publication Data

Woliver, Laura R., 1954–
    From outrage to action : the politics of grass-roots
dissent / Laura R. Woliver.
        p.   cm.
    Includes bibliographical references and index.
    ISBN 0-252-01962-8 (alk. paper).–ISBN 0-252-06311-2 (pbk.)
    1. Local government—Wisconsin.   2. Pressure groups—
Wisconsin.   3. Recall—Wisconsin.   4. Political activists—
Wisconsin—Interviews.   5. Social reformers—Wisconsin—
Interviews.   I. Title.
JS451.W65W75   1993
320.8'09775—dc20   92-14047
                                                                    CIP

FROM OUTRAGE TO ACTION

To Mark Washburn Binkley

Contents

Acknowledgments

I would like to thank Murray Edelman for his guidance and wisdom. I also fondly appreciate the friendships and solidarities provided me through the Political Science Women's Caucuses at the University of Wisconsin and the University of South Carolina. Special thanks go to the members of my dissertation committee, Murray Edelman (the chair), Barbara Hinckley, Leon Epstein, Dennis Dresang, and Martha Fineman, who encouraged me during the earliest stages of this project, offered sage advice, and saw it through to its completion. The Graduate School of the University of Wisconsin–Madison provided me with a small domestic travel grant for my research in Milwaukee.

I was fortunate to have several undergraduate professors at the University of Colorado–Boulder who have meant a lot to me and who have mentored me over the years in countless ways. Anne N. Costain and Douglas Costain have guided me through the mysteries of graduate school, the job market, and the publishing business. Early in my college days I was blessed by the education given me by Dennis R. Eckart. I strive constantly to live up to the examples set by these professors for quality teaching and sterling human character.

I owe much to the members of my community of memory and hope: the Binkley family, Kristin Bumiller, Julie Drucker, Georgia Duerst-Lahti, Beverly Hawk, Karen McCurdy, Deirdre Sullivan Frees, and the Reneau family. My graduate school friends, especially Kristin and Beverly, have nurtured me and my family and helped me survive and enjoy graduate school and the early years of being a professor. Conversations I have had over the years with Shirley Geiger, Paul Raymond, Jerel Rosati, Gordon Smith, David Whiteman, Kenny Whitby, and Richard Zelin have strengthened my teaching and research.

My colleagues in the Department of Government and International Studies at the University of South Carolina–Columbia have been supportive in many ways. Two department chairs, Earl Black and William Mishler, encouraged me with my work and provided resources that allowed me to develop a fledgling's dissertation into a book. The department's staff, especially Sandra Hall, Lori Joye, Becky Deaton, and Sophia Kennedy, have helped me keep up with all the paperwork of a bustling university, a full teaching load, and my research commitments. They manage this gracefully and with humor.

My department is a nice place to work—I recognize that this does not happen by accident. Many people in my department have labored long and hard to create and sustain an atmosphere of collegiality and inclusiveness, and I have benefited greatly from their hard work. In this respect, I am deeply indebted to Ann O'M. Bowman, Natalie Kaufman, and Janice Love. They welcomed me and my family into the department and have helped me through the travails of being an assistant professor in a big university and also being a mother of young children. The addition of Betty Glad to the department, and to my circle of friends, increased the intellectual and personal resources available to me.

Outside of my department, I have learned a lot from my five-year involvement with the brilliant and witty women of the Women's Studies Faculty Development Seminar at the University of South Carolina. These include Joan Gero, Thavolia Glymph, Marjorie Goodwin, Judith James, Diane Johnson, Jenny Kronenfeld, and especially Sue Rosser. These women have expanded my horizons by constantly reminding me that there is wisdom in disciplines besides political science.

Many talented graduate students at the University of South Carolina have helped me teach classes and conduct research. I am grateful for the help I have received from John Cavanaugh, Theresa French, Kenneth Hicks, Kenneth Kitts, Christian Lorrick, Patricia McRae, Suda Radan, Cecile Regner, Colleen Yurkanin, Rebecca Woolston, and Weizhi Xie.

The librarians at the City of Milwaukee Legislative Reference Bureau, the *Capital Times*, and the *Wisconsin State Journal* facilitated my research and made my work much easier. My editor at the University of Illinois Press, Carole S. Appel, recognized the potential in my manuscript and has worked to help me clarify and sharpen my study.

Suggestions from outside reviewers were very helpful and added immensely to the quality of the book. In this regard, I thank particularly Jeffrey Berry of Tufts University and Janet Boles of Marquette University.

I am able to work in relative peace and quiet because of the hard work and loving kindnesses over the years of many day-care providers: Fatima Kahilli, Nilofer Farouqui, Ruth Smyrl, Cecile Regner, and the staffs of the Washington Street United Methodist Church, the Booker T. Washington Child Development Center at the University of South Carolina, and the Montessori Child Development Center.

The people interviewed for this study worked me into their already busy lives, trusted me with their stories and experiences, and taught me a lot about American politics. I thank them for their time and for all the courtesies they extended to me. To paraphrase one interviewee regarding her grass-roots efforts, I hope this book will help make things a little bit easier for people in the future.

Finally, but most important, I thank my husband and friend, Mark Washburn Binkley, for his faith in me, for the sacrifices he has made for my career, and for his love and devotion. Our children, Paul and Sarah, I also thank for the joy they have brought to my life.

1 Introduction: The Flare Up and Cooling Off of Interests

Americans like to believe that theirs is a just society. Yet at the same time a prevalent saying in America is "You can't fight city hall." *From Outrage to Action: The Politics of Grass Roots Dissent* examines the mobilization and results of four ad hoc, grass-roots interest groups formed to challenge local authority. Two groups were recall efforts against local judges. One judge had said that because of the way women dress rape is a normal reaction. The second judge stated that a five-year-old sexual assault victim was the aggressor in the incident and was a "particularly promiscuous young lady." The first judge was recalled; the second was not. The third group formed after an innocent African-American man died while in the custody of arresting police officers. The fourth group arose out of community anger and grief following the murder of a ten-year-old child by a man with a previous criminal record. Analysis of these four groups reveals both strengths and weaknesses in the formation of challenging groups, the potential for reforms, and the subtle ways some voices are silenced.

Throughout American history communities of citizens have periodically expressed political grievances through grass-roots interest groups. Local protest actions have made headlines, made symbolic statements, and then disappeared from center stage. Often, though, these groups are local expressions of larger political grievances. Sometimes they are eruptions of social movements demanding redefinitions of justice and rights. Even when the unrest is simply an attempt by a group to be treated as full adult citizens, the results can be far-reaching. Often only limited, piecemeal results are achieved by group activity. Previous research and theory suggest that local movements of citizens can sometimes be placated and reassured back into quiescence[1] or that the activists will experience frustration and disappointment and retire to the more immediately rewarding private sphere of life.[2] In addition, people engage in group politics even when knowing prospects for immediate success are doubtful. They might respond to their memberships in a variety of potential "communities." These are "communities of memory and communities of hope" as portrayed by Robert N. Bellah and his collaborators:

Communities, in the sense in which we are using the term, have a history—in an important sense they are constituted by their past—and for this reason we can speak of a real community as a "community of memory," one that does not forget its past. . . . The communities of memory that tie us to the past also turn us toward the future as communities of hope. They carry a context of meaning that can allow us to connect our aspirations for ourselves and those closest to us with the aspirations of a larger whole and see our own efforts as being, in part, contributions to a common good.[3]

The political behavior of people in response to a disturbing event or condition in their lives is an important area for research. Because people are in general acquiescent, their activation into a new group is a significant event. As Jeffrey Berry wrote, "The most important decision on a given issue is not the selection of strategy or the choice of the tactics, but the decision to become active on the issue in the first place."[4] Alexis de Tocqueville concluded with bemused wonder that in America people tend to get politically active in groups, whether to promote temperance or to help a neighbor.[5] In fact, an entire school of thought in the empirical study of human behavior argues that the way to understand people is to understand their group affiliations.[6]

The present study accepts as a premise the importance of group activities in American politics and seeks to contribute to the understanding of group political origins, behavior, and results. This book focuses on interpretations of events by the group activists and explores respondents' identification of the injustice and the targets and tactics chosen to achieve justice. The study analyzes theories of group politics, consciousness, and power. The evidence used to carry out these objectives comes from examinations of the mobilization, tactics, and results of four ad hoc, grass-roots interest groups.

    1. The Committee to Recall Judge Archie Simonson, Madison,

Wisconsin, May 1977–September 1977. Judge Simonson, speaking from the bench while sentencing a juvenile in a rape case, remarked on Madison's sexual permissiveness and the provocative clothing worn by women. He asked, "'Should we punish severely a 15 or 16-year-old who reacts to it normally?'"[7] The Committee to Recall formed within twenty-four hours, and three months later Judge Simonson was removed from the bench.

2. The Coalition for Justice for Ernest Lacy, Milwaukee, Wisconsin, July 1981–July 1985. Ernest Lacy, a twenty-two-year-old African-American, was picked up on suspicion of rape (a crime he did not commit) and died while in the custody of the arresting police officers. The Coalition for Justice for Ernest Lacy formed to demand that responsibility for his death be determined and punishment be imposed on the guilty. It achieved "a measure of justice."

3. Concerned Citizens for Children, Grant County, Wisconsin, January–May 1982. Judge William Reinecke speaking from the bench while sentencing a man for sexually assaulting a five-year-old girl said she was "a particularly promiscuous young lady."[8] Concerned Citizens for Children formed in response and succeeded in getting a recall election scheduled. Reinecke survived the recall.

4. Citizens Taking Action, Madison, Wisconsin, March 1982–March 1984. A ten-year-old girl, Paula McCormick, was murdered. Roger Lange, a man with a criminal record, was charged. Citizens Taking Action was formed out of community anger, grief, and fear immediately after Paula McCormick's death but had no clear objective. The group had mixed results. Citizens Taking Action was helpful in getting sexual assault education into the Madison elementary schools but did not succeed in achieving any larger impact on the criminal justice system and eventually disbanded.

The four groups included in this study were selected to represent a range of ad hoc group experiences. Although two of them are from Madison, Wisconsin, they represent two distinct parts of the city. Citizens Taking Action was an East Side group drawn largely from blue-collar residents. The Committee to Recall Judge Archie Simonson, on the other hand, was predominantly a central city and West Side group drawn from the population around the University of Wisconsin and the white-collar families who work for the university or the state of Wisconsin. Although two efforts to recall judges are included, they represent different motivational origins. The Simonson recall sprang from committed feminist roots. The Reinecke recall occurred in a rural and more conservative area of Wisconsin and did not contain any clear feminist elements. It tried to make a stand for silent victims of sexual assault and to assert the value of children in a society that treats them like property. Finally, the Coalition for Justice for Ernest Lacy was a downtown Milwaukee phenomenon based upon African-American neighborhood groups, civil rights activists, and churches.

These four groups, while responding to grievances with the criminal justice system, represent different issues: feminist, victim's rights, civil rights, and law and order. But taken together they raise common questions concerning the nature of political power, the shaping of consciousness of injustice, and the experience of dissenters in American politics. The two most successful groups, the Committee to Recall Judge Archie Simonson and the Coalition for Justice for Ernest Lacy, were responses to catalyzing incidents where leaders and networks from previous reform movement activities were woven together. The two less successful groups, Concerned Citizens for Children and Citizens Taking Action, display the weaknesses of activists unaffiliated to previous movements; the power of public officials to belittle, placate, or blame challenging citizens; and the reluctance of disappointed activists to broaden and sustain their political critiques. There is a need to believe in a just world, even when the evidence points to the contrary. Traces of this psychological need are found in the two disappointed mobilizations.

Despite a penchant for group affiliations in American politics, very few citizens actually get active in local issues. Some modern interest groups lack grass-roots activists altogether and are composed of "checkbook affiliates."[9] Direct, face-to-face adversarial politics is intimidating and alienating to many citizens.[10] One motivation for checkbook affiliation with progressive reform groups, therefore, is "it provides middle-class adults a painless means to remain faithful to their liberal idealism without disturbing their conventional roles in the larger corporate society."[11] The sustained, face-to-face, direct grass-roots conflict the activists in these four sputtering groups engaged in, therefore, is remarkable. As one activist explained, she was not simply "concerned" about the triggering incident in her community but "driven and obsessed." The activists in these four groups volunteered hundreds of hours, spent untold personal resources, took time away from families, children, jobs, and friends to work on their causes.

They took political stances that were sometimes isolating and personally troubling. Many faced community opposition. Their local newspaper editors and letter writers to the newspapers alleged that they were uninformed, undemocratic, intolerant radicals, troublemakers, and zealots. Actually, they were moderate people, sometimes religious, devoted to their families and communities, and believers in the fairness of their governmental system. For some activists, the animosity of neighbors, co-workers, and erstwhile friends was a jarring disappointment. Many, therefore, had to reconcile their faith with their experiences in these protest groups. Each activist filtered his or her interpretation of events through previous political experiences and commitments to alternative communities or ideologies (religious, civil rights, feminist). Those without these connections found solace in a faith in public education and healing through satisfaction of their expressive incentives.

Equally remarkable is the formation of these four groups. Examining their experiences leads to suggestions for explaining why other outrageous, tragic, and unjust incidents might not trigger a sputtering group. McGlen and O'Connor document necessary ingredients for the rise of a women's movement: "(1) a sense of collective oppression; (2) an extant organizational base; (3) a communicating network; and, (4) a critical mobilizing event." [12] Groups might be politically aroused by the lack of official reassurances, symbolic concessions, or reforms. The success of mobilized interests may also be tempered by the response of opposing groups. [13] The convergence of these factors assists in group formation. When a communication network is lacking, for example, or when officials placate and calm down upset citizens, group formation is difficult.

I used three approaches to examine these interest groups: in-depth interviews with the group activists; examination of local newspaper accounts of the group efforts and the written record (if any) of the group; and integration of the findings into debates over the dimensions of political power and the impact of social movements. Taking interest group members themselves as subjects of analysis is a useful contribution to understanding interest mobilization. [14] I conducted forty-two interviews between June 1984 and July 1985. I chose people to interview on the basis of their leadership roles as I could determine these through a review of newspaper accounts of the triggering incident and the group response. The interviews were between one and two hours long and were conducted in the interviewees' homes or offices. I promised confidentiality to assuage concerns about possible repercussions from the interviews and thus assure more open and spontaneous responses. Activists are identified in this book only in statements they made to the press, where the press identified them. Direct quotations from interviews will be given throughout the book without explicit references.

I conducted the most interviews with the Committee to Recall Judge Archie Simonson. Between June and October of 1984 I met with eighteen people. Fifteen people were interviewed from the Coalition for Justice for Ernest Lacy between January and March of 1985. A smaller number of interviews were conducted with group members from Citizens Taking Action and Concerned Citizens for Children. Four people from Citizens Taking Action were interviewed in May of 1985. I conducted five interviews between May and July of 1985 with leaders from Concerned Citizens for Children.

Some explanation for the small number of interviews conducted with Citizens Taking Action and Concerned Citizens for Children members is necessary at this point. These two groups were very small, with a tiny number of dedicated activist leaders. Citizens Taking Action had five leaders; Concerned Citizens for Children had six. I interviewed all the leaders of both groups with two exceptions. One leader in Citizens Taking Action died. One activist in Concerned Citizens for Children never returned my phone calls or acknowledged my letters. Another activist in Concerned Citizens for Children told me that he probably didn't want to be included in my study since he was trying to forget and get over his disappointing experiences in the Reinecke recall. My small number of interviews does not indicate a lack of importance of these two groups in comparison to the Simonson recall and the Lacy case. Rather, it is in the nature of the groups. Although they were very small groups, they were significant organizations during their short lives. Concerned Citizens for Children forced a judge into a recall election; Citizens Taking Action mobilized hundreds of upset citizens who attended a public meeting to voice their dissent. Present at the Citizens Taking Action forum were virtually all the key leaders of the criminal justice system in Madison. Interest-group scholarship should include small, short-lived groups such as these.

These unobtrusive interviews were primarily retrospective, focusing on the interviewee's recollection of responses at the time they were experienced.[15] The questions focused on issues such as the respondent's reasons for involvement in the issue, the past political activity of the respondent, the role the respondent played in the group, and the respondent's assessment of the group's efficacy. Complete interview schedules for each group are in Appendixes 1–4.

Previous research has suggested that interest groups are partially shaped and influenced by the media attention they attract.[16] In addition to in-depth interviews, therefore, I examined the print media accounts of the triggering incident and the sputtering group. Media coverage of these incidents and group efforts was extensive. I was concerned about treatment of the groups by the media and asked questions in the interviews about both the effects media coverage had on the group and the efforts the group exerted to get such coverage.

I have integrated materials from the interviews and newspaper accounts of the group efforts in this study in an attempt to offer what Clifford Geertz describes as "thick description."[17] Vital to understanding sputtering interests is a sense of the local political context in which they either flourish or die. Local circumstances—history, leadership, and past conflicts—provide cultural filters through which an injustice is defined and possible responses are shaped.[18] The perspective of this study is what Parenti calls "from the bottom up,"[19] with attention paid to the local political circumstances of power and powerlessness.

I have also integrated normative questions with historical and philosophical dimensions into the analysis of these four sputtering groups, in the spirit of seeing "social science as public philosophy,"[20] in order to include the whole of society. Bellah and his coauthors advocate such an approach because

social science is not a disembodied cognitive enterprise. It is a tradition, or set of traditions, deeply rooted in the philosophical and humanistic (and, to more than a small extent, the religious) history of the West. Social science makes assumptions about the nature of persons, the nature of society, and the relation between persons and society. It also, whether it admits it or not, makes assumptions about good persons and a good society and considers how far these conceptions are embodied in our actual society.[21]

This study challenges simplistically optimistic views of American politics. The interviews reveal how difficult participating in a challenging group can be in American politics. Examination of these four groups reaffirms the role of leadership, co-optable networks, coalitions, and political consciousness derived from a larger social movement identity in the success or failure of challenging interests. These four sputtering interests were also shaped by issue definition and agenda setting. In addition, the response of government officials, the media, and countermovements influenced the fortunes of the challenging groups.

Examination of these four sputtering groups adds to research on interest groups, social movements, protest, agenda setting and political power in America. The experiences of group participants adds to discussions of how some interests arise and sustain a voice while other, perhaps equally legitimate, interests remain silent. To place these four interest groups within this ongoing debate on political power in America, the next chapter discusses pluralist theory and the role pluralism has played in evaluating the openness of the political process, especially for challenging groups like these four. Chapters 3 through 6 are in-depth studies of each ad hoc protest group. The final chapter weaves together the findings from the four sputtering groups back into the discussions from chapter 2 on group politics and official responses to challenging groups.

NOTES

1. Murray Edelman, *Politics as Symbolic Action: Mass Arousal and Quiescence* (Chicago: Markham, 1971).

2. Albert O. Hirschman, *Shifting Involvements: Private Interest and Public Action* (Princeton, N.J.: Princeton University Press, 1982).

3. Robert N. Bellah, Richard Madsen, William M. Sullivan, Ann Swidler, and Steven M. Tipton, *Habits of the Heart: Individualism and Commitment in American Life* (Berkeley: University of California Press, 1985), 153. See also Donald Downs's portrait of the Jewish community of memory and hope in *Nazis in Skokie: Freedom, Community, and the First Amendment* (Notre Dame, Ind.: University of Notre Dame Press, 1985).

4. Jeffrey M. Berry, *Lobbying for the People: The Political Behavior of Public Interest Groups* (Princeton, N.J.: Princeton University Press, 1977), 271.

5. Alexis de Tocqueville, *Democracy in America, Vol. 1.* (New York: Vintage Books, 1945).

6. For example, see Arthur F. Bentley, *The Process of Government* (Cambridge, Mass.: Belknap Press, 1967).

7. Anita Clark, "West High Rapist Given Year of Supervision," *Wisconsin State Journal* (Madison), May 26, 1977.

8. "Gays' Mills Man Sentenced for Sexual Contact with Child," *Telegraph Herald* (Dubuque, Iowa), Dec. 31, 1981.

9. Michael T. Hayes, "Interest Groups: Pluralism or Mass Society?" in *Interest Group Politics*, ed. Allan J. Cigler and Burdett A. Loomis (Washington, D.C.: Congressional Quarterly Press, 1983), 110–25; see also Michael W. McCann, *Taking Reform Seriously: Perspectives on Public Interest Liberalism* (Ithaca, N.Y.: Cornell University Press, 1986), 207–8.

10. McCann, *Taking Reform Seriously*, 208.

11. Ibid., 191.

12. Nancy E. McGlen and Karen O'Connor, "An Analysis of the U.S. Women's Rights Movements: Rights as a Public Good," *Women and Politics* 1 (Spring 1980): 65–85, the quotation is on p. 65; see also McGlen and O'Connor, *Women's Rights: The Struggle for Equality in the Nineteenth and Twentieth Centuries* (New York: Praeger, 1983).

13. McGlen and O'Connor, "An Analysis," 65–85; see also McGlen and O'Connor, *Women's Rights;* and Jane J. Mansbridge, *Why We Lost the ERA* (Chicago: University of Chicago Press, 1986).

14. Terry M. Moe, *The Organization of Interests: Incentives and the Internal Dynamics of Political Interest Groups* (Chicago: University of Chicago Press, 1980), 165, 219–21, 228–29.

15. Robert K. Merton, Marjorie Fiske, and Patricia L. Kendall, *The Focused Interview: A Manual of Problems and Procedures* (Glencoe, Ill.: Free Press, 1956), 24.

16. See Todd Gitlin, *The Whole World Is Watching: Mass Media in the Making and Unmaking of the New Left* (Berkeley: University of California Press, 1980); and Richard B. Kielbowicz and Clifford Scherer, "The Role of the Press in the Dynamics of Social Movements," in *Research in Social Movements, Conflicts, and Change*, ed. Louis Kriesberg (Greenwich, Conn.: JAI Press, 1986), 71–96.

17. Clifford Geertz, "Thick Description: Toward an Interpretive Theory of Culture," In *The Interpretation of Cultures* (New York: Basic Books, 1973), 3–30.

18. D. Garth Taylor, *Public Opinion and Collective Action: The Boston School Desegregation Conflict* (Chicago: University of Chicago Press, 1986), 64; see also Gary Delgado, *Organizing the Movement: The Roots and Growth of Acorn* (Philadelphia: Temple University Press, 1986), 135, 142.

19. Michael Parenti, "Power and Pluralism: A View from the Bottom," *Journal of Politics* 32 (Aug. 1970): 507–8.

20. Bellah, et al., *Habits of the Heart*, 297–307.

21. Ibid., 301.

2 Pluralism and Its Critics: From Narrow to Broader Views of Interests

Research on interest groups has shifted the emphasis of many studies of politics away from romantic, disembodied notions of democracy and sovereignty to the empirical reality of political power.[1] In addition, analysis of group-based political activities, such as that of these four ad hoc groups, often involves discussion of the advantages and disadvantages of the pluralist approach.

Pluralism

In American scholarship the study of the group nature of politics led to a subfield called pluralism. Pluralism, as defined by John F. Manley, "asserts that the American power structure is made up of many competing elites, not just one. Different elites with low elite overlap operate in different issue areas. Political and economic power are by no means evenly distributed among the population, but inequality is 'noncumulative,' i.e., most people have some power resources, and no single asset (such as money) confers excessive power."[2] David Truman defines an interest group as one that, on the basis of one or more shared attitudes, makes certain claims upon other groups in the society.[3] The pluralist world is not necessarily stagnant. Truman argues that group politics is dynamic, with continuous shifts in relative influence.[4] New groups form after disturbances in the habitual relationships of groups. Truman's disturbance theory of group formation posits a wavelike development of groups mobilizing to counter the pressure of other groups.[5] Truman recognizes that governmental structure influences the variety of channels of influence open to interest groups and that groups have differential access. Formalities, for example, are never neutral. He concludes, nevertheless, that there is a wide diffusion of access in the long run resulting in fair representation of group interests to government.[6]

Robert Dahl also sees the organization of American politics as inhibiting concentrations of power. He argues that issue-related oligarchies rule. Dahl maintains that "in this sense the majority (at least of the politically active) nearly always 'rules' in a polyarchal system."[7] The realistic issue to Dahl, therefore, is not majority tyranny but "the extent to which various minorities in a society will frustrate the ambitions of one another with the passive acquiescence or indifference of a majority of adults or voters."[8]

Dahl argues further that in America "all the active and legitimate groups in the population can make themselves heard at some crucial stage in the process of decision."[9] It is a bargaining, nonstatic system surviving through an evolutionary process of adjustment to new group demands.[10]

In the pluralist account, issue-specific minorities rule in an open and active political system where interested people may become politically active. Inactivity by the masses abdicates the political field to interested, particularistic minorities. Although these are reassuring conclusions, there is much debate about their veracity.

Critiques of Pluralism

Interest-group research in America largely focuses on the applicability of pluralist theory to describe politics. During the 1950s and early 1960s, when the surface of American politics was placid, interest-group research was influenced chiefly by the pluralist approach. Indeed, one scholar maintains that today "there is little doubt that pluralism is the dominant theory or paradigm of power among American social scientists."[11] There are, however, many critics of pluralism. It is not that a pluralist society would be unjust, the argument goes, but rather that we do not have a pluralist society. Organization is the mobilization of bias, E. E. Schattschneider argues: "Some interests are organized into politics while others are organized out."[12] Schattschneider observes that the pluralists' "heavenly chorus sings with a strong upper-class accent."[13] The civil rights movement alleged that the chorus was white; the antiwar movement that the chorus was deaf; and the women's movement that the chorus sang for a private male club. Recent scholarship shows the extent of business and elite dominance of interest-group politics in America. Schlozman and Tierney's study of organized group politics in the early eighties, for example, reveals that "in spite of the growth over the past two decades in the number of organizations designed to represent the disadvantaged and broad publics, the heavenly chorus continues to sing with an upper-class accent."[14]

The result of interest-group politics, given the unrepresentative pattern of group mobilization and the behind-the-scenes nature of policy formation and implementation, is to make politics less accountable and democratic.[15] Theodore Lowi's well-received *The End of Liberalism* documented the conservatizing influence of "policy without law," vague laws that organized interest groups could shape along with their "captured" implementing bureaucracies to fit their needs. Politics by interest groups resists reform while pluralist theory justifies the process and, therefore, bolsters the status quo.[16]

There have been recent modifications in pluralist's theories of power in America, with the recognition that some groups, particularly businesses, are more powerful than balanced interest-group pluralism had argued.[17] These later works John Manley calls "Pluralism II," and offers the following critique: "Pluralism II now tries to hold in balance severe criticisms of the system's performance, the need for major structural reforms, support for redistribution of wealth and income, and more government ownership of private enterprise, at the same time that it supports social pluralism as necessary for democracy, denies the special importance of class, reconfirms the inevitability and value of incremental change, and sees incrementalism as a way of achieving major structural reforms."[18] Thus, Manley continues, Pluralism II defends "many features of the system that perpetuates the social results it now deplores."[19] Pluralism could become, then, a reassuring account of a society where inequalities are cumulative,[20] access is limited, acquiescence is not necessarily acceptance, and agendas are set outside the public scrutiny of affected groups.

Michael Rogin argues that "the mundane language of interest group liberalism" rationalizes popular disenfranchisement and turns political weakness into strength.[21] By reifying the group and linking the interest of the group with its ruling elite, pluralist theory isolates and stigmatizes dissenters. Rogin describes the suppression of interests at the prepolitical stage. He explains, "The tyranny of public opinion, the ideology of domesticity, and the creation of the asylum all limited political dissent in scarcely measurable ways. Insofar as they succeeded, they did not simply intimidate political opposition already formed but inhibited the formation of new opposition."[22] This is partially achieved by "the transformation of potentially political discontent into problems of personal life" and social adjustment.[23] Local political initiatives, for example, are interpreted as signs of alien power where dissenters are stigmatized as social pariahs. In what Rogin sees as "America's demonological tradition," communism gets confused with terrorism and political opposition with crime, drugs, and disease.[24] These characterizations make it easier to practice political repression and avoid personal responsibility for the consequences.

"Underinvolvement" in politics caused by institutions that inhibit citizens from expressing the intensity of their political beliefs also preempts some interests from being represented. Voting, for example, corrals participation into this comparatively harmless and reactive activity.[25]

Pluralism sometimes evolves from a descriptive model of politics to a prescriptive, normative model of how politics should be. Pluralism provides no guidelines for social change and views major social conflicts and social movements as aberrations rather than as normal aspects of politics. Furthermore, pluralism ignores the problems of unorganized groups, unarticulated demands, and non–decision making as policy-making.[26] By ignoring nondecisions, pluralists fail to study the possibility of dominant forces limiting the public agenda.[27]

In addition to debates about normative aspects of the pluralist model to describe American politics, some scholars question the empirical basis of some pluralist research. Group approaches to politics are most useful when analysis includes recognition of the limits of a strictly group approach. Murray Edelman argues that although studying public policy as the interplay among groups is useful, "groups which present claims upon resources may be rendered quiescent by their success in securing nontangible values. Far from representing an obstacle to organized producers and sellers, they become defenders of the very system of law which permits the organized to pursue their interests effectively."[28] Signs and symbols, then, are "the only means by which groups not in a position to analyze a complex situation rationally may adjust themselves to it, through stereotypization, oversimplification, and reassurance."[29] Edelman's theory suggests "a tie between the emergence of conditions promoting interests in symbolic reassurance and widened freedom of policy maneuver for the organized."[30] Lowi showed how pluralism practiced by the large administrative state avoids difficult policy choices in legislative arenas and delegates and defers the important details of policy-making to interest-group politics. The result is unrepresentative procedures and unanticipated consequences from policies.[31] Edelman's observations of what actually happens in American government, as opposed to "what we wish would happen," lead to several propositions; among them, symbolic reassurance that the state recognizes the claims and status of the group as legitimate.[32]

The symbols evoked in a controversy are important to its outcome. Those that can manipulate symbols and set the agenda, for example, can redefine police brutality to be laudable examples of cracking down on criminals, or peaceful protests can be discussed as threatening.[33] Similarly, defining social problems as individual problems, requiring reform of individuals instead of social reform, has a narrowing, conservative influence on politics.[34]

In addition to the often overlooked symbolic dimensions to politics within a pluralist approach, much of the debate about pluralism has been over differing views of political power. Pluralist scholarship on interest groups in American politics uses what Steven Lukes labels a "one-dimensional approach" to power.[35] The one-dimensional approach accepts as an adequate explanation of political power a description of the groups that are active on an issue, the questions that the contending groups raise, and the process by which decision is reached.

The critique of pluralism can be pursued with what Lukes calls the "two-dimensional approach."[36] Groups outside the dominant system of power document their exclusion and petition to be admitted to the group political process. The second dimension of power is analyzed by Bachrach and Baratz in their work on "nondecisions and power." Dominant groups can exercise power without any overt evidence of doing so. Examples include setting the agenda of public discourse and exclusion of issues from public debate.[37] Similarly, Matthew Crenson shows that a group's "reputation for power" can preempt government officials from acting against the powerful group and can prevent some topics from ever becoming official issues.[38]

Although Lukes believes the two-dimensional approach is a valid critique of the one-dimensional approach, its explication of political power is inadequate because account is not taken of the way people can be prevented from defining their problems as political and, therefore, appropriate for government redress. Lukes calls this "three-dimensional approach" the most comprehensive description and explanation of political behavior.[39]

Steven Lukes's third dimension of power is evident in the suppression of interests at the prepolitical stage: obstructing recognition of the group nature of problems, their political implications, and their power dynamics. "A may exercise power over B by getting him to do what he does not want to do, but he also exercises power over him by influencing, shaping or determining his very wants" through the control of information, the mass media, and socialization.[40] This may occur in the absence of actual, observable political conflict.

The three- (and even the two-) dimensional approach to political power has been questioned by those who doubt the ability to document the second and third dimensions.[41] Difficulties in defining and observing instances of "power" and "decision" have been pointed out.[42] In addition, the three-dimensional approach is criticized for its potential to become nonfalsifiable; a scholar could claim that happy, contented people are just unknowing victims of the third dimension of power, which works to keep them quiescent, and that those who claim otherwise are victims too.

Even while accepting these warnings, the three-dimensional approach to power results in telling analyses of cultures and systems of power. For example, John Gaventa's study of the power of coal interests in Appalachia is a perceptive application of the three-dimensional approach to power. Gaventa displays how Appalachia's poor are prevented from seeing their problems as political and mobilizing. Gaventa's study displays how some voices are taught to be still. Gaventa "began to wonder if [he] would not do better to turn [his] traditional political science around: to ask not why rebellion occurs in a 'democracy' but why, in the face of massive inequalities, it does not."[43] He found that coal miners did not take up opportunities to challenge inequities: "the miner showed no particular interest. His response did not seem one of apathy or ignorance. It seemed to grow from past experiences in the Valley, as well as from his situation in the present. The miner understood something of powerlessness, of power, and of how the two could serve to maintain inaction upon injustice, even in a 'democracy.'"[44] People cognizant of political injustices still might remain inactive out of a fear of dire consequences. Schlozman and Tierney point out, "When those to whom political interests might reasonably be imputed do not in fact pursue those interests, it may not reflect lack of awareness of their 'true' interests. Sometimes the absence of political activism reflects what might be called a calculated quiescence, a conscious choice in the face of awareness of the potential costs involved in position taking."[45]

Recent feminist theorists have begun to describe the way language, science, and public/private distinctions often exclude the experiences and concerns of women. Susan Griffin, for example, weaves together a portrait of patriarchal thought to include "all that women know of naming feeling while we live in a culture that misnames and mistakes what we experience."[46] One result is the powerless learn "that our speech is unholy . . . and we seek dumbness . . . and we practice muteness."[47]

Elisabeth Noelle-Neumann offers a theory for the phenomenon of opinion silenced by majority views, "the spiral of silence":

People "dread isolation more than error," de Tocqueville wrote when he wanted to explain why no one in France defended the church anymore toward the end of the eighteenth century. Tocqueville's description of the "spiral of silence" was as precise as a botanist's. Today it can be proved that even when people see plainly that something is wrong, they will keep quiet if public opinion (opinions and behavior that can be exhibited in public without fear of isolation) and, hence, the consensus as to what constitutes good taste and the morally correct opinion speaks against them.[48]

Based on her studies of European public opinion, Noelle-Neumann defines the "spiral of silence" as when views that receive vocal support appear stronger than they really are and the opposing view weaker. This conformity, Noelle-Neumann argues, comes from our social nature, which "causes us to fear separation and isolation from our fellows and to want to be respected and liked by them."[49] She continues, "To run with the pack is a relatively happy state of affairs; but if you can't, because you won't share publicly in what seems to be a universally acclaimed conviction, you can at least remain silent, as a second choice, so that others can put up with you."[50] People's silence, though, can be misinterpreted as agreement, which is one reason people are tempted to remain mute.

Scholarship such as that of Gaventa, Noelle-Neumann, and Griffin supplements the pluralist approach by examining reasons why some groups might find it difficult to organize, pressure, and succeed. The three-dimensional theory of power informs the research in this examination of the formation of ad hoc, grass-roots interest groups and the sense of injustice on which the group is based. Questions are raised, for example, about why once-active people fade into inactivity and believe that their political setbacks were deserved. In this way, the research adds to previous work on interest groups and their relation to power.

Origins of Interest Groups

This study of the rise and fall of interests explores theories about group political strengths and weaknesses. There is a large subfield within the study of interest groups that addresses itself to questions of their origins and longevity. Truman advances the "disturbance theory": groups form out of a disturbance in the political environment and often work to reinstitute the prevailing power equilibrium.[51] Robert Salisbury, in testing Truman's theory, finds constant disturbances among American farmers between 1867 and 1900. Entrepreneurs, Salisbury asserts, are a better explanation for group origin, maintenance, and demise.[52] The rational motivation to minimize costs yet reap gains, in Mancur Olson's view, explains why groups form or do not form.[53] The existence of the "free rider" inhibits the formation of certain large groups. People benefit from public goods even when they do not work to achieve them. It is logical, then, not to join groups pressuring for a nondivisible, public good. Groups lobbying for a public good, where they can't offer material incentives to induce membership, therefore find it difficult to organize and maintain their memberships. Olson calls large, diffuse groups "latent" groups because they have a latent power or capacity for action that can be realized or "mobilized" only with the aid of selective, material incentives.[54] Clark and Wilson also argue the rational nature of group formation and maintenance, positing that group membership is based on either solidary, purposive, or material incentives.[55]

Olson, as succinctly put by Terry Moe, strikes "at the heart of pluralism in denying its logic of membership."[56] But, rational choice arguments such as these, while offering insight into lack of mobilization for some interests, do not adequately explain formation of groups like the four in this book. Olson's assumptions of rational decision making by informed individuals calculating economic costs and benefits to membership, Moe points out, "is also susceptible to criticism, largely because its behavioral expectations derive from highly restrictive assumptions about the information and values that structure individual choice."[57] Moe offers a different perspective on group membership:

(1) When an individual acts on his subjective estimates of the costs and benefits of political success, he may well think that his contributions "make a difference" for political outcomes. He may, in other words, have a perception of *efficacy*. If so, he may have every rational incentive to join and contribute, even if his efficacy appears (to us) entirely unjustified by the objective context. (2) The individual's decision may be shaped by incentives other than economic gain. For simplicity, these incentives can be classified as "solidary" or "purposive."[58]

Solidary incentives include friendship and social acceptance derived from group memberships. Purposive incentives are more political in nature, since they can shape the individual's evaluation of collective goods and may outweigh any economic gains the person expects to receive. Second, when someone believes in a group's political goals,

he may also gain a purposive sense of satisfaction from the act of contributing itself; he may feel a responsibility to do his part or do what is right, for example, and he may receive satisfaction from following through. These satisfactions are selective incentives; the source of benefits is not the actual provision of collective goods, but the individual's expression of support for them. Purposive bases of motivation are singularly important, therefore, because they can operate to connect collective goods and selective incentives in the individual's membership calculus. As a result of this connection, collective goods can actually generate their own selective incentives, producing direct inducements for membership.[59]

Moe wants to lead the discussion of the formation of groups away from Olson's nonpolitical perspective and "to a broader view that leaves a good deal of room for political action and that outlines the theoretical roles of perceptions and values in explaining why political action occurs."[60] The four groups in this book confirm the need for a broader view of interest groups, one that encompasses disappointing experiences as well as instances of empowerment. Although these theories are not mutually exclusive, they emphasize different explanations for the origin of groups.

Surprisingly, government has a hand in the formation of many interest groups. A 1983 study found that leaders of groups with a public-interest agenda built organizations not by inducing large numbers of new members to join through the manipulation of selective benefits but by securing funding outside the immediate membership through foundation or government support.[61] Sometimes through the encouragement of patrons, group mobilization occurs from the top down. Therefore, Walker finds,

A pressure model of the policymaking process in which an essentially passive legislature responds to petitions from groups of citizens who have spontaneously organized because of common social or economic concerns must yield to a model in which influences for change come as much from inside the government as from beyond its institutional boundaries, and in which political entrepreneurs operating from bases in interest groups, from within the Congress, the presidency, or many private institutions, struggle to accommodate citizen discontent, appeal to emerging groups, and strive to generate support for their own conceptions of the public interest.[62]

Similarly, Salisbury's research shows the need to amend the pressure group model to include the powerful role institutions, such as corporations and local governments, play in American national politics.[63] Ad hoc groups pose important questions about these theories since not all disturbances trigger group formation. The impact of pluralism on studies of challenging groups and the critiques of pluralism show that many voices might remain silent even when injustices exist.

Communities of Solidarity:
How Interests Gain and Sustain a Voice

Two of the challenging groups studied here, the Committee to Recall Judge Archie Simonson and the Coalition for Justice for Ernest Lacy, were shaped by larger social movements. For the Lacy Coalition the civil rights movement provided a political stance, seasoned leaders, access to co-optable networks such as the African-American church, and a long-term time frame in which to place their struggles. The Committee to Recall was stitched together by previously active women who identified with feminism and utilized skills obtained from their previous social movement activities (civil rights and antiwar). The two groups that sputtered out, Concerned Citizens for Children and Citizens Taking Action, were weakened by their independence from larger social movements.

Social movements can sometimes overcome the obstacles challengers face in the political system. A social movement provides a language with which to describe injustice, connections to like-minded individuals, networks of interests aligned with the movement, experienced leadership, and a sense that change is possible. Understanding social movements, therefore, is integral to the analysis of the fortunes of ad hoc, grass-roots interest groups.

Social movements exert enduring influences on interest-group behavior. McFarland, for example, writes, "Social movements have clearly falsified an unalloyed plural elitist theory of power structure."[64] A social movement is "a set of opinions and beliefs in a population which represents preferences for changing some elements of the social structure and/or reward distribution of a society."[65] Garson, for example, criticizes Bentley and other group theorists for constituting "a force in the divergence between interest-group theory and the study of collective behavior," including studying social movements and social change.[66] The segmentary, polycephalous, and reticulate structures of social movements enable them to be effective, adaptive, and innovative when pressuring for social change and surviving established order opposition.[67] Social movement structures lend themselves to linkages, or networks, of communication among adherents.

The resource-mobilization approach to social movements deals directly with Olson's logic about the formation of diffuse groups. It stresses the role of the selection of incentives, cost-reducing mechanisms, and career benefits leading to collective behavior.[68] It also offers a further critique of pluralism.

McCarthy and Zald recognize that "grievances and discontent may be defined, created, and manipulated by issue entrepreneurs and organizations."[69] In addition, the potential for resource mobilization is affected by public officials and counter groups. Important to movement success is the strength of the opposition. In addition, authorities can frustrate or assist social movement partisans. The actions of public officials affects the readiness of bystanders, adherents, and constituents to commit to the movement or work against it. Resources important to social movements include "communication media and expense, levels of affluence, degree of access to institutional centers, preexisting networks, and occupational structure and growth."[70]

Cognitive Liberation

One power social movements have is the reshaping of consciousness of injustice and rights for adherents. Recognition of problems as political, not simply personal or individual, and identification with some of the goals of a movement means a social movement can have an impact much broader than displayed by the people actively participating. What Gusfield calls a "fluid social movement" perspective acknowledges the powerful influence social movements have on people's hearts and minds. Gusfield explains:

A more fluid perspective toward the meaning of movement emphasizes the quickening of change and the social sharing of new meanings in a variety of areas and places. It is less confined to the boundaries of organizations and more alive to the larger contexts of change at the same time as it is open to awareness of how the movement has consequences and impacts among nonpartisans and nonmembers as well as participants and devotees. Rather than success or failure of a movement, it is more likely to lead to questions about consequences: What happened?[71]

Some feminist scholarship explores such broad influences on public opinion traced to the modern women's movement.[72] McAdam reminds us that such "cognitive liberation" is a group phenomenon: "Segments of society may very well submit to oppressive conditions unless that oppression is collectively defined as both unjust and *subject to change*."[73] These group identities build cultures of solidarity and support.[74]

Cognitive liberation, though, is not alone a sufficient condition for successful social movement formation. Movement potential is also shaped by the extant organizational base, communications and networking resources, issue definition, and the response of authorities and opposing groups.[75] Sometimes a critical mobilizing event is a catalyst for potential leaders to act. In the four ad hoc protest groups studied here, a crisis quickly mobilized potential leaders along with latent fellow travelers to address the perceived injustice.

Networks

Social movement activists are often recruited from previous social, religious, or political reform efforts.[76] In her study of the origins of the modern women's liberation movement, for example, Freeman points out that

the development of the women's liberation movement highlights the salience of such a network precisely because the conditions for a movement existed *before* a network came into being, but the movement did not exist until afterward. Socioeconomic strain did not change for women significantly during a twenty-year period. It was as great in 1955 as in 1965. What changed was the organizational situation. It was not until a communications network developed among like-minded people beyond local boundaries that the movement could emerge and develop past the point of occasional, spontaneous uprising.[77]

Indigenous organizations such as churches represent what Freeman describes as a co-optable network for new groups.[78] Lack of previous organizational involvements leads to weaknesses in leadership, communication networking, and membership recruitment, often sufficient to keep potentially contentious group mobilization at bay.[79]

The Impact of Reform Movements

There are various ways to assess the impact of social movement tactics. Symbolic reassurance and placating policies sometimes result.[80] Some analysts view incremental reforms as inadequate answers to the politics of the powerless.[81] Others see incremental change as indicative of success in attracting outside support. One study on women and public policy, for example, maintains "that feminists in politics have conformed to both the scope and bias of the system and simultaneously, by virtue of their presence and demands, have expanded the range of decision making to include a broader segment of the populace." [82] These changes occur through feminist's "reformist as opposed to radical techniques." [83] Whether incremental changes and working through the system is to the benefit of challenging movements or not is a still unsettled political debate. As Freeman points out, when social movements enter politics, the dilemma of those involved is the necessity to play by the rules to accomplish objectives.[84] But rules and procedures often weaken movements for social change. One dilemma is that members of challenging movements such as feminism often recognize the need for large-scale social change. But broad changes of a public goods nature are strongly resisted by public officials and help generate the mobilization of counter groups. Social movements are less likely to succeed in achieving these broad changes than they are more piecemeal, incremental reforms.[85]

Protest Politics
There is disagreement in studies of protest about its effects. One position holds that protest offers a useful mechanism for future organization and that through organization powerless groups can attain power.[86] Another position holds the opposite: protest occurs for its own

sake and is, as a disruption of the peace of powerful groups, the only power the weak possess.[87] Other studies of the impact of protest fall between these positions. Michael Lipsky claims that protest is useful in that it might awaken a sympathetic, latent public.[88] Eisinger shows how pervasive knowledge of the usefulness of protest is, even among middle-class, "respectable" African-Americans in Milwaukee.[89] One study of national organizations found that protest is a tactic most likely used by organizations with roots in social movements, for example, civil rights and women's groups.[90]

One power that authorities have is the interpretation and meaning attributed to protest politics. The four groups of the present study used protest in different forms and degrees. Many times their protests were seen as potentially threatening by public officials. Actually such "disorderly behavior" is a valued tradition in American politics, helping to keep the system effectual.[91] As we will see by the analysis of the protest tactics of the Simonson Committee, the Lacy Coalition, Concerned Citizens for Children, and Citizens Taking Action, the result of protest depends on the social movement–based strengths of participants, their ability to deflect negative interpretations of their "disorderly behavior," and the symbols evoked during issue definition. The experience of people in these sputtering interests also displays how narrowly legitimate political behavior is defined. We will also see how searing the experience of challenging the status quo can be for people without the community and solidarity offered by a social movement.

NOTES

1. Arthur F. Bentley, *The Process of Government* (Cambridge, Mass.: Belknap Press, 1967), 5–6, 176, 204.
2. John F. Manley, "Neo-pluralism: A Class Analysis of Pluralism I and Pluralism II," *American Political Science Review* 77 (June 1983): 368–69.
3. David B. Truman, *The Governmental Process: Political Interests and Public Opinion* (New York: Alfred A. Knopf, 1959), 33.
4. Ibid., 65.
5. Ibid., 79.
6. Ibid., 325.
7. Robert A. Dahl, *A Preface to Democratic Theory* (Chicago: University of Chicago Press, 1956), 132. Nelson W. Polsby similarly argues that ruling minorities are issue related in *Community Power and Political Theory* (New Haven, Conn.: Yale University Press, 1963), 88.

8. Dahl, *A Preface to Democratic Theory*, 133; see also Polsby, *Community Power and Political Theory*, 123–24.

9. Dahl, *A Preface to Democratic Theory*, 137.

10. Ibid., 149–50.

11. Manley, "Neo-pluralism," 368.

12. E. E. Schattschneider, *The Semi-sovereign People* (New York: Holt, Rinehart, and Winston, 1960), 71; see also 35–40.

13. Ibid., 35.

14. Kay Lehman Schlozman and John T. Tierney, *Organized Interests and American Democracy* (New York: Harper and Row, 1986), 117; see also 58–87; and Kay Lehman Schlozman, "What Accent the Heavenly Chorus?: Political Equality and the American Pressure System," *Journal of Politics* 46 (Nov. 1984): 1006–32.

15. Theodore J. Lowi, *The End of Liberalism: The Second Republic of the United States* (New York: W. W. Norton, 1979).

16. Ibid.; see also Jeffrey M. Berry, *The Interest Group Society* (Glenview, Ill.: Scott, Foresman/Little Brown, 1989), 11.

17. See Robert A. Dahl and Charles E. Lindblom, *Politics, Economics, and Welfare* (Chicago: University of Chicago Press, 1976); Robert A. Dahl, *Dilemmas of Pluralist Democracy* (New Haven, Conn.: Yale University Press, 1982); and Charles E. Lindblom, *Politics and Markets* (New York: Basic Books, 1977).

18. Manley, "Neo-pluralism," 371–72.

19. Ibid., 372. Dahl and Lindblom defend their later works in Robert Dahl, "Comment on Manley," *American Political Science Review* 77 (June 1983): 386–89, and Charles E. Lindblom, "Comment on Manley," *American Political Science Review* 77 (June 1983): 384–86.

20. See Richard Sennett and Jonathan Cobb, *The Hidden Injuries of Class* (New York: Alfred A. Knopf, 1972); and Jay MacLeod, *Ain't No Makin' It: Leveled Aspirations in a Low-Income Neighborhood* (Boulder, Colo.: Westview Press, 1987).

21. Michael Rogin, *"Ronald Reagan," the Movie, and Other Episodes in Political Demonology* (Berkeley: University of California Press, 1987), xvii; see also C. Wright Mills, *The Power Elite* (New York: Oxford University Press, 1956), 323, 336.

22. Rogin, *"Ronald Reagan,"* 58–59.

23. Ibid., 59.

24. Ibid., xv.

25. Albert O. Hirschman, *Shifting Involvements: Private Interest and Public Action* (Princeton, N.J.: Princeton University Press, 1982), 106, 112; Murray Edelman, *Constructing the Political Spectacle* (Chicago: University of Chicago Press, 1988), 97; see also Peter Bachrach, *The Theory of Democratic Elitism: A Critique* (Boston: Little, Brown, 1967).

26. Schattschneider, *The Semi-sovereign People*, 28; Peter Bachrach and Morton Baratz, *Power and Poverty: Theory and Practice* (New York: Oxford University Press, 1970), 46; Grant McConnell, *Private Power and American Democ-*

racy (New York: Alfred A. Knopf, 1966); Roger W. Cobb and Charles D. Elder, *Participation in American Politics: The Dynamics of Agenda-Building* (Boston: Allyn and Bacon, 1972), 7.

27. Cobb and Elder, *Participation in American Politics*, 8; see also Bachrach and Baratz, *Power and Poverty*, 15, 55; and Bachrach and Baratz, "Two Faces of Power," *American Political Science Review* 56 (Dec. 1962): 947–52.

28. Murray Edelman, *The Symbolic Uses of Politics* (Urbana: University of Illinois Press, 1964): 39–40.

29. Ibid, 40.

30. Ibid, 42.

31. Lowi, *The End of Liberalism*.

32. Edelman, *The Symbolic Uses of Politics*, 193.

33. Charles D. Elder and Roger W. Cobb, *The Political Uses of Symbols* (New York: Longman, 1983), 130–31; Cobb and Elder, *Participation in American Politics*.

34. Barbara J. Nelson, *Making an Issue of Child Abuse: Political Agenda Setting for Social Problems* (Chicago: University of Chicago Press, 1984); Edelman, *Constructing the Political Spectacle*, 99.

35. Steven Lukes, *Power: A Radical View* (London: MacMillan, 1974), 11–15.

36. Ibid., 16–20.

37. Bachrach and Baratz, "Two Faces of Power," 947–52.

38. Matthew A. Crenson, *The Un-politics of Air Pollution: A Study of Nondecisionmaking in the Cities* (Baltimore, Md.: Johns Hopkins University Press, 1971), 177–78.

39. Lukes, *Power*, 21–25.

40. Ibid., 23.

41. See Richard M. Merelman, "On the Neo-elitist Critiques of Community Power," *American Political Science Review* 62 (June 1968): 451–60; Geoffrey Debnam, "Nondecisions and Power: The Two Faces of Bachrach and Baratz," *American Political Science Review* 69 (Sept. 1975): 889–907.

42. Polsby, *Community Power and Political Theory*, 103.

43. John Gaventa, *Power and Powerlessness: Quiescence and Rebellion in an Appalachian Valley* (Urbana: University of Illinois Press, 1980), vi.

44. Ibid., v.

45. Schlozman and Tierney, *Organized Interests and American Democracy*, 22.

46. Susan Griffin, *Woman and Nature: The Roaring inside Her* (New York: Harper and Row, 1978), xi.

47. Ibid., 19–20.

48. Elisabeth Noelle-Neumann, *The Spiral of Silence: Public Opinion—Our Social Skin* (Chicago: University of Chicago Press, 1984), ix.

49. Ibid., 41.

50. Ibid., 6–7.

51. Truman, *The Governmental Process*.

52. Robert H. Salisbury, "An Exchange Theory of Interest Groups," *Midwest Journal of Political Science* 13 (1969): 1–32.

53. Mancur Olson, Jr., *The Logic of Collective Action* (Cambridge: Harvard University Press, 1965).

54. Ibid., 51.

55. Peter B. Clark and James Q. Wilson, "Incentive Systems: A Theory of Organizations," *Administrative Science Quarterly* 6 (Sept. 1961): 129–66.

56. Terry M. Moe, "Toward a Broader View of Interest Groups," *Journal of Politics* 43 (May 1981): 533.

57. Ibid., 535.

58. Ibid., 536. Moe used the concepts of solidary and purposive incentives of Clark and Wilson they defined in "Incentive Systems," 219–66.

59. Moe, "Toward a Broader View," 536–37.

60. Ibid., 537.

61. Jack L. Walker, "The Origins and Maintenance of Interest Groups in America," *American Political Science Review* 77 (June 1983): 397; see also Georgia Duerst-Lahti, "The Government's Role in Building the Women's Movement," *Political Science Quarterly* 104 (1989): 249–68.

62. Walker, "The Origins and Maintenance," 403.

63. Robert H. Salisbury, "Interest Representation: The Dominance of Institutions," *American Political Science Review* 78 (Mar. 1984): 64–76.

64. Andrew S. McFarland, "Recent Social Movements and Theories of Power in America," paper presented at the annual meeting of the American Political Science Association, Aug. 31, 1979, 9.

65. John D. McCarthy and Mayer N. Zald, "Resource Mobilization and Social Movements: A Partial Theory," *American Journal of Sociology* 82 (1977): 1217–18.

66. G. David Garson, "On the Origins of Interest-Group Theory: A Critique of a Process," *American Political Science Review* 68 (Dec. 1974): 1514.

67. Luther P. Gerlach, "Movements of Revolutionary Change: Some Structural Characteristics," in *Social Movements of the Sixties and Seventies*, ed. Jo Freeman (New York: Longman, 1983), 133–34; see also Luther P. Gerlach and Virginia H. Hine, *People, Power, Change: Movements of Social Transformation* (Indianapolis, Ind.: Bobbs-Merrill, 1970). For an insightful analysis of the advantages and disadvantages of these structural characteristics of social movements see Janice Love, *The U.S. Anti-apartheid Movement: Local Activism in Global Politics* (New York: Praeger, 1985).

68. McCarthy and Zald, "Resource Mobilization and Social Movements," 1216.

69. Ibid., 1215.

70. Ibid., 1217.

71. Joseph R. Gusfield, "Social Movements and Social Change: Perspectives of Linearity and Fluidity," in *Research In Social Movements, Conflicts, and Change*, ed. Louis Kriesberg (Greenwich, Conn: JAI Press, 1981), 323.

72. Claire Knoche Fulenwider, *Feminism in American Politics: A Study of Ideological Influence* (New York: Praeger, 1980); see also Virginia Sapiro, "News from the Front: Intersex and Intergenerational Conflict over the Status of Women," *Western Political Quarterly* 33 (June 1980): 260–77.

73. Doug McAdam, *Political Process and the Development of Black Insurgency, 1930–70* (Chicago: University of Chicago Press, 1982), 34; see also 48–51.

74. Rick Fantasia, *Cultures of Solidarity: Consciousness, Action, and Contemporary American Workers* (Berkeley: University of California Press, 1988).

75. Nancy E. McGlen and Karen O'Connor, "An Analysis of the U.S. Women's Rights Movements: Rights as a Public Good," *Women and Politics* 1 (Spring 1980): 65–85; McGlen and O'Connor, *Women's Rights: The Struggle for Equality in the Nineteenth and Twentieth Centuries* (New York: Praeger, 1983); McAdam, *Political Process;* Gary Delgado, *Organizing the Movement: The Roots and Growth of Acorn* (Philadelphia: Temple University Press, 1986), 221–24.

76. McAdam, *Political Process,* 47–50; Gerlach and Hine, *People, Power, Change;* Maurice Pinard, *The Rise of a Third Party* (Englewood Cliffs, N.J.: Prentice-Hall, 1971); Jo Freeman, *The Politics of Women's Liberation* (New York: David McKay, 1975), 48–53; Duerst-Lahti, "The Government's Role"; McGlen and O'Connor, *Women's Rights.*

77. Freeman, *The Politics of Women's Liberation,* 66–67.

78. Freeman, "The Origins of the Women's Liberation Movement," *American Journal of Sociology* 78 (Jan. 1973): 792–811; see also McAdam, *Political Process;* Aldon D. Morris, *The Origins of the Civil Rights Movement: Black Communities Organizing for Change* (New York: Free Press, 1984).

79. D. Garth Taylor, *Public Opinion and Collective Action: The Boston School Desegregation Conflict* (Chicago: University of Chicago Press, 1986), 102; see also Charles Tilly, *From Mobilization to Revolution* (New York: Random House, 1978); William A. Gamson, *The Strategy of Social Protest* (Homewood, Ill.: Dorsey, 1975); Delgado, *Organizing the Movement.*

80. Edelman, *The Symbolic Uses of Politics.*

81. Frances Fox Piven and Richard A. Cloward, *Poor People's Movements: Why They Succeed, How They Fail* (New York: Vintage Books, 1977); see also Piven and Cloward, *Regulating the Poor: The Functions of Public Welfare* (New York: Vintage Books, 1971).

82. Joyce Gelb and Marian Lief Palley, *Women and Public Policies* (Princeton, N.J.: Princeton University Press, 1982), 4–5.

83. Ibid., 5.

84. Freeman, *The Politics of Women's Liberation,* 6.

85. McGlen and O'Connor, "An Analysis," 69, 82; see also McGlen and O'Connor, *Women's Rights;* McAdam, *Political Process,* chap. 8; Saul Alinsky, *Rules for Radicals: A Pragmatic Primer for Realistic Radicals* (New York: Vintage Books, 1971); and Alinsky, *Reveille for Radicals* (Chicago: University of Chicago Press, 1946).

86. Alinsky, *Rules for Radicals.*

87. Piven and Cloward, *Poor People's Movements.*

88. Michael Lipsky, "Protest as a Political Resource," *American Political Science Review* 62 (Dec. 1968): 1144–58.

89. Peter Eisinger, *Patterns of Interracial Politics: Conflict and Cooperation in the City* (New York: Academic Press, 1976). For further treatment of the per-

vasiveness of protest in American politics see Michael Useem, *Protest Movements in America* (Indianapolis, Ind.: Bobbs-Merrill, 1975).

90. Schlozman and Tierney, *Organized Interests and American Democracy*, 182.

91. Freeman, *The Politics of Women's Liberation*, 3.

3 Feminism at the Grass Roots: The Committee to Recall Judge Archie Simonson

In May of 1977 a Madison, Wisconsin, newspaper reported that Judge Archie Simonson said from the bench during a dispositional hearing in a juvenile sexual assault case that given the way women dress, " 'should we punish severely a 15 or 16-year-old who reacts to it normally?' " [1] Three juveniles were involved in the sexual assault in a city high school. Simonson was presiding over a hearing involving one of the juvenile offenders when he made his infamous remark. Simonson's statement and subsequent elaborations triggered a hard-fought, successful recall campaign by an ad hoc, grass-roots interest group, the Committee to Recall Judge Archie Simonson.

The Committee to Recall was a local manifestation of a larger social movement, the modern women's liberation movement, which attempts through education, or, in present-day language, "consciousness-raising," to change dominant beliefs about justice, rights, and the boundaries of political issues. Rape reform efforts, in general, have attempted to change the public's perception of rape from a crime of passion to a crime of violence. This definitional change represents a shift in the rules of public discourse that is at the heart of the Simonson recall. The Simonson recall is part of such consciousness-raising by changing the issue of rape from an exclusively personal event that is the victim's private problem to one with power implications for gender politics.

Although the definitional attitude toward rape was the impetus for the feminist reaction to Simonson's statements, it alone was not enough to recall Simonson. Success was achieved only because a convergence of factors kept the issue broad enough. This can be seen most clearly when the Simonson recall is contrasted with the recall attempt against Grant County Judge William Reinecke discussed in chapter 6.

Feminist theorists have begun to describe the way language, science, and public/private distinctions often exclude the experiences of women. Reanalysis of rape is an example of feminist influence. In the past, rape was treated as a personal crime, a private problem for the victim. The state exercised the police powers of investigation, trial, and punishment. Feminists assert that rape is not merely a private victim's problem but also an act with power implications for every woman. "Rape," Susan Brownmiller wrote, "keeps all women in a state of fear."[2]

Feminist scholarship supplements the pluralist approach to interest groups by examining reasons why some groups might find it difficult to organize, pressure, and succeed. The Simonson case displays the convergence of factors necessary for interest group success given the potential difficulties these groups, especially feminist ones, must surmount. Because the facts were clear, the target tangible, and the agenda specific, the issue became political. Political conflict occurred because feminist social movement partisans organized, sustained, and targeted the public opposition to Simonson's remarks.

I conducted eighteen interviews with activists and protagonists in the Committee to Recall Judge Archie Simonson between June and October 1984. Fourteen women and four men were interviewed. I also interviewed people who, though outside the group, were important to the efforts of the group. For example, I spoke with members of the district attorney's office, with a newspaper reporter, and with former judge Archie Simonson.

The interview material is supplemented by analysis of newspaper accounts of the entire incident, which was extensively covered by the media, national as well as local. The uproar over the statements Simonson made in court and the efforts to recall him were front-page news in the two Madison newspapers (the *Wisconsin State Journal* and the *Capital Times*) for weeks on end. Research into the archives of the newspapers uncovered more than 560 articles and letters to the editor concerning the Simonson recall. Both Madison papers ran scores of these letters, which were nearly ten to one against Simonson.[3] Early into the controversy the *Wisconsin State Journal* announced it was going to cease publication of letters to the editor regarding Simonson because they were so numerous and repetitive. Until its announcement, the newspaper had received 109 letters critical of Simonson and 13 supporting him.[4]

Background of the Recall

Although the Simonson recall was a manifestation of the social movement of feminism in America, it is also important to understand the local context in which the recall took place, in order to provide a "thick description" of the events. It is a commonplace of political wisdom that "all politics is really local politics." The Simonson recall is no exception.

The Judge

Archie Simonson was a respectable local lawyer and politician in Madison for over twenty years before he made his infamous remarks. He was a member of the Madison City Council from 1953 to 1955 and was elected a judge in the county court in 1972. Ironically, both Madison newspapers endorsed Simonson's judicial candidacy over the incumbent judge, citing the incumbent's lack of judicial temperament.[5]

In 1976 Simonson was elected to the Dane County Circuit Court, although the local bar association had rated him unqualified. His judicial record until his fateful remarks in 1977 was marked by praise as well as controversy. Simonson was known as an innovative judge who occasionally punished, scolded, and fined people in his court for tardiness and delays. He displayed a predilection to exercise wide judicial discretion and a concern for procedural propriety in criminal cases. From the beginning of his judicial career Simonson's style was to speak out rather than be an unobtrusive judge. His honest, outspoken judicial style carried through into the recall campaign against him at a time when a silent tone of judicial decorum might have been a wiser course.

The Feminist Community

Madison, located in Dane County, is a liberal, white-collar, university town with an active, diverse feminist community. The Simonson recall occurred when agencies and groups concerned about sexual assault were already in existence. In Dane County there was a Rape

Crisis Center; a university student-run and operated Women's Transit Authority, providing rides home at night for women as a rape prevention program; the Whistle Stop Program, providing whistles so people could raise an alarm if attacked; and a feminist bookstore, A Room of One's Own, willing to serve as a downtown drop-off and pickup point for recall petitions. Although these organizations were not officially "activists" in the Simonson recall, they disseminated information about where to get petitions. The Rape Crisis Center also responded to the Simonson remarks by explaining that rape is a crime of violence and that such victim-blaming remarks were exactly what the Crisis Center was trying to overcome.

These various agencies and groups were supported by an active, progressive, feminist community in Madison. Indeed, a statement by the local chapter of the National Organization for Women about the Simonson remarks argued that such things should not be tolerated in liberal Madison. In addition, the women's community had been grappling with a high number of rapes in the downtown university area and Wisconsin's rape laws had recently been changed to a new sexual assault statute. The public and media discussions about these issues were still fresh in the minds of the recall activists when Simonson made his controversial remarks.

The Strongest Challenger

One candidate opposing Simonson helped make it the perfect test case. The first aspirant to announce against Simonson was a young attorney, Moria Krueger. At a Legal Association of Women luncheon the day after Simonson's statements were publicized at least three women, including Krueger, expressed interest in running against Simonson. In fact, Krueger announced only six days after the first publicity of Simonson's remark. She was highly qualified, a graduate with honors of the University of Wisconsin Law School, and a respected, bright attorney specializing in juvenile and family matters.

Several female attorneys interviewed for this study revealed that Judge Simonson was establishing a reputation for disrespectful, disparaging attitudes toward female attorneys. Indeed, Krueger and others like her had speculated before the recall on the chances of unseating him in the next regularly scheduled election. She first started thinking about running against Simonson, she said, when she had "'the misfortune to practice in front of him.'"[6] After her victory,

Krueger maintained Simonson's entire judicial record, and not just the rape case, was the issue.[7]

Krueger had a distinct advantage in being the only woman in a crowded field of six and certainly became a symbolic candidate. As one commentator remarked at the time, "She claims it is not an issue, but considering the time and place, considering the circumstance, and considering that presently there are *no* women judges in this state the significance of an able woman in Madison replacing Archie Simonson cannot be overstated. In the eyes of many, justice would be done. Poetically."[8]

Krueger's status as the only woman was sometimes used against her. At a candidate forum, for example, Daniel Moeser (another challenger) said, "'If I thought I represented a special interest group or cause, I would not be running.'"[9] Krueger objected to the implication that women are only a "special interest":

"At the forum . . . I was accused of representing a special interest group— which at first I thought meant something like Exxon—and it turned out that the special interest group, according to Moeser, meant women. I'm not saying that women are an interest group per se—I'm only addressing myself to his definition—but I really resent that. I've never appealed to women any more than I've asked for everyone's support, and I really object to someone saying so. No one has accused the male candidates of representing the special interest group of men."[10]

She stressed that she was running on her qualifications and did not emphasize that she was the only female candidate. Krueger's balanced approach, placating fears that she might be a Trojan horse for the women's movement, yet not appearing to be antifeminist, was evident throughout her campaign.

As one analysis in a Madison weekly pointed out, although Simonson had the incumbency advantage, Krueger had endorsements by many of Madison's political opinion leaders. Krueger's endorsements included the mayor, the local NOW chapter, and the Dane County Women's Political Caucus.[11] Krueger's campaign stationery listed many liberal, Democratic, progressive political activists in Madison and Dane County (including future governor Tony Earl). She also spent more than any other candidate in the recall election.[12] A poll of Dane County Bar Association members, though, rated both Simonson and Krueger "unqualified."[13] Krueger's endorsements and tempered campaign were in stark contrast to those of Simonson.

Wisconsin's Recall Law

In most recalls an official or officials have disturbed a certain segment of the community through being "excessively rude, extravagant, unresponsive, or incompetent."[14] The response of government officials to these protest groups partially determines the results the groups achieve. Sponsors of a recall election bear the burden of proof for justifying removal and must overcome voter resistance to change and affections for the status quo.[15] The ability of citizens to address this issue was aided by the institutional mechanism of recall in Wisconsin. In 1977 Wisconsin was one of only eight states providing for the recall of judges, and no judge had been recalled in the United States since 1940.[16] At the time of the Simonson recall, a Wisconsin judge could be recalled if a petition by at least 25 percent of the number of voters who participated in the previous gubernatorial election was filed within sixty days from the beginning of the recall drive.[17] For the Simonson recall this translated into 21,000 signatures.[18] The Committee to Recall obtained about 17,000 signatures in the first two and a half weeks and ultimately filed 36,343 signatures.[19] Within ten days after the petitions are submitted the judge has the choice of resigning or facing a special election to be called within forty-five days.[20] At the time of the Simonson recall, no run-off was required; the candidate with a plurality in the nonpartisan recall election won the seat.[21] The Wisconsin recall law was passed in 1926 and had not been successfully utilized until the Simonson recall.[22]

Inclusion of judges in the 1926 law was opposed by Wisconsin's judges and lawyers. In fact, one report pointed out, Simonson and his lawyer harkened back to earlier arguments against judicial recall laws when they maintained, "'If the courts are to be tyrannized by interest groups, indeed even by the majority of the people, the ultimate victim will be the liberty of the individual.'"[23] Simonson argued that the fate of an independent judiciary was at stake in the election.

The Chronology of Events

From examination of the Simonson recall, three broad lessons can be drawn for citizen participation: first, the central importance of issue construction; second, the strength derived from previous political activities and from connections with other groups; and third, the difficulty of achieving success.

Issue Construction

The public reaction to Simonson's remarks reflected years of feminist public discussion about rape. Before the modern women's movement, isolation of rape victims was one poignant part of their experience. Reformulating personal experiences to expose their political dimensions is central to the feminist approach. Jo Freeman sums up the significance of these political activities:

Social movements are one of the primary means of socializing conflict; of taking private disputes and making them political ones. This is why a successful movement provides an *intersection* between personal and social change. Personal changes can be a *vehicle* to more concrete social changes, and are also often a result; but if a movement restricts itself to change purely on the personal level, its impact on society remains minimal. It is only when private disputes that result from personal changes are translated into public demands that a movement enters the political arena and can make use of political institutions to reach its goals of social change.[24]

Elshtain makes a related point: "Feminist analysts—radical, liberal, Marxist, and psychoanalytic—share at least one overriding imperative: they would redefine the boundaries of the public and the private, the personal and the political, in a manner that opens up certain questions for inquiry. They would 'break the silence' of traditional political thought on questions of the historic oppression of women and the absence of women from the realm of public speech."[25]

Western feminism is influenced by changes in social values and structures, including the gradual extension of the ideology of individual rights to women.[26] The resurgence of feminism in America in the 1960s is based on time-honored role equity traditions emphasizing individual merit and equality of opportunity. In a similar manner, Barrington Moore argues that only when people stop believing that all their misfortunes are inevitable or individual can they recognize injustice and begin to address it.[27]

Intellectual and Cultural Antecedents

There were other intellectual and cultural antecedents of the feminist movement. American women active in the abolition movement had found that the extensions of citizenship rights after the Civil War did not apply to them. Industrialization, World War II, and the pressures of the "feminine mystique" helped spark a new women's movement. The civil rights movement also had a strong influence.

Women's frustrations in the civil rights and antiwar movements exacerbated feelings of relative deprivation, helping them to realize their common interests as women. Relative deprivation is developed and defined by Gurr as a perceived discrepancy between your value expectations and your value capabilities.[28] As Freeman points out,

No single group or organization among these protest movements directly stimulated the formation of independent women's liberation groups. But together they created a "radical community" in which like-minded women continually interacted or were made aware of each other. This community consisted largely of those who had participated in one or more of the many protest activities of the 1960s and had established its own ethos and its own institutions. . . . The values of their radical identity and the style to which they had been trained by their movement participation directed them to approach most problems as political ones that could be solved by organizing. What remained was to translate their individual feelings of "unfreedom" into a collective consciousness.[29]

Evans corroborates these findings of incipient feminism within the civil rights and antiwar movements:

The stage was set. Yet the need remains to unravel the mystery of how a few young women stepped outside the assumptions on which they had been raised to articulate a radical critique of women's position in American society. For them, a particular set of experiences in the southern civil rights movement and parts of the student new left catalyzed a new feminist consciousness. There they found the inner strength and self-respect to explore the meaning of equality and an ideology that beckoned them to do so. There they also met the same contradictory treatment most American women experienced, and it spun them out of those movements into one of their own.[30]

Some scholars see an inevitable pressure in America for increasing equality of treatment given the political culture's basis of individualism and equality. Alexis de Tocqueville, after pointing out how democracy levels various social inequalities, asked, "But is that the end of the matter? . . . May it not ultimately come to change the great inequality between man and woman which has up till now seemed based on the eternal foundations of nature?"[31] Women involved in the abolition movement, for example, based their opposition to slavery and their budding feminism on an ideology of individual natural rights.[32]

Louis Hartz developed a thesis, similar to Tocqueville's, that America's lack of a feudal history allows the philosophy of John Locke full flower. Hartz believed there is a general consensus in American political thought on individualism, natural rights, and equality of opportunity. He saw it as an atomistic social freedom.[33]

The impetus for the women's movement stems partially from this philosophical tradition. A liberal legal reform approach to expanding rights reflects and encourages, however, less concern for addressing structural economic maladies and fundamental social change.[34] Within the tradition of liberal feminism though, Zillah Eisenstein asserts, there is potential for radical political mobilization as feminist reformers discover the limits to liberal reform within a patriarchal capitalist system.[35]

When "the word was spoken," Evans reports, it was as if a dam had broken. "When they heard the message—sometimes simply in the form of the words 'women's liberation'—their first response, over and over again, was exhilaration and relief."[36] Women experiencing ambiguity and strain in their roles, sharing a new left history, and acquiring an intellectual perception of sexual inequality discovered each other and realized they were not alone.[37]

The women active in recalling Simonson come from similar roots: experience in the civil rights and antiwar movements. They described vague feelings of dissatisfaction. They realized life was different for their brothers, husbands, and male co-workers. Often, they felt resentments toward disparity in treatment when they were growing up. Even as little girls, they noticed the inequities and bristled against them. Housework, one woman recalled, was done by the girls in her family, not the boys. They didn't have a language to describe these feelings until the women's movement supplied the concepts for them. The women's movement provided a source of strength enabling them to act on behalf of others, a connection Holsworth also found in feminist anti–nuclear weapons activists.[38] Several women reflected that they had always been feminists. As one woman stated, she was always a feminist although she "didn't have a name for it then." When feminism touched their lives, just as in Evans's study, these women felt relief.

One woman, a young mother of two, with her graduate studies truncated by children and her husband's career moves, was isolated with her thwarted ambitions until the women's movement. She was fascinated by feminist authors and hungrily read book after book, recognizing within them her own dreams and disillusionments. Emerging from her self-imposed reading program, she joined NOW, was a leader in the Simonson recall, and thus started a long-term public, political life.

Rape and the Rights of Women: Political Issue Mobilization

The treatment of rape cases in American law is a glaring example of the disparate treatment of women. Feminism tries to reorient discussions on rape from an individual's trauma and victimization to a group political issue. Women's movement literature and rhetoric emphasize the potential for every woman to be a rape victim. Discussions also focus on the ways in which women incorporate the "rape culture" into their lives (such as avoiding solitary nighttime errands).

Throughout this process the central theme is redefinition of rape, through statutory revision as well as public education, as not a crime of passion but a crime of violence. Susan Brownmiller's *Against Our Will* is probably the most famous example of this argument. If rape is a crime of violence, analogous to other forms of assault, then hospital, police, and trial procedures that blame the victim are inappropriate and inconsistent. In other words, if rape is no longer treated as a sex crime but as a violent assault, the victim's attire or actions are irrelevant. The definitional change, originating from the women's movement, is the driving force behind statutory reform in state laws eliminating Lord Hale instructions (where the judge reminds the jury that rape is easily accused, hard to prove, and "'harder to be defended by the party accused though ever so innocent'"),[39] corroboration requirements, the admissibility of victims' past sexual activities, and, ultimately, replacing the legal language to call it not "rape" but, "first-degree sexual assault" or "second degree sexual assault." The conceptual change pushed by the women's movement that rape is a crime of violence, not passion, was very visible in the grass-roots response to Simonson's remarks.

The modern women's movement addresses the issue of rape in two ways: through statutory reforms and public education. Throughout the late sixties and the seventies there was widespread discussion of rape and its impact on victims. Scholarly journals as well as the popular press and entertainment media reported the high incidence of rape, the low reporting rates, and the way that victims were "twice victimized," once by the rape and once by the legal system. Even network television, in made-for-TV movies as well as in episodes of popular series, portrayed rapes and the shabby treatment victims received at the hands of health-care professionals, police, courts, family, and friends.[40]

Redefining rape, reformers hope, will mean victims will no longer be readily blamed. Interviews with the leaders of the Committee to Recall Archie Simonson revealed that this redefinition of rape was central to their sense of injustice. The informants stated that Simonson did not understand the crime; rape is a crime of violence, not passion, so it does not matter how the victim (or any woman) dressed. Indicative of this view was the following response:

Well, [Simonson] didn't understand, he was evidently under the misapprehension that rape is a crime of passion rather than a crime of violence. And that it can be provoked by what he considered to be a state of undress or provocative clothing. But it didn't even make sense in context because it turned out that the girl had been wearing a turtleneck sweater and corduroy pants. But it's a ridiculous proposition even if she'd been wearing a bikini. That it's a normal reaction to see someone in a halter and shorts, or whatever, to rape them. To attack them sexually. I don't think I had ever heard anything so outrageous. The whole subject of rape was a subject upon which, one upon which many men had views that I found fairly outrageous, also. But this was the worst thing that I ever heard anybody say on the subject. And to hear it from the bench was just unbelievable.

Recalling Simonson was seen, then, as an educational, consciousness-raising exercise for the entire community. One activist said, "It seems so obvious to me and it was a revelation to me that . . . people did not understand that sexual assault is a crime of violence. So many people really believe it to be a crime of passion. Of lust. As opposed to what I think it really is. . . . One of the good things, I think, about the campaign is that there was then a public dialogue about what is this all about."

The process of education was an important theme in the political work of these activists. Dolores Grengg, a committee leader, remarked, "'Even if we don't get rid of Simonson—God forbid—I think it all will have been worth it in terms of consciousness-raising. Many people— many men—have changed their attitudes about sexual assault.'"[41]

The activists shared the pragmatic American reformers' tradition that problems can be solved through education and the proper programs and policies, without, at the same time, requiring large-scale social reform. Nelson makes a similar point concerning a witness to U.S. Senate hearings on child abuse. The witness, Jolly K., was an abusive parent and had founded Parents Anonymous: "Jolly K. was the perfect witness, cutting through academic pieties to convince the assembled senators, witnesses and journalists of the gravity of the problem. She was, figuratively, a sinner who had repented and been saved by her own hard work and the loving counsel of her friends. But, more importantly, she embodied the American conception of a social problem: individually rooted, described as an illness, and solvable by occasional doses of therapeutic conversation." [42] This construction of social problems as individually based and requiring individual reform, not social reform, has a limiting, conservative influence on policy-making. The result is to "erase structural conditions from notice." [43] One recall leader, asked why the Committee to Recall did not dispute the sentence given to one of the juveniles accused, answered that such an orientation would have been merely vengeful. "It wouldn't have done anything as far as consciousness-raising. It wouldn't have helped change any attitude, it would have just given a severe sentence. It would have been meaningless as far as I would have been concerned. And I wouldn't have spent my time on that. It wouldn't have been a feminist issue that way. And it wouldn't have been a consciousness-raising exercise." The recall movement's feminist orientation recognized the many insidious ways that women are denigrated. Asking for reform in gender relations, therefore, requires large-scale reforms. These changes are often in the "personal is political" arena, not necessarily resulting in a new political agenda.

Some activists, in retrospect, doubted the efficacy of their many years of attempting to educate the public through their community activities. For example, one activist whose political history included anti–Vietnam war and civil rights involvements spanning nine years said upon reflection, "We used to have these lofty ideas. . . . But, as far as really changing things, especially now, particularly the way things are now, you know, I think we've just gone backwards."

The activists responded to the injustice in the judge's statement as opposed to the case disposition. The juvenile convicted in this particular dispositional hearing received one year of home supervision. Although the recall leaders all made a distinction between the sentence and the statement, opposition to the perceived "light" sentence was an element in the general public assessment of the case. This is evident in numerous letters to the editors of the *Wisconsin State Journal* and the *Capital Times*. The distinction made from the very beginning by the Recall Committee between the disposition and the judge's statements was later important when questions of race prejudice were raised. A press release by the Committee to Recall summarized their position: "'We do not believe that a judge has the "freedom" to:

(1) not understand an important new law—the Sexual Assault Law, (2) be ignorant of the nature of a serious crime—rape, nor (3) believe that the victims of that crime are responsible for their own victimization.' "[44]

The activists, therefore, constructed a symbolic case of injustice. One activist explained her feelings: "I just have a conception of a young woman being raped by a nonentity and that somehow society said that it was okay because of the way she was dressed." Justice to them would entail more judicious language, the same policy decision, but no insults or victim-blaming. In the words of one woman, "You can give a short sentence and still make it very hard depending on how you present it to the person. But the way he presented it to this kid was sort of like, 'Well, I have to do this.' You can give the same length of sentencing and have it different. You can say, 'Well, you really did bad. But, you are a juvenile.' And, you know, and I don't, I don't have that much problem, it was the way it was handled, you know." As another woman cogently stated, "When women said they were outraged by the sentence it was not outrage by the individual kind of thing, it was a symbol, it was a symbol. I don't think that they felt that this particular individual should have been punished more. It was the way, [pause] the feeling I had of the people is the way it was done, and it wasn't against the boy who had done it. There was *no* talk of him."

In addition to the feminist support for the recall, some people were insulted by what Simonson said about men—that they cannot control themselves and rape is a normal reaction. The activists, therefore, framed the issue in the context of individual rights and toned down what might be considered "feminist rhetoric."

The Simonson recall aimed at broad support not only because of the issues but because of the facts of the case. Because the victim and the accused were juveniles, their identities were not revealed. The usual public debate over the relationship of the victim to the accused, then, was not prominently discussed. The recall issue was framed as the rape of any woman. Issue definition was a central ingredient in the Simonson recall. As McGlen and O'Connor show, when a good is defined as a public bad, women's reform efforts fail (for example, ratification of the Equal Rights Amendment); when reform can be defined as a limited public good, success is more likely.[45] It was a perfect test case for public education about the new construction of the definition of rape. One informant said, "In a way, it was perfect. If you want to show people that rape is not caused by women in see-through blouses hanging out in bars, you show them a girl in a turtleneck in high school."

One potentially divisive question arose when it was revealed that the victim was white and the accused juveniles black. Recall supporters, then, were forced to defend themselves against charges of racism. In addition, some of their supporters fell away. Most important was the *Capital Times*'s reversal of its editorial position on the recall. The editorial advocated that Simonson apologize instead of be recalled, among other reasons, because

not everyone who is after Simonson's hide objects to his statements. A sizeable body of opinion, including that of some of this state's newspapers, has focused on the leniency of the sentence Simonson imposed on a 15-year-old boy charged along with two other teenagers in the rape of a girl at West High School. . . . It is the sentence that has brought out the ugly side of this controversy. The three boys involved in the incident were black. The girl was white. There are those who are trying to fan the fires of racial hate, those who are falling back on old racist stereotypes, who are demanding vengeance.[46]

There was an immediate response from the Committee to Recall:

Organizers of the recall drive against Judge Archie Simonson have accused *The Capital Times* of raising "false issues" and indulging in a "white liberal guilt trip" in its editorial opposition to the recall effort.

Committee to Recall said, "The Recall Committee did not reveal, and most of the community did not know, that it was a black-white incident. . . . That revelation was made by the very people now calling the [recall] campaign racist. The press is responding to panic in them."[47]

One recall leader labeled the racism issue diversionary, charging that the *Capital Times* "'appears to be more concerned about racism than it is about sexism.'"[48]

The editorial position of the *Capital Times* was endorsed by the president of the local NAACP who explained,

"I know [a recall leader] is not a racist. But the charge that *The Capital Times* reacted as a white liberal guilt trip is viewed by myself and numerous black men and women as being insensitive to the concerns of blacks. Clearly, Simonson's remarks were sexist, and ought not to be condoned. There is no question about that. But at the same time he did not act in a sexist manner in sentencing the youth, and that's a hard thing to separate. I think the whole thing shows there is a need for women and minorities on the bench in Dane County."

He added that the time to replace Simonson was during the regularly scheduled election, not with a special recall.[49] Opinion was not united, though, in the African-American community. Madison's one African-American city council member, for example, publicly opposed the editorial stance of the *Capital Times*.[50]

In their interviews activists described the issue of race as a "red herring," used to deflect the opposition to Simonson's remarks. They maintained that the race of the juveniles was largely unknown, only to be revealed by the very people who alleged racist motives. Indeed, the first mention in print of the race of the juveniles was in an article describing the concerns of one case worker that race prejudice was an element in the recall.[51] The recall leaders separated themselves from the issue of the propriety of the sentence, concentrating instead on Simonson's remarks about women.

The media response varied. Some papers saw the issue of race in the case as "negligible,"[52] while others, notably the *New York Times*, gave the issue much greater weight and credence. A *New York Times* writer noted that Madison was plagued by a series of rapes; Madison police said one African-American was involved in several. "Leaders of the 4,000 black residents among Madison's population of 172,000 are not so sure that sexism is the only issue," the reporter wrote. The same article also included a statement from one recall leader and NOW member, who "said they took issue with the judge's statement before they knew the races of the students in the case."[53]

Coals were added to the fires of discontent when a week before the recall election a juvenile offender in the West High assault was charged with stealing a bicycle. His probation was eventually revoked and he was sent to the state reformatory.

Many people were critical of Simonson's light sentence in this and previous cases.[54] Criticism was also leveled at Simonson for his lack of judicial decorum on the bench. Eventually an official transcript of the sentencing hearing was released. Instead of vindicating Simonson as he had predicted, it made matters worse for him. One article noted that the official transcript showed Simonson's remark that rape was a normal reaction "followed a stream of steamy comments by the judge concerning what parts of the human anatomy could be viewed for free on State Street or for a couple of dollars at a local nude dance club."[55] In addition, a handful of former litigants criticized Judge Simonson for his treatment of their cases, which added to the bad impression of

Simonson's rulings.[56] In the Simonson recall, though, these people did not receive a lot of attention, whereas in the Grant County recall, as we shall see, the Reinecke recall activists were falsely accused of being former litigants and were not able to cast aside that image. The differences are partially based on the political legitimacy and experience of the Simonson recall activists. The Grant County activists were political innocents, so Grant County opinion leaders could more easily discredit them and focus on alleged ties to disgruntled ex-litigants.

The construction of the issue, then, was as broad as possible. The Committee to Recall argued that it was a rational, technical question of removing a judge who does not understand a crime, who blames victims, insults men, and is injudicious. It was a symbolic rape wherein Simonson personified their worst-case scenario. One woman told a reporter, "'If you lay awake at night and try to think up the most sexist thing a person could say, this is what you would come up with.'"[57]

Although the activists' stance was that the issues were sharply delineated, with no shading of gray, there was a small sliver of agreement between Simonson and the women's community. It is best illustrated by Susan Brownmiller's assessment of the Simonson controversy. Brownmiller, in an interview with the *Milwaukee Journal*, agreed with Simonson's remarks on pornography when he called for "'an elimination from the community of the sexual gratification business.'" "'It may surprise you,'" she said, "'but I happen to agree with him. . . . I think he has stumbled upon a glimmer of the truth. Yes, pornography does help promote rape.'" She disagreed with Simonson, though, on where responsibility should be placed. Simonson blamed women, but she saw a larger, societal responsibility. She maintained that rape is not a normal reaction because rape is violence, not eroticism.[58] If Simonson, therefore, was saying that society bears a responsibility for the existence of rape, some feminists agree. But they part company with him over the definition of rape and the responsibility for its occurrence.

Networks: Previous Grass-Roots Activities

Important to the success of the Simonson recall was the membership of the activists in other political organizations and interest groups. The women were connected to an active communications network of feminists in community politics and the women's movement. The central importance of communication networks is summed up in Freeman's propositions for social movement beginnings: the need for a preexisting communications network, which is co-optable to new ideas of the incipient movement, and a galvanizing crisis or cadre of dedicated organizers.[59] A critical mobilizing event, like Simonson's remarks, can actually help an incipient social movement. Whether mobilization occurs, though, also often depends on the facilitation provided by a preexisting social movement.

There was such a network quality to the Simonson recall. The print media portrayed the activists as primarily consisting of angry feminists from the National Organization for Women. As one interviewee pointed out, the media focus on the recall was partially on "battle of the sexes" aspects. Many commentators noted the skewed treatment of the women's movement by the press. As Freeman succinctly summarizes, "The press treated women's liberation much as society treats women—as entertainment not to be taken seriously."[60] *Time* magazine quipped, for example, that Simonson "became the feminist equivalent of Anita Bryant."[61]

Although the Committee to Recall was an ad hoc, grass-roots interest group, it was also a practical, issue-specific coalition of people from other interest groups. Previous research shows that ad hoc, issue-specific coalitions of women's groups can achieve lobbying successes at the national level.[62] The ad hoc coalition within the Committee to Recall was similarly important for the success of the recall effort.

Many related organizations responded to news of Simonson's remarks. The initial story in the *Wisconsin State Journal* went out on the wire services the afternoon before publication in the next morning's *Journal*. The wire service story was picked up by the local television, and many people first heard about Simonson's remarks from their local late-night television news. Immediately, a NOW member started calling people on the NOW telephone tree, soliciting people to attend an impromptu demonstration outside the City-County Building the next day. The day after his comments were aired on the local news, therefore, and the day the *Wisconsin State Journal* ran its original story, a small, but colorful, demonstration took place outside Madison's City Hall. Two of the younger demonstrators, students at the University of Wisconsin, wore clothing that covered them from head to toe (one in a nun's habit) and carried signs saying "Is This What You Had In Mind, Judge?" Pictures of their photogenic parody were carried by newspapers nationwide.

Five women at the demonstration, known to each other from previous political activities, decided to talk to the judge. They were hoping to get an explanation from Simonson that would cool down the discontent. Ironically, there was a film crew from Chicago in Simonson's offices to interview him about his innovative use of videotaped testimony. They were on hand, then, to film the "angry feminists" in action. Simonson agreed to see the five emissaries from the street demonstration. Instead of reassuring them, however, Simonson elaborated further on his philosophy about rape and women's attire. The delegates left his courtroom incensed at his arrogance and insensitivity, and in the hallway they decided that "he had to go." They reasoned that among alternative routes to oust him (impeachment, legislative removal, defeat at his next general election), recall was the only viable option, even though a judge had never been recalled successfully before.

In the spirit of this determination a meeting was called jointly by the Madison chapter of NOW, the Women's International League for Peace and Freedom, and the Madison Rape Crisis Center. The meeting, held at the feminist bookstore, A Room of One's Own, was well attended. The same day, at a previously scheduled luncheon of the Legal Association of Women, the assembled female attorneys discussed Simonson and his remarks. They issued a statement calling his comments an "'insult' and an 'embarrassment to the community.'"[63] At this same meeting, Moria Krueger mentioned that she was considering running against Simonson in a recall election.

The recall was achieved through the coalition efforts of three groups of people: members of the local chapter of the National Organization for Women, members of the local chapter of the Women's International League for Peace and Freedom (WILPF), and local Democratic party activists and elected officials. These categories were not mutually exclusive. Several of the women had been campaign office workers (and even campaign chairs) for various political races in addition to being active in the WILPF or NOW. Many of them also had extensive experience in the local chapter of the League of Women Voters. There was no overlap, though, between NOW and the WILPF. Their ad hoc alliance was issue specific. One WILPF leader, for example, pointed out that NOW's position on a military draft was too conservative for the WILPF. Many WILPF members maintained that compulsory drafts are inherently wrong. NOW, in contrast, seemed more concerned with the gender-specific nature of American conscription. One activist, who came to the Committee to Recall from the WILPF, explained, "It was interesting because the Women's International League for Peace and Freedom always had this identity crisis. They've been around since 1915 and other groups tend to get the publicity. And so, the national press kept saying, 'NOW had organized this' and it was just, it was mainly NOW and the Women's International League and the Rape Crisis Center." The WILPF, she continued, had always seen a connection between peace and women's issues, "but, if they're asked to choose a priority, it's almost always the peace issue." [64]

In combination, the coalition was a formidable political team. As in McGlen and O'Connor's study of women's rights, the Simonson recall displays how previous movements provide training for later movement leaders. [65] The activists brought to the Simonson recall all of the organizational skills learned through previous political activities. Of four committee leaders interviewed, for example, their other memberships included NOW, WILPF, the League of Women Voters, the Women's Political Caucus, Rape Crisis Center, Women's Transit Authority, involvement with A Room of One's Own, the Freedom from Religion Foundation, pro-choice abortion groups, and various election campaigns, including being campaign chairs. Other activists in the recall included members of the Dane County Board of Supervisors, the Board of Education, and the Madison City Council. The leaders of the recall effort were highly political women. They had been active for years in getting various politicians (usually men) elected; this time they used those skills to "dis-elect" one. They knew how to become an officially registered committee, issue press releases, deflect potentially damaging issues, and take care of mundane matters, such as getting notaries public to various drop-off locations for the recall petitions.

They organized one big downtown demonstration in front of the City-County Building. They created T-shirts and buttons with the message "React Normally—Recall Simonson." The Committee to Recall focused its attention on recalling Simonson and deliberately did not endorse a candidate, although they favored Krueger. They wanted to protect themselves from charges of being a front for Krueger's election. They were concerned, though, that Simonson in a crowded field of candidates would win, especially since he needed only a plurality.

Communities of Memory

There was also a very personal dimension to the motivation for activism for some of the interviewees. Of the fourteen women interviewed for the Simonson recall, three revealed that they had been victims of sexual assault. The attacks occurred when they were much younger (two were fourteen) and the women's movement had not yet touched their lives. They remembered how they blamed themselves in various ways for the assaults. These women neither reported the attacks nor took any public action. Rape was a hushed-up crime. One older woman said about women she knew who were raped, "It was much better if you just swallowed your pain and hid yourself and healed yourself." One activist explained, "It was a way of women, you know it's like people would come in [to the bookstore, A Room of One's Own] and say, like, 'I had a friend that was raped' or it was a way of them kind of being able to publicly make an announcement about something that had been a secret all of these years. It was almost like, we didn't just take the petitions. We had to hear everybody's, you know [pause] 'my daughter was raped, I was raped.' It was like, it all came out, you know." She said that activity in the recall campaign helped women come to grips with the reality of their rape. They thought that reforms had been achieved, that it wouldn't be as bad for their daughters as it had been for them. When they heard about the Simonson controversy, "they realized that it hadn't changed. It really scared them, you know. It made them, it gave them, the motivation to do that, to do something." In part, their becoming activists was motivated by knowledge of what their victimization had done to them. Working in this recall campaign or counseling other rape victims or driving a car for Women's Transit Authority was a way for them to do something about rape, without identifying themselves as rape victims with all the stigma attached.[66]

In her study of the modern women's movement Jo Freeman noted, "There is a phoenixlike quality to the movement—different groups simultaneously dying, reforming, and emerging—so that it is hard to get an accurate reading on the state of its health."[67] Clearly, the Simonson recall was sparked by a larger social movement including women (and men) from various viewpoints joining in an ad hoc, issue-specific coalition to depose this judge. Interviewees described the range of people bringing petitions into A Room of One's Own. Some of these individuals were never seen in the bookstore before or after.

Convergence of Factors Required for Success
When examining this successful example of citizen participation, one is struck by how easily it all could have passed unnoticed. The same

incident could have become politics as usual. This was certainly not the first time, nor the last, that people would make injudicious comments concerning a rape case. In October 1989, for example, Florida jury members explained their verdict to acquit a man accused of rape because the victim was "asking for it" given the way she was dressed.[68] It requires a convergence of factors for a triggering incident such as these remarks from the bench to become a public issue and elicit an effective response.[69]

First, there must be an initial challenge to authority or the injustice will pass unmarked.[70] The young, female prosecutor, in appearing before Simonson, challenged the judge.

Judge Simonson: And then you are saying that I should be responsive to the community in what their needs and wishes are. Well, how responsive should I be? Should I adopt a double standard? This community is well known to be sexually permissive; look at the newspapers, look at the sex clubs, the advertisements of sex, the availability of it through your escort services, the prostitutes, they are being picked up daily. Go down State Street and the University area. I used to see girls clothed like that and I had to pay a lot of money to go into the south side of Chicago to view what I see down on State Street today. Even in open court we have people appearing—women appearing without bras and with the nipples fully exposed and they think it is smart and they sit here on the witness stand with their dresses up over the cheeks of their butts and we have this type of thing in the schools. So, is that the attitude of the community? Am I supposed to be responsive to that? Are we supposed to adopt a double standard? . . . It is really wide open and are we supposed to take an impressionable person 15 or 16 years of age who can respond to something like that and punish that person severely because they react to it normally? . . . What response do you have?

Prosecutor: Your Honor, with all due respect, I find your remarks about women's clothing particularly sexist.

Judge Simonson: You bet it is. I can't go around walking exposing my genitals like they can the mammary glands.

Prosecutor: You are reflecting the general theory that a woman provokes an assault and I cannot accept that idea.[71]

Second, there has to be a public airing of the event. As luck (or lack of it) would have it there was a newspaper reporter in the courtroom. She had been following the controversial West High School rape case from the beginning. Judge Simonson had an informal agreement with reporters that they could sit in on juvenile matters as long as they did not reveal juvenile identities. Many of the activists in the recall saw this reporter as pivotal to the whole episode. In the words of one activist, "If she had not been there this would have never been, the story would never have gotten out. . . . A man would have let it go over his head because he's heard it all the time. Of course it's the woman's fault."

In an interview for this study the reporter maintained that she didn't do anything important; she just reported accurately what seemed newsworthy, as any journalist should. Further into the interview, though, she said that she was relatively new to the newspaper at the time and another reporter told her later, after the story had broken, "I don't know how you know that is newsworthy, he says things like that all the time." One can only wonder, then, if a more seasoned, acculturated reporter would have considered the exchange between the prosecutor and the judge to be newsworthy.

The initial story was picked up by the wire services, engendering massive coverage across the country. The three major television networks sent reporters to Madison. Each network featured the recall on its national news program. AP and UPI carried lengthy accounts on May 27, 1977. The extent of the national news coverage was duly reported to Madison residents by the local papers. One article discussed coverage by the *New York Times*, Chicago papers, and *People*.[72] Another article noted that ABC had a crew in town to get up-to-the-minute coverage.[73] Pictures of a demonstration against Simonson outside the courthouse made front pages of newspapers as far away as Honolulu, Hawaii.[74] When the Dane County Board of Supervisors' vote of censure against Simonson was taken, it was filmed by NBC and ABC.[75] Editorials critical of Simonson's statements from the Racine and Green Bay papers and the *Los Angeles Times* and *Valley News* (Lebanon, New Hampshire) were recounted. One article noted that at a press conference Simonson faced a virtual mob of reporters and television crews, including all three national networks. In addition, there was an article by George F. Will and a cartoon by Herblock.[76] Simonson appeared on the "Today Show" and the "Phil Donahue Show," was interviewed by *People*, and was quoted in *Time, Newsweek*, and the *New York Times*.

Media coverage at times resembled a circus. One newspaper story indicates the media's attempts to find sexual humor in the situation. Simonson received a package at his office from Hawaii. He called the bomb squad, which discovered the box contained tropical flowers.

The newspaper jeered, "While there was no note with the flowers, several persons noted that the tropical blooms with their prominent pistils looked decidedly Freudian." [77]

This national coverage placed a lot of pressure on the fledgling recall activists. Their experiences in civil rights and antiwar politics, however, had helped prepare them for managing the media. In addition, their feminist awakenings prepared them for the conflict and publicity the Simonson affair sparked. They anticipated that challenging a judge over a comment in a rape case would cause conflict and backlash. They drew strength for the battles from their sense of belonging to a larger feminist community.

In addition, the national visibility of the controversy was used by Simonson's opposition. Moria Krueger's campaign included signs proclaiming "The Whole World Is Watching, Vote." Her campaign literature also drew on the national attention, saying, in part, "All of America has heard Judge Simonson, all of America will hear the results of this election." The wisdom of this adage was demonstrated by the national and international coverage of the recall election results.

Third, the Simonson recall worked because it was the perfect test case. The facts of the crime itself (three juveniles assaulting another juvenile in a back stairway of a public high school in the middle of the afternoon during school hours with the victim wearing jeans, a turtleneck, and tennis shoes) make it possible for the issue to be broadly framed, attracting enough voters to recall the judge.

Another element making this an excellent test case was Archie Simonson's failure to reassure the outraged citizenry. Instead, he continued to elaborate his views, sinking into deeper political trouble. The day after the story on his court comments broke

he said the response [from people supporting him] "reinforces" his opinions and contended that a recall petition drive "only has two chances—slim and none.

"Women's activist groups concerned about rape should follow the old saying that an ounce of prevention is worth a pound of cure. I'm trying to say to women, 'Stop teasing.' There should be a restoration of modesty in dress, and the elimination from the community of the sexual gratification business.

"Whether the women like it or not, they are sex objects." [78]

He labeled his critics "a group of 'strange bedfellows' including lesbians, atheists, Marxists and members of the National Organization for Women." [79] He also called recall petition signers and organizers "'radical feminists or their dupes,'" prompting the Committee to Re-call's response that his "opposition 'encompasses citizens from all shades of the political spectrum, of all ages and both sexes.'"[80] He believed that he was a sacrificial lamb that might have been "'set up.'"[81] He tried to discredit his critics, claiming the controversy was merely a political ploy: "'I think basically it's the ambition of the NOW group . . . who saw an opportunity and a vehicle to gain national attention from the news media to further their views and projects at the expense of me and the kids involved and the residents of this community, the whole bit. I think it's an outrage.'"[82] Simonson con-tinued to expound on this conspiracy even closer to the election.[83] Dolores Grengg, one recall leader, noted, "'Our best ally was Mr. Simonson himself. He crawled out on a limb and just kept sawing himself off.'"[84]

Simonson discussed the West High rape case in a manner that showed he was unfamiliar with the facts of the case. Only a couple days after his infamous remarks Simonson asserted that no "rape" had occurred. The Madison police quickly disagreed with him.[85] He also admitted he was not familiar with all the provisions of Wisconsin's new sexual assault statute.[86] Within a matter of weeks, almost every gov-ernmental organization in the Dane County area and numerous poli-ticians and groups publicly criticized Simonson's remarks; some called for his removal from office.

Simonson did strike a responsive chord in parts of the community, however. Some people supported his views on women's dress, femi-nism, and the causes of rape; but supporters mixed praise with criti-cism of his light sentencing of the juveniles.

The case became, then, the perfect horror story.[87] As Edelman has written, "Political facts that disturb people and produce conflict are often reconstructed so that they conform to general beliefs about what *should* be happening."[88] These women recognized that sexism works in many insidious ways outside the reach of simple legislative reforms. Affirmation of these beliefs is provided by a 1987 study by Susan Estrich, and as Zillah Eisenstein asserts, in a deeply sexist culture women will not achieve equality from reform alone.[89] Remarks like Simonson's reflect personal, ideological, and cultural roots of sexism beyond the reach of legal changes. Usually, though, accountability is not as easily traced.[90] Degrading remarks are a direct challenge to the social prestige or status of the women's movement. As Joseph Gusfield points out, "Conflicts of status in society are fought out in public arenas as are conflicts of class."[91] Reform of law, therefore, is not the only issue. In their study of the impact of Michigan's rape reform, Marsh, Geist, and Caplan point out,

Because old laws were predicated on this degrading and confining view of women, efforts to reform them represent more than a redefinition of the crime. Such efforts are part of a larger statement that, as women move into more autonomous roles in society, their activities deserve to be acknowledged and respected. Reformed rape laws, then, reflect and legitimate increasingly varied and independent roles and styles of behavior for women in society. They define the crime in terms consistent with emerging concerns of women.[92]

The Simonson recall was framed as an unambiguous question of blaming victims and excusing individuals from responsibility for their violent acts against women.

Personal Effects of the Recall Activism

Many of the people interviewed for this study expressed satisfaction that as beleaguered feminists in a sexist society, they had won for a change. Their evaluation of the long-term impact of the recall, though, was tempered and measured.

Three of the activists, in retrospect, were ambivalent. They thought they might have targeted Simonson unfairly and perhaps used him as a scapegoat. One woman said, for example, "He was an outlet for people's anger." Two other women pointed out that ironically some feminists agree with Simonson that society breeds rape, but they still saw the point of distinction between Simonson's remarks and the feminist critics with respect to causality and responsibility in cases of rape.

Their ethos was incrementalism. One woman reflected on her political activities:

Sometimes there's satisfaction. This recall gave me more satisfaction than I've ever got. Because it was an immediate return on some of my efforts. I guess I see things that the women's movement has done and the peace movement. Certainly, when I started working on the peace movement, it was just a dirty word. I mean, we were called communists. I had tomatoes thrown at me the first time when I went on a march. And, it's a lot more respectable now. I suppose that's a victory of sorts for what I consider to be rationality. And, I mean, the civil rights movement: things are not great for blacks, or minorities in general, but they're better. Things are not great for women, but they're better. And so I see progress. It's very slow, discouragingly slow, but I think it exists.

Another woman derived a different lesson from her recall experience. Like Eileen described in chapter 7, she dated her turning away from a public, political role from her leadership role in one of these challenging groups. She remembered her deep involvement in the recall effort to be physically, as well as emotionally, exhausting. More than that, though, was her heartfelt anguish during the debate over the alleged racist nature of the recall. Years later, when she applied for a job with the state of Wisconsin, prospective supervisors received phone calls asking if they knew that she was a racist, alluding to the Simonson recall. She had experienced adversity earlier, as an antiwar activist, for example. But these conflicts, she said, were too personally searing for her to ever publicly engage in politics again.

This woman, like a number of others, now has an administrative and policy-making position in government. They all wonder if being politically controversial now would jeopardize their new jobs. They had dedicated decades of their lives to movements: civil rights, antiwar, and women. Their full-time jobs outside the home, they realized now, left them little time for politics. At the time of the Simonson recall, though, they had little to lose.

Conclusion

There was a high turnout for the special election (48 percent of the eligible voters). In a field of six candidates, Simonson came in second to Moria Krueger. The vote totals were

Krueger	27,244
Simonson	18,435
Daniel Moeser	15,250
William Smith	8,446
Robert Burr	5,190
Worth Piper	3,342.[93]

The activists interviewed for this study all felt that a woman replacing Simonson on the bench was "poetic justice" likened to "doubling our victory." One recall leader summed up the lesson drawn from the Simonson defeat and the Krueger victory as "women are to be taken seriously."[94]

The media frequently attempted to pigeonhole the recall into either a liberal or a conservative movement. Contrast, for example, the messages in *Time*'s and *Newsweek*'s coverage. *Newsweek* reflected Simonson's view that he was recalled because Madison is too liberal and intolerant of other points of view.[95] *Time* was perplexed that Madison, a town it categorized as liberal and easygoing, should have reacted so vehemently and conservatively against a judge who treated the rapists leniently. *Time* expected Madison to be tolerant of the judge, as he was of the rapists, but advocated that some form of law and order was necessary, concluding, "Permissive age or not, it is unwise to be too understanding of rapists even in a relatively liberal university town like Madison, Wisconsin."[96]

It is important to have respect for what these women accomplished. Too often people belittle women's achievements. But this example of citizen participation may be a successful exception that actually proves the rule about the difficulty of fighting city hall. The success of newly emerging groups, such as feminists, at the grass-roots level requires the convergence of many factors. Of central importance is issue construction. As Tocqueville could have predicted, in a society where the majority rules the issue has to be constructed in a way acceptable to the majority. Movements also need ways to address perceived injustices. In this case, Wisconsin's recall laws provided such a mechanism. Many times, though, similar grass-roots movements are weakened in their attempts to challenge authority through reassurance, deflection of issues, or institutional protections from citizen participation.

The Simonson recall activists viewed events in moderate, almost idiosyncratic fashion: Simonson was a bad apple, he had to be made an example, and now that he was off the bench, things were much better. They realized that they could not easily change some people's beliefs, but they could announce their coming of age politically and their demands for more judicious language in the courtroom. As one activist reflected,

I think whenever the community is brought up short against an incident like that, it does a little soul searching. And, hopefully, in the process people have a little more awareness of the problem. A little more understanding. [pause] And every now and again, you're brought up short where you wonder if anybody understood anything. [pause] But, I think on the whole, it has not decreased the number of rapes in the nation. But it has made our handling of the victim's situation maybe a little more humane.

The Simonson recall activists were Lockean liberals in what Louis Hartz called the liberal tradition in America.[97] They were not fomenting revolution, nor advocating widespread social change, but were piecemeal reformers, banking on the potential to improve people through education and seeking extension of the principles of individual rights to women.

NOTES

1. Anita Clark, "West High Rapist Given Year of Supervision," *Wisconsin State Journal* (Madison; hereafter *WSJ*), May 26, 1977.
2. Susan Brownmiller, *Against Our Will: Men, Women, and Rape* (New York: Simon and Schuster, 1975), 15.
3. "Judge's Office Gets Favorable Letters, Too," *Capital Times* (hereafter *CT*), June 3, 1977.
4. "Simonson Mail," *WSJ*, June 8, 1977.
5. "Editorial: Judicial Temperament: Issue," *WSJ*, Mar. 20, 1972; see also "Editorial: Simonson for County Judge," *CT*, Mar. 21, 1972.
6. Lenny Kachinsky, "Krueger to 'Raise Consciousness,'" *Badger Herald* (Madison), July 14, 1977.
7. Mary Beth Murphy, "New Dane County Judge Meets the Press," *Milwaukee Sentinel* (hereafter *MS*), Sept. 9, 1977.
8. Fred Milverstedt, "A Woman's Challenge to Archie Simonson: The Possible Dream," *Isthmus* (hereafter *I*), Aug. 19–25, 1977.
9. Ed Bark, "Judge Candidates Say Transcripts Should Stay Secret," *CT*, Aug. 11, 1977.
10. Milverstedt, "A Woman's Challenge."
11. Ibid.; see also Rosemary Kendrick, "Voters Can Judge Simonson Sept. 7," *CT*, July 28, 1977; "Local NOW Group Endorses Krueger in Recall Election," *CT*, Sept. 1, 1977; Moria Krueger paid political ad, *CT*, Sept. 6, 1977.
12. "Simonson Foe Krueger Defends Campaign Tab," *CT*, Aug. 24, 1977.
13. Whitney Gould, "Victory Brew Had Many Ingredients," *CT*, Sept. 8, 1977.
14. Thomas E. Cronin, *Direct Democracy: The Politics of Initiative, Referendum, and Recall* (Cambridge: Harvard University Press, 1989), 152.
15. Ibid., 153, 197–98.
16. Phil Haslanger, "If Recall Is Successful, Simonson Will Make History," *CT*, June 11, 1977.
17. "Judge's Rape Comment Draws Angry Backlash," *Milwaukee Journal* (hereafter *MJ*), May 27, 1977.
18. Kendrick, "Judge Notes Support, Scoffs at Recall: 'Stop Teasing' Simonson Tells Women," *CT*, May 27, 1977.
19. Kendrick, "C-T Flip-Flop Called 'Guilt Trip,'" *CT*, June 18, 1977; Kendrick, "Simonson Foes Look to September," *CT*, July 26, 1977.
20. "Women's Law Group Blasts Simonson," *CT*, May 27, 1977.
21. Wisconsin amended its recall law a few years later to require the win-

ner to poll a majority or to have a primary. Debate about such reform began immediately after the Simonson recall. See "Candidate Limit in Recalls Urged," *MJ*, Sept. 8, 1977.

22. Haslanger, "If Recall Is Successful."

23. Ibid.

24. Jo Freeman, *The Politics of Women's Liberation* (New York: David Mc-Kay, 1975), 5.

25. Jean Bethke Elshtain, *Public Man, Private Woman: Women in Social and Political Thought* (Princeton, N.J.: Princeton University Press, 1981), 202.

26. Freeman, *The Politics of Women's Liberation*, 12–13.

27. Barrington Moore, Jr., *Injustice: The Social Bases of Obedience and Revolt* (New York: M. E. Sharpe, 1978); see also Charles Tilly, *From Mobilization to Revolution* (New York: Random House, 1978), and Freeman, *The Politics of Women's Liberation*.

28. Ted Robert Gurr, *Why Men Rebel* (Princeton, N.J.: Princeton University Press, 1970), 13.

29. Freeman, *The Politics of Women's Liberation*, 58.

30. Sara Evans, *Personal Politics: The Roots of Women's Liberation in the Civil Rights Movement and the New Left* (New York: Alfred A. Knopf, 1979), 23.

31. Tocqueville, as quoted in Richard Reeves, *American Journey: Traveling with Tocqueville in Search of "Democracy in America"* (New York: Touchstone, 1982), 305.

32. Nancy E. McGlen and Karen O'Connor, *Women's Rights: The Struggle for Equality in the Nineteenth and Twentieth Centuries* (New York: Praeger, 1983), 16.

33. Louis Hartz, *The Liberal Tradition in America* (New York: Harcourt Brace Jovanovich, 1955), 62.

34. Michael W. McCann, *Taking Reform Seriously: Perspectives on Public Interest Liberalism* (Ithaca, N.Y.: Cornell University Press, 1986), 25–26.

35. Zillah Eisenstein, *The Radical Future of Liberal Feminism* (New York: Longman, 1981), 175–76, 206, 220–48; see also Laura R. Woliver, "Review Essay: The Equal Rights Amendment and the Limits of Liberal Legal Reform," *Polity* 21 (Fall 1988): 183–200.

36. Evans, *Personal Politics*, 201.

37. Ibid., 201–2.

38. Robert D. Holsworth, *Let Your Life Speak: A Study of Politics, Religion, and Antinuclear Weapons Activism* (Madison: University of Wisconsin Press, 1989), 94.

39. "Forcible and Statutory Rape: An Exploration of the Operation and Objectives of the Consent Standard," *Yale Law Journal* 62 (Dec. 1952): 56.

40. For a similar illustration of the trickling-down, yet symbiotic, relationship of professional experts' discovery and publication of an issue to the popular press, see Barbara J. Nelson, *Making an Issue of Child Abuse: Political Agenda Setting for Social Problems* (Chicago: University of Chicago Press, 1984).

41. Kendrick, "Simonson Foes." On the role of consciousness-raising in the women's liberation movement see McGlen and O'Connor, *Women's Rights*, 26, 289–90.

42. Nelson, *Making an Issue of Child Abuse*, 2.

43. Murray Edelman, *Constructing the Political Spectacle* (Chicago: University of Chicago Press, 1988), 99; see also Michael Rogin, *"Ronald Reagan," the Movie, and Other Episodes in Political Demonology* (Berkeley: University of California Press, 1987), 135; Charles E. Silberman, *Crisis in Black and White* (New York: Vintage Books, 1964), 311–12.

44. "Recall Committee Finds Flaws in Judge's Remarks," *CT*, Aug. 4, 1977.

45. McGlen and O'Connor, *Women's Rights*, 15–16; see also McGlen and O'Connor, "An Analysis of the U.S. Women's Rights Movements: Rights as a Public Good," *Women and Politics* 1 (Spring 1980): 65–85.

46. Editorial, "Recall Not the Way to Handle Simonson," *CT*, June 17, 1977.

47. Kendrick, "C-T Flip-Flop."

48. Ibid.

49. "Parks Backs C-T's Simonson Editorial," *CT*, June 20, 1977.

50. "Shivers Says He Backs Campbell on Racism, Sexism," *CT*, June 24, 1977.

51. Phil Haslanger, "'He's a Child, Not a Rapist,' Youth Worker Claims," *CT*, June 2, 1977.

52. Donald Pfarrer, "Judge Misinterprets Rape, Experts Say," *MJ*, June 5, 1977.

53. Paul Delaney, "Judge's Remarks in Rape Case Create Tension in Blacks and Whites in Madison, Wis.," *New York Times*, June 15, 1977.

54. Irvin Kreisman, "Simonson Sees Single Election Issue," *CT*, Sept. 3, 1977. For other criticism of the light sentence, see Anita Clark, "Rape Remarks Are Censured," *WSJ*, May 27, 1977; "Simonson Still 'On the Hook' for His Remarks in Rape Case," *CT*, May 28, 1977.

55. Michael Dorgan, "Simonson Still Insists He's Misrepresented," *CT*, Aug. 25, 1977.

56. See Howard Cosgrove, "City Council Calls on Simonson to Resign," *CT*, June 1, 1977; Carole Moore, letter to the editor, *WSJ*, June 7, 1977; Kathleen Begley, "Madison Judge Hits Again: 'Girls Tease like Strippers,'" *Chicago Daily News*, June 25–26, 1977.

57. Kendrick, "Protesters Agree: 'He's Got to Go,'" *CT*, May 26, 1977.

58. Pfarrer, "Judge Misinterprets Rape."

59. Freeman, *The Politics of Women's Liberation*, 48–49; see also McGlen and O'Connor, "An Analysis," 70.

60. Freeman, *The Politics of Women's Liberation*, 112.

61. "There Goes the Judge: Women Rout a Rape-Condoning Wisconsin Jurist," *Time*, Sept. 19, 1977, 26.

62. Anne N. Costain, "Representing Women: The Transition from Social Movement to Interest Group," in *Women, Power, and Policy*, ed. Ellen Boneparth (New York: Pergamon Press, 1982), 19–37.

63. "Women's Law Group Blasts Simonson."

64. For a detailed study of the WILPF see Jeffrey M. Berry, *Lobbying for*

the People: The Political Behavior of Public Interest Groups (Princeton, N.J.: Princeton University Press, 1977), 141–77.

65. McGlen and O'Connor, *Women's Rights*, 20–23.

66. For an insightful study of the reluctance to act in instances of discrimination and, therefore, take on the stigma of a victim see Kristin Bumiller, *The Civil Rights Society: The Social Construction of Victims* (Baltimore, Md.: Johns Hopkins University Press, 1988).

67. Freeman, *The Politics of Women's Liberation*, 143.

68. "Jurors in Fla. Rape Case Spark Outcry by Blaming Woman for Sexy Attire," *Atlanta Constitution*, Oct. 5, 1989.

69. I would like to thank Professor Herbert Jacob for his suggestions on this point.

70. William A. Gamson, Bruce Fireman, and Steven Rytina, *Encounters with Unjust Authority* (Homewood, Ill.: Dorsey, 1982).

71. "Complete Official Transcript," *WSJ*, Aug. 26, 1977.

72. Clark, "Rape Remark Reaction Still Strong," *WSJ*, May 28, 1977; "Simonson Still 'On the Hook' "; "Simonson Faces the Music—in Song," *CT*, May 28, 1977; see also Kendrick, "Judge Notes Support."

73. "Clarenbach Eyes Plan for Removal of Simonson," *CT*, May 31, 1977.

74. Ibid.

75. Kendrick and Bark, "Supervisors Rap Simonson; Recall Drive Third Complete," *CT*, June 3, 1977.

76. "What Other Editors Say: Simonson Reaction Continues," *MJ*, June 10, 1977; see also Bark, "Simonson Breaks Silence in Interview with Chicago Paper," *CT*, June 27, 1977; Bark, "Recall Vote Focuses National Attention on Madison," *CT*, Sept. 6, 1977; Bark, "Election Is Front Page around the Country," *CT*, Sept. 8, 1977; Kendrick, "Simonson Won't Resign; Says Free Speech at Stake," *CT*, July 29, 1977; George F. Will, "Foggy Justice in Madison, Wis.," *Washington Post*, June 2, 1977; Herblock, Political Cartoon, "It's Your Own Fault for Being Built That Way," *CT*, June 3, 1977.

77. "Simonson Calls the Bloom Squad," *CT*, May 31, 1977.

78. Kendrick, "Judge Notes Support"; see also "Judge Won't Resign after Rape Comment," *Denver Post*, May 29, 1977.

79. Begley, "Madison Judge Hits Again."

80. Bark, "*Daily Cardinal* Won't Endorse in Recall Election," *CT*, Aug. 30, 1977.

81. "No Evidence of Rape Presented, Judge Says," *MJ*, June 1, 1977.

82. Pfarrer, "Judge Misinterprets Rape."

83. David Haskin, "Women Out to Get Me: Simonson," *MJ*, Sept. 4, 1977.

84. Gould, "Victory Brew."

85. Phil Haslanger, "Simonson Claims No Rape Occurred: Police Say Otherwise," *CT*, May 31, 1977; Pfarrer, "Judge Misinterprets Rape"; Mike Miller, "Doyle Rips Simonson's 'Version,' " *CT*, June 8, 1977; editorial, "Simonson's Excuses," *WSJ*, June 10, 1977; Bark, "Judge Candidate Burr Accuses Simonson of Lies in Rape Case," *CT*, Aug. 31, 1977.

86. Bark, "Simonson Admits Not Reading Law," *CT,* Sept. 3, 1977; "Law Not Read," *MJ,* Sept. 4, 1977. Wisconsin's new sexual assault statute codified sexual assault by degrees. First-degree sexual assault involved the use of a weapon. Second-degree sexual assault could include intercourse, but also covered sexual contact short of intercourse. The juvenile convicted in the Simonson incident was charged with second degree sexual assault.

87. Martha L. Fineman, "Implementing Equality: Ideology, Contradiction, and Social Change; A Study of Rhetoric and Results in the Regulation of the Consequences of Divorce," *Wisconsin Law Review* (Nov. 1983): 789–886. Fineman shows how use of "horror stories" by divorce reform advocates helped them achieve change in Wisconsin divorce law.

88. Edelman, *Political Language: Words That Succeed and Policies That Fail* (New York: Academic Press, 1977), 37.

89. Susan Estrich, *Real Rape* (Cambridge: Harvard University Press, 1987); Eisenstein, *The Radical Future of Liberal Feminism,* 222.

90. See Dennis F. Thompson, "Moral Responsibility of Public Officials: The Problem of Many Hands," *American Political Science Review* 74 (Dec. 1980): 905–16.

91. Joseph R. Gusfield, *Symbolic Crusade: Status Politics and the American Temperance Movement* (Urbana: University of Illinois Press, 1963), 19. See also Kristin Luker's study of the status conflicts within abortion politics, *Abortion and the Politics of Motherhood* (Berkeley: University of California Press, 1984).

92. Jeanne C. Marsh, Alison Geist, and Nathan Caplan, *Rape and the Limits of Law Reform* (Boston: Auburn House, 1982), 3.

93. Bark, "Krueger Is in, Simonson Out," *CT,* Sept. 8, 1977.

94. Gould, "Victory Brew."

95. "Strong Convictions," *Newsweek,* Sept. 11, 1977, 14.

96. "There Goes the Judge," 26.

97. Hartz, *The Liberal Tradition in America.*

Members of the Committee to Recall Judge Archie Simonson protest in front of the Dane County Courthouse. (Courtesy of the *Capital Times,* June 1, 1977, photograph by David Sandell)

"It's your own fault for being built that way"—from *Herblock on All Fronts* (New American Library, 1980)

Thousands turned out for a march to protest alleged police brutality in Ernest Lacy's death. (*Milwaukee Journal* Photo)

Marchers from the Coalition for Justice for Ernest Lacy continue their efforts to make police respond. (*Milwaukee Journal* Photo, July 21, 1981, photograph by Sherman A. Gesser)

Myrtle Lacy, mother of Ernest Lacy, speaks during a rally at Incarnation Lutheran Church sponsored by the Coalition for Justice for Ernest Lacy. (*Milwaukee Sentinel* Photo, Feb. 8, 1982, photograph by Dale Guldan)

4 A Measure of Justice: The Coalition for Justice for Ernest Lacy

Alexis de Tocqueville predicted the issue of race relations in America would be a serious test of the new democratic experiment.[1] Yet, in spite of the importance of race in American politics, there is relative neglect of the topic among American politics scholars.[2] Despite some progress in race relations, many inequities still exist. W. E. B. Du Bois wrote that to be black and an American is to live a duality: "One ever feels his twoness,—an American, a Negro; two souls, two thoughts, two unreconciled strivings; two warring ideals in one dark body, whose dogged strength alone keeps it from being torn asunder. The history of the American Negro is the history of this strife,—this longing to attain self-conscious manhood, to merge his double self into a better and truer self."[3]

The Coalition for Justice for Ernest Lacy, an ad hoc, grass-roots group mobilized by the death of an African-American man in police custody, illustrates some of the complexities of group formation, agenda setting, protest politics, coalition building, and group results. This study displays how an incident involving racial conflict contributes to black grass-roots political organization and how temporary organizations affect the outcome of an incident and the permanent structure of black political organization at the municipal level. The drawing of an African-American community around a largely symbolic issue merits analysis since inertia and apathy are more frequent alternative responses. Diffuse interests of the unorganized or factionalized are more often than not inactive.[4]

My analysis of this incident is based on fifteen in-depth interviews. I interviewed all the key participants except two. The interviews were conducted in January and February of 1985, before a civil suit filed by the Lacy family against municipal officials was settled. Among those interviewed were prominent activists in Milwaukee's African-American community, lawyers active in the conflict, a Lacy family member, three ministers and three Catholic nuns active in the Lacy Coalition, two Milwaukee city council members, and a Milwaukee newspaper reporter who extensively covered the Lacy case. Eight interviewees were members of the Lacy Coalition Steering Committee. The steering committee had ten to fifteen members (interviewees' accounts vary on the precise number). The interviewees were two African-American women, seven African-American men, three white women, and three white men. Media coverage of the controversy was extensive, with over seven hundred newspaper articles relating to the Lacy incident and aftermath. I supplemented the interview material with the print media accounts of the triggering incident, the group response, and results.

The Chronology of Events

The Triggering Incident

On July 9, 1981, a twenty-two-year-old African-American Milwaukee man, Ernest Lacy, took a break from helping his cousin paint an apartment. On his walk along a busy downtown street, Lacy was stopped by three Milwaukee police officers. The officers, members of the all-white, elite "Tactical Squad," were searching for a rape suspect. Interviewees said a white woman reported being raped by an African-American man. Newspaper accounts of the incident did not reveal the race of the victim. Several interviewees believed these race considerations contributed to the "anger" of the white officers who stopped Lacy.[5] The ensuing events are contested. The officers maintained that Lacy resisted arrest. Witnesses testified that Lacy was roughly treated and denied medical attention after he was apparently unconscious.[6] The result, however, was that Ernest Lacy died that evening while in police custody. It was later determined that Lacy had committed no crime, and another man was arrested for the rape.

When the police notified the family of Lacy's death, they were told that Ernest had "just died." This explanation was met with disbelief by his family. Disbelieving reassurances from the powerful is central to the mobilization of the weak: "Disbelief, then, signals something that the powerful fear, and slight as it may appear, we should not underestimate its force. It is, in fact, the first sign of the withdrawal of consent by the governed to the sanctioned authority of their governors, the first challenge to legitimacy."[7] The power of official explanations and the exceptional circumstances required before many people disbelieve official versions of events is evident in the comment of one close family member: "I probably would have settled for the explanation of Ernest's death if I hadn't seen the body." Lacy's body was badly bruised.

The family called on two sources to help them look into the incident: their minister and an attorney. At the same time, African-American activists heard about the death through the media and contacted the family. Ernest Lacy's death immediately triggered a widespread community response. At least 2,500 people attended his wake and hundreds attended his funeral.

Various organizations were also in place in the African-American community and responded immediately to newspaper accounts of Lacy's death. The night Lacy died, one member of the Lacy family, an acquaintance of Michael McGee, telephoned McGee in the middle of the night to advise him of what had happened. The next day McGee, representing the United Black Community Council, a non-profit, self-help agency, attended an initial meeting in the district attorney's office. He and another United Black Community Council member so adamantly insisted on a more detailed explanation for the cause of Lacy's death that they were thrown out of the D.A.'s office.

The death so galvanized the African-American community that the Coalition for Justice for Ernest Lacy formed within three days of the incident. The Lacy Coalition first sought suspension of the police officers who arrested Lacy. Adding to the outrage in the African-American community were numerous reports that the officers involved in Lacy's death had had other citizen complaints filed against them. In fact, the three arresting officers had a scheduled appearance on a brutality complaint before the Police and Fire Commission postponed just hours before they stopped Lacy.[8] During their careers, though, these officers had performed well in other circumstances.[9]

The Coalition also demanded the coroner's inquest jury be composed of people from African-American and other inner city communities.[10] After the initial suspensions, the Coalition wanted the officers prosecuted on criminal charges.[11]

People involved in the Lacy Coalition experienced numerous delays, setbacks, and partial victories. There were three separate autopsies with inconclusive findings, four large rallies and marches, numerous smaller demonstrations outside the common council and the Fire and Police Commission, and other meetings. Attendance at these meetings was often hampered because rooms were too small for those wanting to attend, and pat-down searches and identification were required for Coalition members. Police Chief Harold A. Breier attended the Coalition's marches, often getting out of his squad car to walk among the crowd. Coalition leaders viewed this as a deliberate attempt to provoke violence. Coalition leaders cited in their interviews the lack of violence in the face of these provocations as an example of the commitment to peaceful protest by people active in the Lacy struggle.

There were numerous delays, such as the substitution of a retired judge for Milwaukee Deputy Medical Examiner Hill after Hill said a coroner's inquest would not result in criminal charges.[12] Further disappointment occurred when charges stemming from a month-long coroner's inquest jury were thrown out because jury members were chosen partially by race (in a concession to Coalition demands).[13] The inquest jury of three African-Americans and three whites had heard from more than one hundred people, over twenty-one days of testimony about an episode lasting approximately twenty-four minutes.[14] The jury recommended charges be brought against the three arresting officers of homicide by reckless conduct. The jury also charged one of the arresting officers and two of the officers in the police van with misconduct in public office for failure to render first aid and failure to inform medical persons of Lacy's condition upon request.[15] The decision of the inquest jury was greeted with favor by the African-American community, especially because it was the first time an inquest into the death of an African-American resulted in charges recommended against Milwaukee police officers.[16]

The strengths in Lacy's case, such as his innocence, the presence of witnesses, and the family's response, made it a good issue for some groups and activists to use in promoting their previously established agendas. One African-American city council member, for example, had often criticized police-community relations, but not until the highly visible Lacy case was he able to win a majority on the common council to block a police department request for Law Enforcement Assistance Administration funding as a protest against Breier's administration.

Coalition tactics included an initial one-day boycott of downtown stores, a sit-in at the district attorney's office to pressure for reissuance of charges, and a second month-long boycott of the downtown area and one shopping mall. Eventually a judge dismissed charges of misconduct in public office, reasoning that police department rules on rendering first aid did not have the force of law.[17] The Coalition then focused on Fire and Police Commission hearings, seeking disciplinary action. The Fire and Police Commission found the five officers guilty of failure to provide first aid to Lacy and found one officer guilty of using excessive force in his attempt to subdue Lacy.[18] The officer found guilty of using excessive force was fired from the force and the four others received suspensions.[19]

After the Fire and Police Commission decision, the Lacy family, represented by the New York–based Center for Constitutional Rights, filed a suit for civil damages against the city, Police Chief Breier, and the five officers involved in the arrest. In the fall of 1985 the City of Milwaukee settled the civil suit out of court. The settlement came on the day jury selection was scheduled to begin in the federal civil suit.[20]

Conditions in the Community

Milwaukee has had a long history of racial conflict, at least in part because of its extreme segregation. From his study of Milwaukee, Eisinger described the extent of the separation:

To the south of the Menominee Valley lie Polish and other Eastern European ethnic neighborhoods. Several bridges, or viaducts as they are known in Milwaukee, span the valley and its railroad yards. The Sixteenth Street Viaduct is the bridge over which the Reverend James Groppi led his black demonstrators in 1967, in quest of open-housing legislation. In Milwaukee a joke has it that the viaduct is the longest bridge in the world: "What else," the comic asks, "could connect Africa and Poland?" There is an edge of tension in the joke, for the physical barrier of the valley is symbolic of the distance between these two ethnic groups in the city.[21]

The Lacy death occurred at a time when police-community relations in Milwaukee were very poor. Indeed, distrust and tension between black citizens and largely white police forces is a nationwide policy concern.[22] Activists within the African-American community had a standing feud with Police Chief Breier over insensitivity to minority concerns, discriminatory practices within the police department, and creation of an atmosphere tolerant of prejudice.[23] Tensions were severe enough during the Coalition's activism so that when an African-American suspect in a robbery shot and killed two Milwaukee police officers in December 1981, Roy Nabors, an African-American city council member, commented that the suspect was probably afraid for his life and shot in self-defense; a sixteen-hour police walkout strike resulted. Nabors explained, "'I said that two of our finest lives had been lost because we have not dealt effectively with the root causes of our problems.'"[24] In the aftermath of the incident, demands made by the police union for a comprehensive police-community relations program to improve the image of the police were seen as both criticisms of Breier's policies and a response to Nabors.[25] The extent of Breier's reputation for prejudice is reflected in a 1984 statement by the Milwaukee Police Association president: "'Harold Breier is a racist and he emulates the community he serves.'"[26]

There had been a number of lawsuits concerning personnel practices in the Milwaukee Police Department. For example, the African-American police officers' association, the League of Martin, filed a discrimination suit against the city in 1981, singling out Breier as an instigator of many discriminatory practices. The League argued such practices resulted in the lack of African-Americans in high ranks and the absence of black officers on the white, south side of town and on elite police squads, such as the tactical unit. In 1983 the League suit was consolidated with a similar 1974 suit. In 1983 the League won its suit and settled on an agreement with the city wherein a court-ordered schedule of promotions and assignments of African-American officers in the police department would be implemented.[27]

At the time of Lacy's death the city was also involved in a well-publicized suit for civil damages from the heirs of Daniel Bell.[28] Bell, an African-American, was shot to death in 1958 by a Milwaukee police officer after being stopped for a traffic violation. The officer maintained that he shot the allegedly knife-brandishing Bell in self-defense. Subsequent police department and Fire and Police Commission investigations cleared the officers involved in the Bell death of any misconduct. More than twenty years later one of the officers revealed that the knife found in Bell's hand had been planted to make the incident look like self-defense. The revelations implicated the Milwaukee Police Department in a two-decade-long cover-up.[29]

The Bell case was widely debated throughout these years. In October 1979, the common council adopted a resolution, signed by Mayor Henry Maier, requesting a United States Department of Justice investigation into past incidents of beatings and deaths at the hands of Milwaukee police. The United States Attorney, Joan Kessler, found twenty-two persons (all males) had died in police custody or while being apprehended from January 1, 1975, through December 31, 1979. Fourteen of the victims were white, eight were black. Six involved suicide in jail; sixteen involved shootings. In addition, there were 140 citizen complaints filed against the Milwaukee police with the Fire and Police Commission during that same period. The Justice Department received no assistance from the police department when gathering information for this investigation. In fact, Chief Breier indicated he would have to be subpoenaed before he would release any police department records. The investigation proceeded, therefore, without police department records. The Justice Department concluded there was no basis to pursue the case in the federal courts.[30]

This conclusion was referred to as a "white wash" by several African-American activists interviewed in relation to the Lacy study. The memorandum by U.S. Attorney Kessler reflected the investigators' lack of information about the extent and nature of complaints against Milwaukee police. The federal statute of limitations limited the study to the years 1975 to 1979 to establish a pattern of abuse. The investigation was further confined by an exclusive reliance on public records because investigators reasoned "that if there was a civil rights violation, there was probably a citizen complaint about the conduct."[31] Such an assumption overlooked the possibility that many people might not make their complaints official and part of the public record. The tip-of-the-iceberg character of the incidences should have been clear to the investigators, especially since they themselves reported, "When our jurisdiction in the civil rights area was publicized in the local media, we began to receive more than the ordinary number of complaints. One Assistant U.S. Attorney was assigned to screen all of the call-in or walk-in complaints so that they would be handled in a somewhat uniform and consistent fashion."[32]

Milwaukee residents had been making mental note of the numerous questionable deaths at police hands, a disproportionate number of them minorities. One Milwaukee council member listed at least twenty-three persons unjustifiably beaten or killed by Milwaukee police between February 1958 and July 1979.[33] All of the informants for the present study mentioned the Bell case as evidence of the history of excessive use of force and lack of accountability by the Milwaukee police. In addition, one Milwaukee newspaper reporter, interviewed for this study, stated that his editors told him to cover the Lacy controversy extensively because the Milwaukee media had so seriously "messed up" on the Daniel Bell case. At the same time, Milwaukee papers pointed out that although the police had a bad record on excessive use of force, "there were fewer complaints leveled against Milwaukee officers than in some other major cities."[34]

Several ad hoc, grass-roots groups in the African-American community had formed in response to some of these previous questionable deaths. Throughout the marches, speeches, and protests conducted by the Lacy Coalition, constant references were made to these previous deaths, especially the cases of Daniel Bell, Clifford McKissick (1967), and Roger Lyons (1977). Lacy's death, then, for some of these groups and activists, was one more grievance to be added to a long list.[35] Combined with a sympathetic victim, a modest agenda, and experienced leaders, the Lacy Coalition was able to garner significant support.

Ten years after Lacy's death, the deep-rooted nature of Milwaukee police insensitivity was shockingly revealed in an incident concerning a serial killer, Jeffrey Dahmer. In July 1991 Milwaukee police discovered the dismembered bodies of eleven men in the north side apartment of Jeffrey Dahmer. Dahmer quickly confessed to seventeen murders. Almost all of his victims were African-Americans. Milwaukee residents were shocked and saddened by the gruesome mass murders. A few days after the murders were discovered, an aspect of the case was revealed that further outraged many area residents.

In May of 1991 Milwaukee police officers had been called to Dahmer's street by a resident concerned about a naked, bleeding, confused young Asian man in the alleyway and another man seemingly trying to drag him down the alley. When police arrived they talked to Jeffrey Dahmer, who convinced them that the naked youth, Konerak Sinthasomphone, was Dahmer's nineteen-year-old boyfriend who had had a little bit too much alcohol to drink. The officers went to Dahmer's apartment with Sinthasomphone, and after further discussion, left. Dahmer later told investigators that he murdered Sinthasomphone minutes after the police left. He killed five more men before he was caught that July.

While responding to the call that night, the officers discounted repeated questions and comments from neighbors who had come out to observe the scene. The citizen who initially called the Milwaukee 911 emergency number about Sinthasomphone called the police again and tried to press her point that the Asian was "a boy" and not an adult man. The officers responding to her telephone queries, as well as the officers on the scene that night, quickly dismissed her concerns.

The officers did not run a routine background check on Dahmer during their May visit to his apartment. If they had, they would have learned that he was on probation for an earlier sexual offense involving Sinthasomphone's brother. Nor did the officers ask to see any of Sinthasomphone's identification. If they had asked for some ID, they might have learned that he was fourteen years old. The officers left the scene believing Dahmer's story that this was a domestic disturbance, that Sinthasomphone was nineteen and had had too much to drink. Even at that, the legal drinking age in Wisconsin at that time was twenty-one.

To many area residents this incident displayed deep insensitivity and double standards on the part of the Milwaukee police. Gwendolynee Moore, an African-American state legislator from Milwaukee commented, "'It was sort of like, pulling a scab off a very, deep wound.'"[36] The citizen who called in the complaint about the naked youth was an African-American woman; the other witnesses were also African-American. Sinthasomphone was Laotian. Dahmer and the officers were white. Residents said that any person of color suspected of even the slightest infraction in that neighborhood would have had incurred a background check and would have been questioned more closely than the officers questioned Dahmer that night. Gay and lesbian citizens were outraged over the insensitivity police displayed that May night when they decided nothing needed their attention in the Sinthasomphone incident. Further insults were displayed in transcripts of the radio transmissions between the officers and their station when they said, among other things, that they needed to be "deloused" when they returned to the station.

Police Chief Philip Arreola, upon learning of the police mishandling of the Sinthasomphone incident, immediately suspended the officers involved and eventually fired them. In contrast to Chief Breier's denial of police wrongdoing in the Lacy case, Arreola tried to heal community outrage over the police department's handling of the Sinthasomphone and Dahmer encounter.

African-American, Hispanic, and gay and lesbian groups that mobilized in 1991 in reaction to the Dahmer murders and the insensitivity displayed in the Sinthasomphone case were largely pleased with Arreola's response and concerned that his plans for increased police sensitivity training and recruitment of minority officers to the force not be sabotaged by the police officers' association or officers on the beat. Other groups organized at the same time to support the police and oppose the Arreola administration.[37]

Over the years since the Lacy Coalition's struggles, council member and activist Michael McGee has been frustrated by the slow pace of reform in Milwaukee race relations. Despite his involvement in forums and marches protesting police behavior in the Dahmer case, he has seen few results. He has recently advocated the formation of a black militia to take violent action if his demands for racial parity are not met within five years. McGee stated, " 'We've done things the nonviolent way, and it hasn't gotten us anywhere.' "[38] McGee was also a leader in the public forums and marches protesting police behavior in the Dahmer case.

Agenda Politics

The most important thing to know about an interest group, according to Moe, is its goals.[39] The media and those in power often focus attention upon a group's failure to achieve its primary objectives to the exclusion of related, but less visible, accomplishments. Such negative evaluations, Janeway argues, serve to perpetuate beliefs among the weak that they cannot change society: "Devaluing the everyday, the personal, the ordinary, is one way that the judgments of the powerful trivialize the lives of the governed, and so promote the indecision and lack of ambition for which the governed are then criticized. If the weak agree, they will go on distrusting themselves, assuming that the committees or sodalities or clubs they found can never really accomplish anything, merely add a pinch of spice to their drab existence."[40] When attempts by the weak fall short of their goals, "the powerful can laugh at these fools, and the weak themselves have to admit that their clumsy efforts at influencing events don't work well."[41]

Through their period of involvement, the people in the Coalition felt they were viewed by Milwaukee officials and part of the public as doing something wrong. Although the Coalition's actions during the four years following Lacy's death were legal and peaceful, the Coalition and its ability to marshal widespread African-American community support was portrayed as potentially dangerous.

One example lending support to this perception of the Coalition is an editorial in the *Milwaukee Journal* published shortly after Lacy's death. The editorial criticized Chief Breier for his quick pronouncement of his officers' innocence. The editorial cautioned:

Meanwhile, a similar duty to avoid hasty judgment rests on the black community and others in the larger community who suspect that police officers behaved improperly in the Lacy case. Thus, leaders of a mass march that is planned for Monday have a responsibility to restrain rhetoric that assigns guilt before all the facts are known.

It is not unreasonable of Milwaukee's black community to insist upon a thorough investigation into Lacy's death. No one familiar with the generation-long coverup of the police killing of Daniel Bell would expect that community to do less. However, a temperate search for justice will best serve the interests of blacks and the total community.[42]

There were repeated allusions to the 1967 civil rights demonstrations and riots in Milwaukee and the fears of more unrest. One article, for example, ended by reminding readers, "But local and national leaders, in assessing the potential for trouble in a community, have repeatedly said it is trouble with police—particularly the death of a black under questionable circumstances involving the police—that can set off a reaction."[43]

Similarly, when Wisconsin Attorney General Bronson La Follette announced the State Justice Department would assist the Lacy investigation, it was reported that "he had been concerned about racial tensions in Wisconsin communities since racial disturbances erupted in Milwaukee in 1967 and civil rights demonstrators marched through city streets. . . . He feared that 'the Lacy affair could cause similar tensions and be a potential for violence. Nobody gains when that kind of thing happens.' "[44] La Follette remarked that Lacy's death and the emotions it aroused had the "'potential for breeding violence such as that seen in the 1960s.' "[45]

Conjuring up the same memories of the sixties riots, but placing causal emphasis on the police, are the comments by the Reverend

Jesse Jackson. He said he was concerned about the Lacy case because police abuse of force might spread and emphasized that every riot in the sixties had started because of police overreacting.[46] Public officials, editors, and reporters, however, raised the specter of violence again and again in connection with the activities of the Coalition for Justice for Ernest Lacy.[47] A Chicago account says, in part, that the death "spurred community charges of police brutality and fears that Milwaukee could turn into another Miami, where riots erupted after white policemen killed a black man."[48]

In these simple and subtle ways, the weak are "deterred from challenging the powerful by advance persuasion—persuasion which plays on the natural doubts of the governed in order to convince them that they can't trust their own motives when they try to improve their lot."[49] The implication is that voting is the limit of legitimate citizen participation: "In subtle ways the public is constantly reminded that its role is minor, largely passive, and at most reactive."[50] One influence elites retain, then, even during periods of stress and disorder, is defining what is legitimate.[51]

Although the Lacy Coalition leadership attempted to keep larger issues of world racism off the ad hoc group's agenda, the activists recognized that the issue had to be expanded to include a public larger than the African-American community. Protest sometimes expands issues by mobilizing sympathetic, latent publics.[52] The Coalition kept the issue focused on justice for Lacy, while enlarging the targeted public from police and elected officials to what the activists described as "the real power brokers in this town," the business community. This expansion was attempted through two separate boycotts, primarily of downtown stores. McGee explained, "'We're doing this because we're running out of places to vent our anger and frustrations. We feel business has an obligation not to just take our money, but to speak out' about racial injustice."[53] In one member's assessment of lessons learned from the Lacy Coalition, this attempt to expand the issue to the larger society was seen as a tactical mistake.[54] Previously supportive Milwaukee newspaper editors, for example, quickly condemned the boycotts for targeting innocent parties.[55] Definition of the Lacy case beyond the individual officers' excessive use of force and Breier's insensitivity met resistance. Expanding the issues and arguing that Lacy's death was indicative of larger social problems was unsuccessful partly because of the pervasive American belief that problems and solutions should focus on individuals. Deflecting attention from the larger implications of social problems, though, has a conservative influence on the results protest groups might achieve. Yet, if a movement seeks to broaden the scope of its conflict it runs the risk of confusing its unifying symbols and losing support.[56] The Coalition's issues, then, continued to be constructed as illegal police conduct exclusively.

Definition of the Situation

The facts of the case were a major aid to the Coalition. Although the police department and other Milwaukee officials tried to raise questions about Ernest Lacy and blame the victim for his own demise, the facts surrounding Lacy's death kept the focus largely on police conduct. Accounts of previous deaths at the hands of police have often shifted attention onto the victim's conduct; for example, a suspect shot during a chase often is considered to have been engaging in questionable conduct, for why else run from police? But asking about the victim's contribution to the incident deflects attention from the police behavior that dominated its outcome. The police maintained in their defense that Ernest Lacy, after being stopped for questioning, was uncooperative, requiring officers to subdue him. All witnesses to the arrest agreed that Lacy did struggle with police. The question became why: to avoid arrest or to avoid pain?

A 1991 instance of police brutality highlights the importance of the initial battle over the facts of a case between police accused of wrongdoing and outraged citizens. On March 3, 1991, a citizen with a video camera filmed a gang of white Los Angeles, California, police officers beating and kicking an African-American man. The man, Rodney King, had been stopped for a traffic violation. The videotape was incontrovertible evidence of police misconduct. The gut-wrenching footage of a prone, unresisting man being beaten and kicked by four officers while at least eleven other officers looked on was repeatedly broadcast nationally and locally.

Although Rodney King had attempted to evade officers, led them on a high-speed chase, was perhaps intoxicated, and was on parole for previous misdeeds, none of this became the issue in the community outrage over his beating. The police behavior recorded on the videotape seemed indisputable. In the Rodney King case, the issue was from the beginning what the officers on the scene did and whether Los Angeles Police Chief Daryl Gates's leadership set a tone that fed that kind of behavior in the police force.

The Rodney King case ignited citizen mobilization for Gates's resignation. The grass-roots pressure was channeled through preexisting community groups such as the National Association for the Advancement of Colored People, the Brotherhood Crusade, the Urban League, and the American Civil Liberties Union of Southern California.[57] The Los Angeles police had long been a sore point for the African-American and Hispanic communities. The videotape corroborated much of the concerns voiced over the years by these groups against the Los Angeles police. As Karol Heppe, executive director of the Police Misconduct Lawyers Referral Service, told the *New York Times*, "'It's horrible [the Rodney King beating], but I must tell you that we receive complaints in this office of that kind of conduct on a weekly basis, if not on a daily basis. The difference this time is that there was somebody there to videotape it. That's the only difference.'"[58]

In the Rodney King case, Chief Gates suspended the officers involved and charges were brought against them. Under intense community criticism of his management, Gates also announced that he would soon retire.[59] In the spring of 1992 four of the officers were tried for their violations of the law when they arrested Rodney King. A change of venue had been granted for the trial. The jury chosen from Simi Valley consisted of ten whites, one Hispanic, and one Asian-American. In the lengthy trial, defense attorneys for the accused officers portrayed Rodney King as uncooperative and threatening to the arresting officers. The jury's verdict acquitting the officers of all charges (except one that resulted in a hung jury) shocked many people worldwide. In Los Angeles the verdict triggered the deadliest and costliest riots in twentieth-century America.

In the Milwaukee case, in contrast, Ernest Lacy, according to the police, harmed himself. From the first news article on his death, the facts that Lacy had been receiving full disability payments because of an emotional handicap, was treated for mental illness, and had been on medication were mentioned as mitigating factors in his death.[60] In fact, two days after his death a *Milwaukee Sentinel* headline read "Fright May Have Caused Man's Death after His Arrest." The same *Milwaukee Sentinel* article quoted the medical examiner: "Asked if it was possible that Lacy might have been scared to death, Erwin said 'something like that. We wouldn't call it that . . . but we're talking about the same thing.' "[61] The paper also quoted Warren B. Hill, the deputy medical examiner, who "said of the possibility that fright caused the death: 'Doctors don't like to use the term, since you can't see it at an autopsy. But it's a possibility, sure, especially since the family has indicated he had a strong fear of police and being confined in enclosed places.' "[62] Fear was still advanced as a plausible cause of death a few days later when Erwin stated that his earlier theory that Lacy might have been "'frightened to death' " remained a strong possibility.[63]

Later reports showed that Lacy had been diagnosed and treated as schizophrenic and psychotic.[64] Speculation about Lacy's failure to take prescribed tranquilizers raised issues of personal culpability in his own death.[65] One leader of the Coalition recalled and interpreted such statements as follows: "Initially, they came out and said that he was on drugs; and then when that was proven not to be true, then they said he should have been. So, you know, they wanted to have it both ways." In addition, Ernest's mother described him as a peaceful, docile, emotionally troubled young man. She added, "'He was petrified of the police. And he would never, never, never ever try to harm one, because he was so petrified.' "[66]

The outcome of the battle between contradictory renditions of the events leading up to Lacy's death (the police story of a suspect resisting arrest and being subdued or the Coalition's story of a frightened young black man roughed up and killed by white officers) was central to the outcome of the conflict. The symbolic definition of an incident is a powerful political resource. Defining situations and manipulating symbols mean, for instance, "questionable applications of coercive force may be applauded in the name of 'law and order,' while unpopular but peaceful protests are defined as 'violent.' "[67]

Lacy's acknowledged innocence and the inability of the police to offer an adequate explanation for his death helped the Coalition maintain broad-based support. As one Coalition activist saw it:

We had the religious support, the political, and [pause] it ended up in a really firm foundation where there really wasn't any negatives from our side of the fence and everyone was united against a common enemy which was seen as the police. With clear facts for the first time this time, too. It was clear that Ernie Lacy wasn't doing anything. Some of the families, say their son stole a car and he was killed in the process, they might get tired of hearing that he was a thief, 'he stole this and he stole that.' In the Lacy case, her son was innocent and he was proven innocent. And this was the first time that it was a clear-cut case of an innocent person without any shadow of a doubt to his being guilty. And so it was a lot of different things going for this that was absent from the others.

Adding to the outrage in the African-American community were numerous reports that the officers involved in Lacy's death had had other citizen complaints filed against them.[68] One African-American minister explained in his interview, "All the wrongs that we had been used to seemed to be evident in this case." The Coalition was never deflected by a need to defend or explain Lacy's behavior prior to his arrest. Had Lacy been guilty of the rape he was stopped for, the activists doubted that the Coalition would have drawn the same level of support, or even formed at all.

This assessment corroborates Garrow's discussion of how any taint of criminality, violence (even in self-defense), or "badness" on the part of victims alters the public's interpretation of conflicts. The victims of police aggression must be pure or the focus shifts to how they brought this on themselves and are undeserving of public concern. The suffering of a sympathetic victim can attract public outrage, while the equally unjust suffering of a less-than-pure victim might not.[69]

Anti-Breier Aspects

Police Chief Harold Breier had long been a severe problem for the African-American community in Milwaukee. It was not the only group with grievances against Breier. Milwaukee feminists were treated offhandedly by Breier when they attempted to create more police department services for victims of sexual assault. Some activists in the Lacy Coalition had been active throughout the seventies in attempts to "oust Breier." Breier further damaged his reputation by announcing almost immediately after the report of Lacy's death that his officers were " 'guilty of no wrongdoing.' "[70] The Milwaukee media had also been critical of Breier. A *Milwaukee Journal* editorial prompted by the Lacy case and the police beating of a white businessman, James Schoemperlen, repeated its earlier proposal that Breier retire for the good of the community.[71]

Throughout the months of investigation and public uproar, Breier showed no sympathy for advocates of better police-community relations. In a meeting with Christine Belnavis, president of the Milwaukee branch of the NAACP, Breier said, "'I don't think you can evaluate your officers on the basis of complaints made against them. I think that you have to remember one thing: that when officers make arrests, people must submit. They cannot resist.'"[72] He antagonized protesters by his presence at marches, reluctantly implemented orders to suspend the officers while awaiting a decision regarding complaints of excessive use of force, and called the members of the Coalition for Justice for Ernest Lacy various derogatory names. Breier called them "radicals" and pointed out that communist and socialist groups were included in the Coalition.[73] He said Coalition leader Howard Fuller was a "Marxist" spewing hate for the police.[74] He also contrasted the Coalition with the "good people" of Milwaukee who supported the police.[75]

Other groups also renewed their calls for Breier's retirement in the light of his behavior in the Lacy controversy. A Fire and Police Commission member, the heads of the Milwaukee police union, and the League of Martin all agreed that to have a true police-community relations program in Milwaukee, Breier had to step down or be removed.[76]

Leadership Roles

One factor in the formation of the Coalition was the presence in the African-American community at the time of Lacy's death of active, politically seasoned leaders ready to add the Lacy death to their list of grievances against the city. Salisbury's discovery of the importance of activists from old groups in founding new ones is substantiated in the Lacy Coalition.[77] For example, activists were quickly recruited from the Save North Division High School Coalition (a neighborhood school controversy) and the Coalition to Oust Breier into the Lacy Coalition. In addition, the dynamics of an ad hoc protest group diminished the conservative tendencies of organizational leaders found by Piven and Cloward. From their study of long-term, sustained and organized poor people's movements they assert that while organizations are not futile,

the more important point is that by endeavoring to do what they cannot do, organizers fail to do what they can do. During those brief periods in which people are roused to indignation, when they are prepared to defy the authorities to whom they ordinarily defer, during those brief moments when lower-class groups exert some force against the state, those who call themselves leaders do not usually escalate the momentum of the people's protest. They do not because they are preoccupied with trying to build and sustain embryonic formal organizations in the sure conviction that these organizations will enlarge and become powerful.[78]

The Lacy leaders were not trying to build organizations but rather to annoy and shame city leaders enough that they would investigate the Lacy death and punish those responsible. These specific goals had a ripple effect by hastening the retirement of the police chief, increasing the pressure on the Wisconsin legislature for police reform, and influencing votes in the common council on police funding.

Two leaders in particular, Howard Fuller and Michael McGee, were instrumental in keeping the Coalition together. Previous group responses to excessive use of force in Milwaukee were hampered by division between what one Lacy activist called "the old guard black elite" and "the younger blood." The lack of such divisions in the Lacy struggle was partly attributable to the experience and eloquence of these two individuals. Howard Fuller, for example, has been active in African-American politics for more than twenty years. He worked as a community organizer in Chicago and as a poverty program director in North Carolina. He also founded Malcolm X Liberation University in Greensboro, North Carolina, in the 1970s.[79]

The leadership made one decision that interviewees saw as central to minimizing divisiveness: the group would focus exclusively on Ernest Lacy's death and leave alone outside issues and statements about world racism, imperialism, the Reagan administration, and South Africa. The leadership knew this would effectively preempt left-wing groups from joining the Lacy bandwagon to promote their own interests. In fact, at the first few Coalition meetings, people from the All African's Revolutionary People's Party criticized the emerging leaders for their inclusion of whites on the steering committee of the Coalition. The leaders had seen this before and waited out the radicals. Eventually, one leader said, the troublemakers just got tired and bored and went back to where they came from.

The visibility of Fuller and McGee during the Lacy case helped cement their positions as leaders in the Milwaukee African-American community. Their activities in the Lacy Coalition, as well as their previous active commitment to the cause of civil rights, helped each achieve higher office. Fuller later became the secretary of employment relations for the newly elected Wisconsin governor, Tony Earl. McGee, during the early years of the Lacy controversy, was director of the United Black Community Council. He had been a political activist in Milwaukee, well-known for his criticism of the police. After unsuccessful bids in 1976 and 1980, he successfully ran for the Milwaukee Common Council in 1984. In fact, he noted with a touch of irony, it was not his ten years of previous dogged community service that got him elected, but mostly the publicity from the Lacy case.

Networks and Coalition Politics

The details of the incident, the history of race tensions, and police misconduct contributed to the intensity of community response in the Lacy case. The formation of the Lacy Coalition illustrates several aspects of group formation theories. There was a disturbing incident upsetting the power equilibrium, as Truman's theory predicts.[80] In addition, a few leaders played the role of Salisbury's "entrepreneurs/organizers."[81] The difference from Salisbury's entrepreneurs was that his study was on permanently organized farm groups whereas the Lacy Coalition was a temporary, issue-specific alliance. People join groups based on a variety of incentives, including solidary and purposive. Solidary incentives derive from a sense of belonging and include friendships and social acceptance. Purposive incentives arise from moral, ideological, or religious principles.[82] Mancur Olson distinguishes between the rational reasons to join a group offering selective incentives and the rational reasons not to join a group where goals are nondivisible collective goods.[83] Olson's scholarship challenges researchers to explain entities like the four ad hoc groups examined in this book. Free riders, people who do not contribute to a cause but will nonetheless share in any benefits the group achieves, probably weakened the potential public response for all four groups, since their goals were public goods. Obtaining a measure of justice for Lacy and inhibiting similar police behavior, for example, would be public goods, available to the entire community. Although certainly there were free riders and the Lacy Coalition was not as big in formal organization as its adherents in Milwaukee might have been, the group was mobilized and sustained its pressure for four years because the Lacy Coalition drew upon the resources and community-mindedness of the civil rights movement, a long-term social movement in America. As pointed out by Terry Moe, "values other than economic self-interest are often important determinants of individual behavior."[84] People have heterogeneous value structures motivating them to participate in group politics.

Numerous established groups joined the Lacy Coalition. The un-

derlying reason spurring the growth of the Coalition was summed up
by one Baptist minister: " 'You mean to tell me we can't even go to the
store and get something to eat without showing up missing.' "[85] Or, as
the president of the Milwaukee branch of the NAACP said, " 'There
comes a point where you don't take any more. The Lacy case was the
straw that broke the camel's back. He is the 23d victim in the last
10 years who has lost his life at the hands of our police.' "[86] The Coalition for Justice for Ernest Lacy became one of the largest coalitions
in Milwaukee politics, including at its height more than 125 groups
(see Table 1).

Organizing as a coalition of groups under the leadership of Fuller
and McGee had definite advantages for Lacy activists. Costain found
that lobbying through ad hoc issue coalitions won favor with women's
rights supporters because "they found that this method of lobbying
allowed individual groups to retain their autonomy, an important con-
sideration given the diversity of active groups, while it brought together organizations with sufficient resources to lobby effectively."[87]
An ad hoc coalition, as opposed to an umbrella organization, makes
cooperation much easier "when it is structured on an issue-by-issue
basis, permitting a great deal of group autonomy."[88] An ad hoc issue
coalition also permits a wide variety of group members since "groups
only need to agree on a single issue to join."[89]

The coalition structure also allowed for diverse, yet complemen-
tary, political styles. The Lacy Coalition, for example, could pursue a
single course of action (prosecution of the officers) while supportive
and parallel groups devoted time and energy to larger issues and different tactics. The local NAACP chapter, for example, was instrumental
in persuading the mayor to set up a special "Lacy Monitoring Committee." The NAACP presented detailed proposals for comprehensive reforms in police hiring, firing, and promotion practices to the Lacy Committee. The national NAACP was concerned about police-community
relations, and the local branch drew upon previous NAACP research
and recommendations in responding to Lacy's death. The leadership
of the Lacy Coalition saw the NAACP's efforts as paralleling and not
conflicting with their activities, but as an ineffectual blue-ribbon study
committee. Actually, the NAACP performed a role similar to that of
the African-American leadership in Atlanta, where "younger" and
older, "establishment" leaders used the strengths of diverse approaches to pressure for reform.[90] In addition, the protest activities of

Table 1. A Partial List of Organizations within the Lacy Coalition

AFL-CIO
A. O. Smith Steelworkers Union
A. Phillip Randolph Institute
All Afro People's Revolutionary Party
Bread and Roses Health Center
Career Youth Development
Church Inc.
Coalition to Oust Chief Breier
Coalition to Save North Division
Commandos
Communist Party of Wisconsin
Community Advocates
Consumers United
Counseling Center of Milwaukee, Inc.
Cross Lutheran Church
Democratic Socialist Organizing
Committee of Wisconsin
East Side Housing Action Council
(ESHAC)
Electrical Radio and Machine Workers
of America Local 1111
Federal Council for Community
Concerns
Gay Peoples' Union
Harambee Community Center
HOPE
Human Concerns Office of the
Milwaukee Catholic Archdiocese
Inner City Development Project North
Journey House
Justice and Peace Center
Ko Thi Dancers
Latin American Union for Civil Rights
Legal Action of Wisconsin
Local 1055 American Federation of
State, County, and Municipal
Employees
Lutheran Church of America
Marquette University Center for
Interracial Justice
Marquette University Equal
Opportunities Program
Marquette University Upward Bound

Martin Luther King Center
Martin Luther King Coalition
Midtown Neighborhood Association
Milwaukee Area Technical College
Black Student Association
Milwaukee Associates in Urban
Development
Milwaukee Urban League
Mobilization for Survival
NAACP
National Association of Black
Criminal Justice
National Association of Black
Veterans
National Association of Professional
Black Fire Fighters
National Conference of Black Lawyers
Neighbors United
Next Door Foundation
North Side Neighbors Together
Northwest Action Alliance
Northwest Action Council
Office of Black Catholic Concerns
Organization of Organizations
Park West Redevelopment Corp.
People's Anti-War Mobilization
Project Equality
Project Respect, Spanish Center
St. Agnes Catholic Church
16th Street Health Center
Socialist Workers Party
Take Back the Neighborhood
United Auto Workers Local 438
United Black Community Council
University of Wisconsin–Milwaukee
Student Association
Welfare Advocacy
West Side Housing Cooperative
Wisconsin Black Lawyers Association
Women against Rape
Women's Coalition
Worker Rights Institute
Workers World Party.[91]

the Lacy Coalition made it easier for more moderate groups, like the NAACP, to gain access to municipal leaders, a phenomena also noted in Costain's study of women's lobbying.[92] The activities of the Lacy Coalition corroborate Costain's conclusion that "this pattern of cooperative lobbying through ad hoc issue coalitions seems to be one way in which a diffuse interest with few resources can rapidly bring together and hold together sympathetic groups to achieve collective impact on the legislative process."[93]

There are also potential weaknesses for an ad hoc group. Hayes describes the likelihood of noninterference, nondecision, delegation, and symbolic reassurance in policy conflicts where the opposition is weak or unorganized.[94] The problem with an ad hoc group is that officials realize that these challengers are temporary and will fade away, especially if given placating reassurances. At the same time, though, a group such as the Lacy Coalition demarcates a volatile latent public. What government officials might seek is avoiding dramatic, clear-cut, personalized cases of injustice and soothing the aroused public back into quiescence. As Edelman observes, "Restiveness occurs when the state is not symbolically aligned with those who feel threatened."[95]

Impact of Temporary Organizations

Issue of Accountability

In addition to the issue of excessive use of force by the police in Milwaukee, the Coalition raised the issue of local governmental accountability. The lack of accountability of Chief Breier to the public had long been an issue. After reviewing the relevant statutes pertaining to the authority of the mayor, the common council, and the Fire and Police Commission vis-á-vis the police, the 1980 Justice Department investigation concluded, "The end result of this statutory scheme is that the Milwaukee Police Department is effectively accountable to no one."[96] Howard Fuller, one of the two main leaders of the Coalition, said, "'The police are supposed to be servants of the community. But in Milwaukee we have a department, symbolized by its chief, that operates above its community.'"[97]

There is evidence of a cultural ethos within police departments marked by resistance to change, cynicism about people, defensiveness about any criticism of police, assumed omniscience, and hostility to the beliefs of social scientists, courts, and other intruders.[98] Hints of this same ethos were evident in the response of Milwaukee police from the chief down to patrol officers. One officer who arrested Lacy, for example, viewed his and the other two arresting officers' positions as being "pawns in the game of politics."[99] An African-American police officer interviewed by the *Milwaukee Journal* voiced an observation similar to Scheingold's: "'You see, the thing is white cops are afraid of black people. . . . When they stop a black guy, they're overcautious. They got their hands on their guns. I've seen those guys.'"[100] The same officer concluded, "If you're that scared of people, you shouldn't even be in the community."[101] Replacing a chief, in such circumstances, will have only limited effect on changing attitudes and behavior at the street level. The 1991 Dahmer case tragically provides compelling evidence of the extent of the cultural insensitivity within the Milwaukee police force. The behavior of officers in the Rodney King case is further proof of the need for widescale organizational reforms above and beyond replacing police chiefs.

Members of the Coalition who were active in local issues before the Lacy incident also saw the case as further evidence of the frustrating lack of responsiveness by the mayor to African-American community concerns. One long-time local African-American politician, also active in the Lacy Coalition, expressed these frustrations: "The most amazing thing to me is that the mayor has a reputation nation-wide amongst the U.S. Conference of Mayors as a liberal, very liberal, mayor. Yet, in the city of Milwaukee, he's been the mayor since 1960, he has never appointed a black department head." Others pointed out the mayor never challenged Chief Breier and police policy, conveniently blaming his inaction on legislation that made him powerless. The lack of interest by Mayor Maier in African-American community concerns supports Peter Eisinger's finding that Milwaukee's black population is an unnecessary, and to some groups an even undesirable, component of winning political coalitions.[102]

Reforms

Many activists interviewed for this study attributed the June 1984 retirement of the seventy-two-year-old Breier, after twenty years as chief, to the activities of the Coalition for Justice for Lacy; in addition, part of the criteria in the search for a new chief was that he or she work on police community relations. Chief Breier, other observers pointed out, was old and in ill health. These personal circumstances contributed to his decision to step down.

The Lacy case also sparked two successful state legislative changes.

One bill, known as "the Lacy bill," specifically made the abuse or neglect of a suspect in custody a crime. The impetus was the circuit court ruling that the charges against the Lacy officers of failure to render first aid as required by police department rules did not have legal status. Second, the Wisconsin legislature in the spring of 1984 removed the life term for future Milwaukee police chiefs and shifted power from the chief to the city's Fire and Police Commission, the mayor, and the common council. Similar legislation had been introduced yearly, usually by African-American Milwaukee legislators, since at least the early seventies. The Lacy controversy provided more ammunition to those in the legislature arguing for these legal changes. The bill was introduced by two African-American Milwaukee legislators; arguments about the merits of the bill relied heavily on the Lacy case. Although the police officers involved were never tried for Lacy's death, these ancillary developments related to the Coalition's efforts left many of the members with the sense that they had been effective.

The influence of the Lacy struggles was visible in the 1991 Dahmer case when Police Chief Arreola quickly suspended the officers involved in the Sinthasomphone incident. Howard Fuller also noted the entirely different response of the leadership of the police department concerning the Lacy incident and the Dahmer case ten years later.[103] Grass-roots dissent such as in the Lacy struggle adds to a confluence of pressures for accountability and decent human treatment by police officers. Howard Fuller pointed out that by 1991 Milwaukee had a new mayor, a new county executive, and a new police chief, which made a different atmosphere for handling conflicts such as in the Dahmer case.

The response of the Milwaukee police chief in 1991, though, was vehemently opposed by the Milwaukee Police Officers Association and many of the rank-and-file police. Several officers harkened back wistfully to the days when Breier was chief and asserted that Breier would have supported his officers and stood up to these "political" pressures.[104]

In the eighties, the Lacy bills, the rejection of the Law Enforcement Assistance Administration funding request, and the retirement of Breier show the diversity of audiences the Lacy protest group addressed. Garrow points out that protests involve three sets of actors, the protesters, their immediate opponents, and the larger audience that is not directly involved in the conflict at the outset.[105] The Lacy Coalition influenced all three audiences. Media coverage of Lacy's death and Coalition activities were extensive. The Coalition's spotlighting of the Lacy incident, their references to previous cases of questionable police conduct, and their ability to stitch together a broad coalition influenced the third audience of the Milwaukee Common Council and Wisconsin legislature and helped shape the outcome of their political mobilization.

The likelihood that these changes might be mostly symbolic reassurances is strong, given the track record of many reform efforts. Laced throughout newspaper accounts of the Coalition's efforts and prominent in the interviews was activists' explanation that they sought "a measure of justice" for Ernest Lacy. Edelman notes, "Unambiguous failure of a group to achieve a political objective is followed by a lowering of the aspiration level." He continues, "Such moderation of objectives is precisely the contrary of what common assumption would suggest: that failure should increase efforts to attain political goals." [106] The Coalition's agenda reaffirms the work of others that even before conflict is engaged in, challengers might grant concessions to the powerful while the powerful take no overt action. [107] Group goals, though, were partially achieved because of a sense of community and contribution to long-term struggles by members. These are expressive and solidary incentives.

In the long term, memories of the Lacy case and the legitimacy of the Lacy Coalition's grievances became part of the community's political history and were conjured up when new outrages occurred. When it was revealed in 1991 that Milwaukee police had disregarded the concerns of three African-American female citizens and returned a drunk, bleeding, and naked fourteen-year-old Asian boy to Jeffrey Dahmer, the insensitivity of the officers seemed to fit a pattern similar to the issues raised by the Bell and Lacy cases.

Public Education

Many of the people interviewed for this study believe in the potential of public education, or consciousness-raising, to correct inequities in the system. American reformers often believe that social problems can be resolved by education and improved communication. [108] The Lacy case offers a twofold lesson Coalition members sought to teach: Lacy died because of a police force that was unaccountable and there is an unfair double standard of justice.

One Coalition leader said the delays during 1981–82 caused frustration and there were many "lows"; however, she said the delays caused people "to really begin to see what was really going on." Particularly striking is the statement of a decade-long activist, a one-time member of the Black Panthers, who stated during his interview in no uncertain terms that Lacy was murdered by a racist police force: "One thing you have to remember is that as an organizer what you do is you raise people's consciousness through organizing efforts" and "you show up the catch-22" in the system.

Within this view is a faith that "the people," if shown the facts of an injustice, will react righteously. Myrtle Lacy, for example, stated: "'Every time we would go before the people, we would always get justice. When we went to the judiciary system, that's when everything broke down.'"[109] She added that people have to unite, fight injustice wherever they find it, and educate others.

The theme of education is especially evident in the lives of three white Catholic nuns who had been teachers at Catholic elementary schools in what are now African-American neighborhoods. They were very active in the Lacy Coalition; one of them served on the Steering Committee. Each had devoted between thirty-five and fifty years to teaching. They believe education is the avenue to correct prejudicial attitudes and, therefore, achieve social reforms. In a statement more revealing about the public role of women of her generation than she probably realizes, one of them said, of her teaching career, "In my life, that was the only way I could" try to solve social problems. She said it gave her hope to see people fighting back, as in the Lacy Coalition. Through their activities, people learn there are higher values and commitments.

The Community and the Struggles

The African-Americans interviewed for this study consistently used two phrases when talking about their lives and the Coalition for Justice for Ernest Lacy: *the community* and *the struggles*. Even though some led quiet, private lives until their involvement in the Lacy struggle, they placed themselves within the African-American community in Milwaukee and the nation. From this sense of community they believed that their months of activities, such as picketing shopping centers in a Wisconsin winter, were worthwhile and important. These are partially expressive needs, desires to voice identities with a cause, but not necessarily to do more.[110] There are a multitude of expressive groups in a political system because of low membership costs (signing a petition or sending dues), but they will also be highly unstable and transient. Therefore, leaders might engage in solidary building actions, such as protests.[111]

Their community identifications meant that purposive benefits could also serve as selective incentives. People receive purposive benefits not exclusively from achieving a goal but also from the personal satisfaction derived from the act of contributing to worthwhile collective goods. In contrast to Mancur Olson's rational choice analysis, then, collective goods can generate their own selective incentives, and a rational, conscientious person may view the free-rider option as morally reprehensible.[112] In this broader view of interest groups, individuals might feel that their "contributions 'make a difference' for political outcomes," providing a perception of efficacy and personal rationality for joining groups working for collective goods.[113]

For the members of the Lacy family, there were three goals: discover the truth about Lacy's death, punish those responsible, and contribute to the larger African-American community by diminishing the chances that the police would do this again. One family member stated that although Ernest would not have become a lawyer, "or anything like that," she believed his life had importance because his death fit into the long-term "struggles" and would, perhaps, ensure that "other people didn't go through the pain that we had"; and she added: "I think as nothing else in this city, Ernie had a death that brought more people together than anything has. Never before had people joined forces [pause] ah, not only black people, but there were white, people of all colors. [pause] And the Coalition was really like a family to us." During the delays and frustrations this same person drew strength from the group: "You think of all the people who made sacrifices, who marched in the streets and who were—a lot of people were threatened, and yet they were determined to see a measure of justice done. And this is something that you can kind of look back on with a sense of pride. And even though Ernest's death was—was totally, totally, totally wrong, you think sometimes, it brought so many people together. You know, I think about that."

An intertwined theme for these activists was that of "the struggles" for civil rights. They knew that they were within what Bellah and his coauthors call "a community of memory" and hope: knowledgeable about their history and connecting their aspirations to a larger whole.[114]

Seeing themselves and their struggles within such a community of memory places the Lacy controversy in a long-term time frame. One Coalition activist explained, "The struggle continued in spite of tiredness. You go on and on and don't expect success in one day."

The strength derived from knowing they belonged to such a community helped these activists face conflict, hostility, and potential danger. Myrtle Lacy, for example, admitted that fighting the system takes its toll: "'We've received letters from people who've said they were glad [Ernest] was dead and they hoped all my family would be murdered,' she said. 'All we have to do,' she told the group, 'is unite and let people know that we will refuse to take any more of these injustices.' If not, Lacy said, 'they will continue to happen, if we don't decide enough is enough.'"[115] Many people mentioned in their interviews that they received hate mail and threatening phone calls and experienced hostility from people when on picket lines. One long-time African-American activist said this conflict was "a constant" in his life.

These conflicts are not unexpected, for as Robert Coles argues, African-Americans do not need their consciousnesses raised about why they might be unhappy. Black children are taught that life is difficult in the white world. When little children must face angry mobs during school integration confrontations, they draw on their history and the support of their community and families to carry on. African-Americans, therefore, "did not have to become angry; they had to learn how to contain their anger."[116] In this struggle for Lacy, one white participant observed: "You could see the power developing and the confidence that people were beginning to feel, that something was happening. They had felt police brutality for many, many years and they felt that something, at least something, was being done to stay the hand of the police force."

The formation of the Lacy Coalition was augmented by the strength of family members, particularly Lacy's mother, Myrtle. Throughout the years of controversy over the case, the family maintained a dignified presence, which reminded the public that Ernest's death hurt a family; he was not just a police department statistic. From the time the immediate family went to the morgue to identify the body it marshalled a large extended family for support and solidarity. Two days later eighteen members of the family sat through the preliminary investigation on the cause of death. The month-long coroner's inquest was similarly attended daily by family members. Newspaper coverage of the Lacy story was sensitive to their presence and influence, portraying it as a close-knit family.

The Lacy family endured extensive media scrutiny. The details of Myrtle's life, her estrangement from her husband, and her poor financial circumstances (the family received welfare) were included in press accounts of the controversy. Nevertheless, Myrtle's dignity, religious faith (she is a minister's daughter), and visibility as a loving, grieving mother strengthened the Coalition. Ernest's death and Myrtle's anguish symbolized the fears of many families. These symbols are central in political communications and mobilization.[117] The apolitical, private Lacy family drew upon some of the "powers of the weak" described by Elizabeth Janeway:

> To put it at its simplest and briefest, the weak do have to learn to be brave. Or, better, they have to learn to be *brave in a different fashion.* For there is indeed a kind of courage that's very familiar to the weak: endurance, patience, stamina, the ability to repeat everyday tasks every day, these are the forms of courage that have allowed generations of the governed to survive without losing ultimate hope. The knowledge of one's own vulnerability, the choice of restraint in the face of provocation, the ability to hear oneself described as unworthy without accepting the stigma as final—that takes courage of a high order. We do not want to lose it, simply to supplement it, for it's still a source of strength when the time comes to be patient no longer, when direct confrontation with the powerful for independent aims must be risked if not sought.[118]

Religion

One element in the family's perseverance was the deep religious conviction of the Lacys. One of the first people the family called on to accompany them through meetings with lawyers, medical examiners, and district attorneys was their minister. The Lacy family minister, Rev. Harry L. Hendricks, Sr., of the Church of the Living God, became a regular participant in the Coalition. The highly visible involvement of him and another minister, the Reverend Claude Joyner, of Incarnation Lutheran Church, provided an added measure of legitimacy in the eyes of the public to the Lacy Coalition.

Indigenous organizations, such as churches, represent what Freeman describes as a co-optable network for new groups. Inclusion of religious leaders and church activists in the Lacy Coalition strengthened and eased formation of the group since it mobilized such a previously organized and co-optable network. The religious element in the Coalition grew, becoming more than the personal faith of the family, taking on a dimension of its own as more and more clergy and religious activists joined the Coalition. For example, Wisconsin religious leaders representing the eleven judicatories of the Greater Milwaukee Conference on Religion and Urban Affairs asked for suspension of the officers pending a full investigation. Included were influential Lutheran and Catholic leaders.[119] The Coalition, for example, held its meetings either at the Church of the Living God or at Incarnation Lutheran Church.

The religious component of the Lacy Coalition had deep roots in African-American politics. Religious leaders and churches have always been enclaves of freedom, education, and community for African-Americans.[120] Although religion often emphasizes happiness and justice in an afterlife, foregoing advocating justice in this life, a religion such as the Christianity embraced by many African-Americans is a double-edged sword. As Genovese noted in his study of American slaves:

The doctrine, "Render therefore unto Caesar the things which are Caesar's; and unto God the things that are God's," is deceptively two-edged. If it calls for political submission to the powers that be, it also calls for militant defense of the freedom of the spirit and the autonomy of the personality. But the master-slave relationship rests, psychologically as well as ideologically, on the transformation of the will of the slave into an extension of the will of the master. Thus, no matter how obedient—how Uncle Tomish—Christianity made a slave, it also drove deep into his soul an awareness of the moral limits of submission, for it placed a master above his own master and thereby dissolved the moral and ideological ground on which the very principle of absolute human lordship must rest.[121]

Elizabeth Janeway also argues that religion can strengthen the powerful as well as serve the weak, by undermining the legitimacy of oppressors, "by keeping alive for them a sense of their personal significance and value and assuring them that they are seen and judged by a present God. This assurance can indeed keep the weak quiet and satisfied; but it doesn't always work this way. Access to the Godhead can also convince men and women to take issue with the powerful, to denounce the princes of this world as heretics, sinners, or oppressors."[122] Religious faith can also help dissolve the cynicism about collective action, which is so prevalent in modern society.[123]

Reverend Harry L. Hendricks, Sr., drew on these strengths during his sermon at Ernest's funeral:

"I heard on the recent news that Chief Breier does not submit to the demands of the public," Hendricks said. "No, but there's someone he will submit to."

Some of the mourners applauded.

And, Hendricks said, "the same men who took Ernie's life will have to stand before judgment, will have to stand before Jesus." [124]

Another activist, a member of the NAACP reflected that though the police officers were suspended, "nothing else has been done. There has not been a margin of justice, in our opinion, for the Lacy family. We feel that, as a patient people, as a tolerant people, as a strong people, we will bide our time, as in the Bell case." After all, she continued, her people understand justice will prevail in the long run. Like members of the Lacy family, this woman was actively religious.

People take comfort from believing tragic events are explainable and losses are for a higher cause. The anguish felt at the death of a family member can be mitigated if it can be justified. Some families with members killed in the Vietnam War are still struggling with feelings that their loss was senseless. [125] The Lacy family felt lowest when, in the words of Ernest's sister, they thought "he died for nothing." [126]

One member of the immediate family related that her lowest point came after a disillusioning procedural setback. She began to question her faith in a just God. She felt she tried so hard, but had failed to achieve some measure of justice for Ernie. She explained, "I just felt like I had failed [pause] and I said, 'It's over. And we tried and it's like it's always been. There is no justice.' " She only recovered her commitment to continue the struggle when another family member made her read the Psalms of David with him. She then regained her conviction that events, even the most tragic and unjust, have a community meaning: "I knew that, whatever we had to face in the future, that we could do it because you can't give up. Because it's not just Ernie Lacy, or your son, it's all the Ernie Lacy's." She summarized her mixed emotions and how she contained her anger: "I think had it not been for our strong religious belief, that perhaps things would have gotten out of hand at certain points—we are blessed with a belief in God and it carried us through. And I'm grateful for that. It's not easy sitting in a courtroom and hear somebody talk about somebody like they were a nonperson, that they never existed. And not feel some kinds of remorse, or, anger, or whatever. And you have to pray a lot."

This same woman believed that God had a hand in Ernie's death, "his time had come," and that through his death he brought people together into a coalition that became like a family, affirming a sense of community and dignity. She would never have met people like Fuller, McGee, and "the sisters" (white, Catholic nuns who were active in the Coalition), without the tragedy of a family member's death forcing her into action. These people and the community spirit felt at the sit-in at the district attorney's office and prayer meetings for Lacy were, to her, "what true Christian fellowship is all about."

Conclusion

The Lacy Coalition was composed of two elements. One consisted of the formerly private, politically inactive family and friends forced into taking a political stance but able to rise to the occasion with religious and community support. The other element comprised the black and white political activists who saw in Lacy's death further proof of a double standard of justice and came to the aid of the Lacy family through community ties.

The Lacy case shows the utility of a coalition approach to pressure for change. Achieving change is difficult, however, even when a group is well motivated and organized. The people interviewed for this study understood that the likelihood of achieving "justice" for Ernest Lacy was remote. Activists placed the incident into a context of ongoing injustices. Given their historic perspective and their ties to the larger, long-term struggles of the African-American community, they take some comfort from incremental results, "a measure of justice," a faith in public education, and satisfaction of their expressive incentives.

Even in their mobilization, some people temper or moderate their political requests based on realistic assessments of relative chances for success derived from knowledge of past unredressed injustices and recalcitrance by government. The Lacy Coalition realized that its highest goal, seeing the officers involved tried and convicted for murder, would not be achieved. Therefore, they moderated their goal to achieve "a measure of justice" for Ernest Lacy. The measure of justice was a small incremental step in the continuous struggle of African-Americans to gain civil rights.

The Lacy case also shows the ability of government to shape the tone and nature of the issues debated. Individual feelings of political efficacy or alienation depend on the time frame and historical context of the group the person identifies with. Individuals in the Coalition for Justice for Ernest Lacy identified with the historical and continuing struggle for black civil rights in America. Based on such identifications, real "justice" for Ernest Lacy was acknowledged to be unobtainable. Instead, group mobilization was joined and protest waged to notify government officials that a boundary of acceptable or unchallenged grievances had been crossed. The notification demarcated the existence of a latent African-American community interest expecting a modicum of civility and restraint from excessive force from government officials.

The hope was to diminish the chances of future civilian deaths at the hands of police officers. The activists' vision for the future was based on an abiding faith in a potential goodness in the human spirit and faith that through public education racial injustice will gradually disappear. Du Bois found a similar theme in the lyrics of the "sorrow songs," black spirituals: "Through all the sorrow of the Sorrow Songs there breathes a hope—a faith in the ultimate justice of things. The minor cadences of despair change often to triumph and calm confidence. Sometimes it is faith in life, sometimes a faith in death, sometimes assurance of boundless justice in some fair world beyond. But whichever it is, the meaning is always clear: that sometime, somewhere, men will judge men by their souls and not by their skins. Is such a hope justified? Do the Sorrow Songs sing true?" [127] This challenge to unjust authority exemplifies what Barrington Moore described as the desire for decent human treatment. [128] Informants for this study echoed this desire, pointing out that the officers didn't even have the decency to take the unconscious Lacy to the hospital. If they had performed even the simplest act of kindness, "telling him why they were doing this to him," it would have "said a lot for them." Instead, they treated him "like a dog."

Coalition leaders, the family, and clergy gathered yearly at the site of Ernest's death for prayer vigils. The influence of their historic and community point of view should be incorporated into theories of group mobilization and demise, continuing to broaden the view of interest groups. These "communities of memory" from which strength to become active arises are an important element in interest-group politics and help explain the efforts of the Coalition for Justice for Ernest Lacy. The findings reveal a temperate, moderate quest for a "measure of justice" for Ernest Lacy by people who expected to be treated poorly by the system. Their first goal was to demonstrate that an injustice occurred. Their time frame was that of a protracted, long-term "struggle" to teach their fellow citizens that African-Americans are treated unjustly. They recognized they must settle for modest achievements in a system in which they have little influence. They live Du Bois's duality of being black Americans where the pluralists' heavenly chorus continues to sing with a white upper-class accent.

NOTES

1. Alexis de Tocqueville, *Democracy in America, Vol. 1.* (New York: Vintage Books, 1945); see also Richard Reeves, *American Journey: Traveling with Tocqueville in Search of "Democracy in America"* (New York: Touchstone, 1982), 215; Indeed, recent scholarship highlights the centrality of race issues in elections, partisanship, and political party fortunes, see Edward G. Carmines and James A. Stimson, *Issue Evolution: Race and the Transformation of American Politics* (Princeton, N.J.: Princeton University Press, 1989).

2. See Ernest J. Wilson III, "Why Political Scientists Don't Study Black Politics, but Historians and Sociologists Do," *PS* 18 (Summer 1985): 600–607; Hanes Walton, Jr., *Invisible Politics: Black Political Behavior* (Albany: State University of New York Press, 1985); Derrick Bell, *And We Are Not Saved: The Elusive Quest for Racial Justice* (New York: Basic Books, 1987); Jane H. Bayes, *Minority Politics and Ideologies in the United States* (Novato, Calif.: Chandler and Sharp, 1982), 1.

3. W. E. B. Du Bois, *The Souls of Black Folk* (New York: New American Library, 1969), 45.

4. Michael T. Hayes, "The Semi-sovereign Pressure Groups: A Critique of Current Theory and an Alternative Typology," *Journal of Politics* 40 (Feb. 1978): 140.

5. For a history and analysis of race and rape see Jennifer Wriggins, "Rape, Racism, and the Law," *Harvard Women's Law Journal* 6 (Spring 1983): 103–41.

6. Kevin Merida, "Second Autopsy Clouds Case," *Milwaukee Journal* (hereafter *MJ*), July 12, 1981; see also "Police Inaction at Lacy Scene Dismayed Medics," *MJ*, Aug. 23, 1981; "Police Didn't Answer Query on Lacy, Paramedic Says," *Milwaukee Sentinel* (hereafter *MS*), Sept. 24, 1981; Gregory D. Stanford, "Police Silent about Lacy, Fireman Says," *MJ*, Sept. 30, 1981.

7. Elizabeth Janeway, *Powers of the Weak* (New York: Morrow Quill Paperbacks, 1981), 162. Similarly, Howard Ball documents the compelling evidence necessary before Utah and Nevada citizens began to question govern-

ment reassurances about the safety of aboveground atomic testing, *Justice Downwind: America's Atomic Testing Program in the 1950s* (New York: Oxford University Press, 1986), chap. 4.

8. "Three Officers in Lacy Case Face Brutality Charge in '80 Arrest," *MJ*, July 14, 1981.

9. Stanford, "Coalition Urges Suspensions," *MJ*, July 14, 1981; see also Stanford, "Officer in Lacy Case Faces New Complaint," *MJ*, July 17, 1981; "Lacy Probe Asked by Panel Member," *MS*, July 17, 1981. A fourth complaint against one of the officers was filed in late July, see "Three Officers Believed Off Duty," *MJ*, July 26, 1981; followed by "Officer Faces Five Complaints," *MJ*, July 29, 1981.

10. Stanford, "Coalition Urges Suspensions."

11. Karen Rothe, "Lacy Coalition to Press for Prosecution of Three Officers," *MS*, July 27, 1981.

12. John Fauber, "Lacy Inquest Postponed after Report of Hill Quote," *MS*, Aug. 18, 1981; Walter Fee, "Cannon to Hear Lacy Case: Retired Judge to Preside at Inquest," *MJ*, Aug. 31, 1981.

13. "McCann Orders Inquest into Cause of Lacy's Death," *MS*, July 18, 1981.

14. Stanford, "Jury Faces a Puzzling Task," *MJ*, Oct. 13, 1981.

15. Stanford, "Officials Prepare to Arrest Three Officers," *MJ*, Oct. 15, 1981.

16. Merida, "Decision Pleases Black Leaders," *MJ*, Oct. 15, 1981.

17. Fee, "Judge Drops Charges in Lacy Case," *MJ*, Apr. 26, 1982.

18. Ralph D. Olive, "Verdicts Are In, but the Lacy Case Is Far from Over," *MJ*, May 20, 1983.

19. Kenneth R. Lamke, "One Officer in Lacy Case Is Fired; Four Suspended," *MS*, June 17, 1983.

20. Fee and Mark Ward, "Lacy Suit Settled for $600,000: Family Will Get $450,000 from City, Lawyers the Rest," *MJ*, Sept. 30, 1985; Ward and Fee, "Council OKs Lacy Settlement," *MJ*, Oct. 1, 1985; Ward, "It's a Calmer, More Patient McGee Now," *MJ*, Oct. 1, 1985; "Langley, McGee Applaud Lacy Settlement," *MS*, Oct. 2, 1985.

21. Peter K. Eisinger, *Patterns of Interracial Politics: Conflict and Cooperation in the City* (New York: Academic Press, 1976), 43.

22. Mark S. Rosentraub and Karen Harlow, "Police Policies and the Black Community: Attitudes toward the Police," in *Contemporary Public Policy Perspectives and Black Americans: Issues in an Era of Retrenchment Politics*, ed. Mitchell F. Rice and Woodrow Jones, Jr. (Westport, Conn.: Greenwood Press, 1984), 107–21; Robert Sam Anson, *Best Intentions: The Education and Killing of Edmund Perry* (New York: Random House, 1987); Bell, *And We Are Not Saved*, 181–97; Grace Hall Saltzstein, "Black Mayors and Police Policies," *Journal of Politics* 51 (Aug. 1989): 525–44; NAACP Police-Citizen Violence Project, *Police-Citizen Violence: An Organizing Guide for Community Leaders* (New York: NAACP, 1983).

23. See Stanford and Marie Rohde, "Officers Sketch a Racist Force," *MJ*, Mar. 13, 1980.

24. "Nabors Seeks to Quiet Storm over Remarks," *MJ*, Dec. 24, 1981.

25. Nathaniel Sheppard, Jr., "Tension Rises in Milwaukee over Police Conduct," *New York Times* (hereafter *NYT*), Dec. 30, 1981.

26. "Police Chief Breier Ends Twenty-Year Reign Today," *CT*, June 29, 1984.

27. "Suit Alleges Bias in Police Promotions," *MJ*, May 19, 1983; "Milwaukee Police Bias Suit Settled," *CT*, June 12, 1984; Thomas J. Hagerty, "U.S. Moves to Force Breier to Promote More Blacks," *MJ*, Sept. 4, 1982.

28. "Testifies against Police Partner," *NYT*, Oct. 18, 1981; Hagerty, "Award Doesn't End Bell Family's Battle," *MJ*, Dec. 17, 1981; editorial, "Justice for Daniel Bell, at Last," *MJ*, Dec. 18, 1981.

29. "$1.69 Million Settlement Offered in Daniel Bell Suit," *CT*, Sept. 28, 1984; "Bell Family Willing to Pay Back Some Welfare," *CT*, Nov. 22, 1984.

30. Joan F. Kessler, U.S. Attorney, Memorandum to Drew S. Days, Assistant Attorney General, "Milwaukee Common Council Resolution: Observations and Recommendations," Mar. 27, 1980.

31. Ibid., 4.

32. Ibid., 5.

33. "Incomplete List of Shootings and Severe Beatings by Milwaukee Police in Instances Where Such Police Behavior Was or May Not Have Been Warranted by the Surrounding Circumstances," undated memorandum from the files of Roy Nabors.

34. Gregory D. Stanford, Barbara Dembski, and James Romenesko, "Lacy Death Puts Spotlight on Police Conduct," *MJ*, July 26, 1981.

35. Rothe, "Chanting Crowd Recalls Three Deaths," *MS*, July 21, 1981; "U.S. Panel Will Monitor Lacy Investigations," *MJ*, July 29, 1981; "Minorities See Police as Brutal," *MJ*, July 30, 1981; Merida, "Advisor to U.S. Panel to Expand Lacy Probe," *MJ*, Sept. 22, 1981

36. "Serial-Murder Aftershocks," *Newsweek*, Aug. 12, 1991, 28.

37. Tom Held, "Chief Suspends Three: Boy Reportedly Left by Officers," *MS*, July 27, 1991; Tom Vanden Brook, "Gay Response: Linking Deaths to Homosexuality Is Unfair," *MJ*, July 24, 1991; William Celis III, "Slayings Point Up Lapses by Milwaukee's Agencies," *NYT*, July 30, 1991; "Serial Murder Case Exposes Deep Milwaukee Tensions," *New York Times*, Aug. 2, 1991; "Serial-Murder Aftershocks,"· 28–29; Lisa Sink, "Angry Blacks at City Hall Forum Want Three Officers, Norquist Out," *MS*, Aug. 2, 1991; Matthew Stelly, "Black Leaders Speak Out on Dahmer Slayings," *Milwaukee Courier*, Aug. 3, 1991; "Union Demands Arreola Resign," *MS*, Aug. 8, 1991; Gregory C. Brundage, "Were Dahmer Killings Motivated by Racism?" *Milwaukee Community Journal* (hereafter *MCJ*), Aug. 7, 1991; Scott Feldmeyer, "Hispanic March Offers Support to Chief Arreola," *South Side Spirit*, Aug. 18, 1991; "Gays/Lesbians Respond to Press," *In Step*, Aug. 15–28, 1991, 13–15; Mikel Holt, "Activists Vow 'Civil Disobedience' If Three Police Officers Are

Not Fired," *MCJ*, Sept. 4, 1991; "Firing of Officers Hailed by Some as Restoring Police Accountability," *MJ*, Sept. 7, 1991; La Mer Riehle, "Gay Community Poorly Served by Milwaukee Police," *Milwaukee Advocate*, Oct. 1991; "Commission in Milwaukee Finds Discrimination by Police Officers," *NYT*, Oct. 16, 1991.

38. Isabel Wilkerson, "Call for Black Militia Stuns Milwaukee," *NYT*, Apr. 6, 1990.

39. Terry M. Moe, *The Organization of Interests: Incentives and the Internal Dynamics of Political Interest Groups* (Chicago: University of Chicago Press, 1980).

40. Janeway, *Powers of the Weak*, 171.

41. Ibid., 204.

42. Editorial, "Quest for Truth in Lacy Case," *MJ*, July 16, 1981.

43. Rothe, "Chanting Crowd Recalls Three Deaths."

44. "State to Join Lacy Probe," *MJ*, July 23, 1981.

45. Marilyn Kucer, "Maier Names Panel to Study Lacy Case," *MS*, July 24, 1981.

46. Stanford and Merida, "Jesse Jackson Urges Boycott in Lacy Case," *MJ*, Aug. 30, 1981.

47. See editorial, "City Needs Dialogue about Lacy Incident," *MS*, July 25, 1981.

48. Monroe Anderson, "Milwaukee Man's Death at Hands of Cops Sparks Furor," *Chicago Tribune*, Aug. 16, 1981.

49. Janeway, *Powers of the Weak*, 90.

50. Murray Edelman, *Constructing the Political Spectacle* (Chicago: University of Chicago Press, 1988), 97.

51. Frances Fox Piven and Richard A. Cloward, *Poor People's Movements: Why They Succeed, How They Fail* (New York: Vintage Books, 1977), 14; see also John Gaventa, *Power and Powerlessness: Quiescence and Rebellion in an Appalachian Valley* (Urbana: University of Illinois Press, 1980).

52. Michael Lipsky, "Protest as a Political Resource," *American Political Science Review* 62 (Dec. 1968): 1144–58; see also Roger W. Cobb and Charles D. Elder, *Participation in American Politics: The Dynamics of Agenda-Building* (Boston: Allyn and Bacon, 1972); David J. Garrow, *Protest at Selma: Martin Luther King, Jr., and the Voting Rights Act of 1965* (New Haven, Conn.: Yale University Press, 1978).

53. Michele Derus, "Lacy Coalition Begins Picketing Three Locations," *MS*, Apr. 2, 1982.

54. Al Nichols, "Some Lessons from the Struggle for Justice for Ernest Lacy," unpublished paper, Summer 1982.

55. Editorial, "Lacy Boycott Aims at Wrong Target," *MS*, Aug. 13, 1981; editorial, "Boycott Leaders Load Blunderbuss," *MJ*, Mar. 24, 1982; editorial, "Lacy Case Secrecy Advanced Boycott," *MS*, Mar. 24, 1982.

56. Charles D. Elder and Roger W. Cobb, *The Political Uses of Symbols* (New York: Longman, 1983), 117.

57. "Pressure by Bradley, Others on Gates Grows," *Los Angeles Times* (hereafter *LAT*), Mar. 20, 1991; Andrea Ford, "King Beating Reunites Civil Rights Groups," *LAT*, Apr. 29, 1991.

58. Seth Mydans, "Tape of Beating by Police Revives Charges of Racism," *NYT*, Mar. 7, 1991. See also "Brutality on the Beat," *Newsweek*, Mar. 25, 1991, 32–33; "Videotaped Beating by Officers Puts Full Glare on Brutality Issue: Details Heighten Sense That It Was No Aberration," *NYT*, Mar. 18, 1991; Jerome H. Skolnick, "It's Not Just a Few Rotten Apples," *LAT*, Mar. 7, 1991; Sheryl Stolberg, "Scholars File Brief against Gates Ruling," *LAT*, June 4, 1991.

59. This analysis was aided by my telephone interviews with *LAT* reporters Sheryl Stolberg (Dec. 18, 1991) and Richard A. Serrano (Dec. 20, 1991).

60. James Romenesko, "Rape Suspect, Twenty-two, Dies in Police Van," *MJ*, July 10, 1981.

61. Bruce Gill and Rothe, "Fright May Have Caused Man's Death after His Arrest," *MS*, July 11, 1981.

62. Ibid.; see also Stanford, Merida, M. I. Blackwell, and Thomas Heinen, "Witnesses Describe Man's Arrest," *MJ*, July 11, 1981.

63. Kucer, "New Autopsy Fails to Reveal Cause of Lacy's Death, *MS*, July 13, 1981.

64. Sheppard, "Death of Black Man in Police Custody Leads to Bitter Protests in Milwaukee," *NYT*, Aug. 16, 1981.

65. Gill, "Medicine Linked to Lacy Reactions," *MS*, July 29, 1981.

66. "Lacy's Family Mourns Shocking Loss," *MJ*, July 12, 1981.

67. Elder and Cobb, *The Political Uses of Symbols*, 130–31.

68. "Three Officers in Lacy Case."

69. Garrow, *Protest at Selma*, 168–69, 216, 228; see also Susan Estrich, *Real Rape* (Cambridge: Harvard University Press), 1987.

70. Gill and Rothe, "Fright May Have Caused Man's Death after His Arrest."

71. Editorial, "Crux of the Problem Is Breier," *MJ*, Oct. 23, 1981.

72. "Unrest Unjustified, Breier Tells Group," *MJ*, July 30, 1981. For similar quotes see Rothe, "Mayor Protests Breier's Remarks," *MS*, Aug. 18, 1981; Ron Elving, "Lacy Panel Hears a Terse Breier," *MJ*, Aug. 18, 1981; Alex P. Dobish, "Breier Tells of Dismay at Allegations," *MJ*, Nov. 20, 1981.

73. "Suspensions Legal, Breier Told—Chief Apparently Will Abide by Order in Lacy Case," *MJ*, July 25, 1981; Kucer, "Police Won't Give Lacy Report to D.A.," *MS*, July 28, 1981; "Unrest Unjustified, Breier Tells Group," *MJ*, July 30, 1981.

74. Elving, "Breier Rips Activist Fuller For 'Marxist' Past," *MJ*, Mar. 18, 1982.

75. Rothe, "Mayor Protests Breier's Remarks," *MS*, Aug. 18, 1981.

76. "Panelists Say Breier Should Quit," *MJ*, Apr. 19, 1982.

77. Robert H. Salisbury, "An Exchange Theory of Interest Groups," *Midwest Journal of Political Science* 13 (1969): 1–32.

78. Piven and Cloward, *Poor People's Movements*, xxi-xxii.

79. Merida, "Howard Fuller: '60's Activist Still Alive," *MJ*, Mar. 21, 1982; William H. Chafe discusses the increasing militancy of young African-American activists, including Howard Fuller, in North Carolina during the sixties in *Civilities and Civil Rights: Greensboro, North Carolina, and the Black Struggle for Freedom* (New York: Oxford University Press, 1980).

80. David B. Truman, *The Governmental Process: Political Interests and Public Opinion* (New York: Alfred A. Knopf, 1959).

81. Salisbury, "An Exchange Theory of Interest Groups," 1–32.

82. Peter B. Clark and James Q. Wilson, "Incentive Systems: A Theory of Organizations," *Administrative Science Quarterly* 6 (Sept. 1961): 129–66.

83. Mancur Olson, Jr., *The Logic of Collective Action* (Cambridge: Harvard University Press, 1965).

84. Moe, *The Organization of Interests*, 113.

85. Stanford, "Coalition Urges Suspensions."

86. Monroe Anderson, "Milwaukee Man's Death at Hands of Cops Sparks Furor," *Chicago Tribune*, Aug. 16, 1981.

87. Anne N. Costain, "The Struggle for a National Women's Lobby: Organizing a Diffuse Interest," *Western Political Quarterly* 33 (Dec. 1980): 478–79.

88. Ibid., 480.

89. Ibid., 490.

90. Jack L. Walker, "Protest and Negotiation: A Case Study of Negro Leadership in Atlanta, Georgia," *Midwest Journal of Political Science* 7 (May 1963): 121–22; Hanes Walton, Jr., notes similar tensions in a grass-roots group protesting the shooting of African-Americans by police in Savannah, Georgia, in *Invisible Politics*, 256–61. See also Charles E. Silberman, *Crisis in Black and White* (New York: Vintage Books, 1964), 139–42.

91. "Black, White, Young, Old Gathered at Rally," *MS*, July 31, 1981.

92. Costain, "The Struggle for a National Women's Lobby," 490–91; see also Costain, "Representing Women: The Transition from Social Movement to Interest Group," in *Women, Power, and Policy*, ed. Ellen Boneparth (New York: Pergamon Press, 1982), 19–37.

93. Costain, "The Struggle for a National Women's Lobby," 491.

94. Hayes, "The Semi-sovereign Pressure Groups," 144–58.

95. Murray Edelman, *The Symbolic Uses of Politics* (Urbana: University of Illinois Press, 1964), 167.

96. Kessler memorandum, 15.

97. Elving, "Panel Shelves Police Plan: Groppi, Breier Clash at Committee Hearing," *MJ*, July 22, 1981.

98. See Stuart A. Scheingold, *The Politics of Law and Order: Street Crime and Public Policy* (New York: Longman, 1984); Michael Lipsky, *Street-Level Bureaucracy: Dilemmas of the Individual in Public Services* (New York: Russell Sage Foundation, 1980).

99. William Janz and Robert H. Edelman, "Officers Defend Actions, Call Suspensions Unfair," *MS*, July 28, 1981.

100. Stanford and Rohde, "Officers Sketch a Racist Force."

101. Ibid.

102. Eisinger, *Patterns of Interracial Politics.* Similarly, the central importance of electoral political strength to advance minority concerns was found by Rufus P. Browning, Dale Rogers Marshall, and David H. Tabb in their study of ten California cities, *Protest Is Not Enough* (Berkeley: University of California Press, 1984). A study of 1,200 cities revealed the role of governmental structure, levels of residential segregation, and the election of minority representatives to city councils in influencing the distribution of public resources, particularly jobs; see Kenneth R. Mladenka, "Blacks and Hispanics in Urban Politics," *American Political Science Review* 83 (Mar. 1989): 165–91.

103. Telephone interview with Howard Fuller, Jan. 6, 1992.

104. See, for example, "Officers See Police Chief as Non-supportive," *MS*, Aug. 9, 1991.

105. Garrow, *Protest at Selma*, 4, 212.

106. Edelman, *The Symbolic Uses of Politics*, 157.

107. These works include ibid., 152–57; Matthew A. Crenson, *The Unpolitics of Air Pollution: A Study of Non-decisionmaking in the Cities* (Baltimore, Md.: Johns Hopkins University Press, 1971); Steven Lukes, *Power: A Radical View* (London: MacMillan, 1974); Gaventa, *Power and Powerlessness;* Jay MacLeod, *Ain't No Making It: Leveled Aspirations in a Low-Income Neighborhood* (Boulder, Colo.: Westview Press, 1987).

108. Robert D. Holsworth, *Let Your Life Speak: A Study of Politics, Religion, and Antinuclear Weapons Activism* (Madison: University of Wisconsin Press, 1989), 66.

109. Gene Conrad, "Fight Injustice, Lacy's Mother Urges," *CT,* Apr. 29, 1985.

110. Elder and Cobb, *The Political Uses of Symbols*, 117; Edelman, *The Symbolic Uses of Politics*, 22–43.

111. Salisbury, "An Exchange Theory of Interest Groups."

112. Moe, *The Organization of Interests*, 118–19.

113. Moe, "Toward a Broader View of Interest Groups," 536.

114. Robert N. Bellah, Richard Madsen, William M. Sullivan, Ann Swidler, and Steven M. Tipton, *Habits of the Heart: Individualism and Commitment in American Life* (Berkeley: University of California Press, 1985), 153.

115. Conrad, "Fight Injustice."

116. Robert Coles's observations from his study, *Children of Crisis: A Study of Courage and Fear* (1967) as described by Barrington Moore, Jr., in *Injustice: The Social Bases of Obedience and Revolt* (New York: M. E. Sharpe, 1978), 112–13.

117. Elder and Cobb, *The Political Uses of Symbols*, 9, 116–17.

118. Janeway, *Powers of the Weak*, 292.

119. "Religious Leaders Ask Suspension of Officers," *MJ,* July 24, 1981; see also "Twenty Lutheran Ministers Back Lacy Coalition," *MJ,* Feb. 20, 1982; Ron Elving and Amy Rabideau Silvers, "Breier's Tough Stance Stuns Religious Leaders," *MJ,* Feb. 18, 1982.

120. See Du Bois, *The Souls of Black Folk*, chap. 10; Robert Booth Fowler,

Religion and Politics in America (Metuchen, N.J.: American Theological Library Association and Scarecrow Press, 1985), 293–313; Eugene D. Genovese, *Roll, Jordan, Roll: The World the Slaves Made* (New York: Vintage Books, 1976), 161–284; Charles V. Hamilton, *The Black Preacher in America* (New York: William Morrow, 1972); Hart M. Nelsen, Raytha L. Yokley, and Anne K. Nelsen, eds., *The Black Church in America* (New York: Basic Books, 1971); Doug McAdam, *Political Process and the Development of Black Insurgency, 1930–70* (Chicago: University of Chicago Press, 1982); Aldon D. Morris, *The Origins of the Civil Rights Movement: Black Communities Organizing for Change* (New York: Free Press, 1984); but see the boundaries in this environment for women in Jacquelyn Grant, "Black Women and the Church," in *All the Women Are White, All the Blacks Are Men, but Some of Us Are Brave: Black Women's Studies*, ed. Gloria T. Hull, Patricia Bell Scott, and Barbara Smith (Old Westbury, N.Y.: Feminist Press, 1982), 141–52.

121. Genovese, *Roll, Jordan, Roll*, 165.

122. Janeway, *Powers of the Weak*, 132.

123. Holsworth, *Let Your Life Speak*, 79.

124. Alicia Armstrong, "Pain Lingers at Lacy's Funeral," *MJ*, July 19, 1981.

125. Grappling with doubts about these cultural and religious reassurances is evident in the popularity of books like Rabbi Harold S. Kushner's *Why Bad Things Happen to Good People* (New York: Schocken Press, 1981).

126. "Lacy's Family Mourns Shocking Loss."

127. Du Bois, *The Souls of Black Folk*, 274.

128. Moore, *Injustice*.

5 Citizens Taking Action: Outsider Dissent for Healing and Reassurance

When details of the murder of a ten-year-old girl became known in Madison, Wisconsin, there was a ground swell of anguished citizen outcry that such a heinous crime had not been prevented. Citizens wanted to believe their community was protected from such acts. If they occurred, there must be a rational reason, perhaps a governmental mistake. On the crest of the outrage about the crime, a small ad hoc group formed, calling itself Citizens Taking Action.

Political activities sometimes teach the futility of trying to reform society as opposed to pursuing specific goals. Failed outcomes are more predictable when the involved individuals are not connected to a larger, nurturing community. Two instances of ad hoc, grass-roots mobilization provide examples of this phenomenon. During the activities of both Citizens Taking Action and Concerned Citizens for Children, issues were deflected, victims blamed, and once-active people retreated in the face of seemingly insurmountable social problems and the critical voices of the majority.

Citizens Taking Action searched for a correctable mistake by government officials prior to the little girl's death in order to prevent future tragedies. They discovered, however, how quickly momentum dissipates with the realization of the enormity of social issues. Analysis of their efforts is drawn from in-depth interviews I conducted in May 1985 with all four of the surviving leaders of the group. A fifth leader died shortly after Citizens Taking Action disbanded. In addition, I attended the two public meetings Citizens Taking Action organized. My role was that of an unobtrusive observer.

The Chronology of Events

The Triggering Incident

In March 1982 ten-year-old Paula McCormick was assaulted and murdered in Madison, Wisconsin. Classes had ended early that day for parent-teacher conferences and teacher preparation. When Paula did not return to her home, a block and a half away from her school, her parents notified police. The news that she was missing was prominently reported in area papers. The police eventually questioned Roger Lange about the child's disappearance. Lange, age twenty-seven, lived in the neighborhood and was known to the police. He told police he was a psychic and that he had a "vision" of where the child's body was. He led them to a miniwarehouse to which he had the key; inside was her body. He was immediately arrested. When Paula McCormick's death was revealed, the public was also informed that Lange, a man with a previous criminal record, had been charged.[1]

At the time of his arrest, Lange was on two years' probation for a 1981 conviction for fourth-degree sexual assault of his live-in girlfriend. He had initially been charged with second-degree sexual assault for that incident. A trial was never held because the couple reconciled. Assistant District Attorney Steve Bablitch had decided to plea bargain to a charge of fourth-degree sexual assault, since without the victim's cooperation the case was unprovable.[2] Lange was ordered to undergo psychological counseling concerning his abusive sexual conduct as a condition for probation.

Lange had been involved in other incidents: shoplifting, harboring juvenile runaways, needing a court-appointed "spendthrift guardian," and being loud and disorderly in the City-County Building. There was also evidence of a troubled childhood.[3] A vocational rehabilitation counselor who had worked with Lange recalled he had a "'horrendous, horrible childhood,'" but, she said,

"That doesn't excuse his behavior. What it means is he needed more treatment than he was given."
The social services system fails to help some people and then they are left on their own, she said. "And these are the people who should be watched," she said.
"We're dropping through the system these people who are anti-social, dangerous, unable to function. These are the very people who should be supervised, and they aren't. . . ."
"There's nobody watching the Roger Langes. . . . They're left on their

own after springing them from our institutions. That's deranged, it's just not right. That dear little girl paid the price."[4]

A long, front-page newspaper article related the child abuse and neglect Lange and his brothers had suffered. His two brothers were murdered by his mother. After his mother's institutionalization, he was placed in foster homes from the age of four and a half.[5] As a juvenile in the late 1960s, he had been committed to Winnebago Mental Health Institute for about eighteen months. It was noted that all the Lange children had suffered a great deal of abuse and that Roger had been a very disturbed adolescent.[6] One of his foster mothers stated, "'What happened before he was four, is what's causing this now.' "[7] Despite all that had happened "Lange was left pretty much on his own."[8]

Six weeks before Lange killed Paula McCormick, his girlfriend had made a second assault complaint against him. After Paula's murder, two Wisconsin state employees were temporarily suspended for failure to act on that assault complaint. A probation agent was suspended for three days and the agent's supervisor was suspended for five days without pay.[9] Rules required that a person who is on probation for assault and is involved in another incident must be taken into custody and detained pending an investigation. The two employees appealed their suspensions. One of their attorneys called the charges "'outrageous' " and said the two were being made "'scapegoats' for the failure of the system to deal with Lange before the McCormick killing."[10] The probation agent was later cleared of the charges.[11]

In the McCormick case Roger Lange was charged with six offenses: first-degree murder, kidnapping, first-degree sexual assault, enticing a minor into a building for immoral purposes, and two counts of attempting to entice children for immoral purposes. The police investigation found that Lange had tried to entice two other girls on their way to school to come babysit for five minutes for a dollar. Both girls had hurried on to school. The two incidents with other girls occurred February 2 and February 23. One child told her teacher about the incident; the other child did not mention it to anyone until police started questioning Lincoln elementary children following Paula's disappearance.[12]

The reactions of the families near Paula's elementary school to the news of her death and the arrest of Lange were described as "grief because a young girl was abducted and murdered, . . . shock because the incident took place so close to home and school, with so many people nearby to help. And . . . anger because the suspect in custody has a history of a sexual offense."[13] The grief of Paula's parents, according to one report, included a sense of helplessness that the incident had happened so close to home and school.[14]

The day after her body was found, area parents were urged to increase their children's security measures. These steps included warning children about strangers and initiating a "Helping Hand" program wherein children could go to predesignated safe places, houses where adults are home, when the child has a problem. At the same time, the superintendent of Madison schools defended the district's early release time for parent-teacher conferences and teacher preparation.[15]

The child's death also sparked concern because it was the first such case within memory for Dane County, although there had been reports of children being approached by strangers on their way home from school. The Paula McCormick case became "a community tragedy."[16]

Paula McCormick's parents filed a $600,000 lawsuit against the City of Madison and the school district, based on school officials' failure to notify police of the first enticement incident near Lincoln School. The suit claimed, "'If law enforcement authorities had been properly notified of the Feb. 23 criminal act, Roger Lange would have been arrested and incarcerated for violation of conditions of his probation.'"[17]

Lange was eventually tried, convicted, and sentenced for first-degree murder, sexual assault, kidnapping, enticement, and two charges of attempting to entice a child for immoral purposes. When arguing for the maximum sentence for each offense, District Attorney James E. Doyle, Jr., said "Lange had 'hurt a single family terribly and he has hurt a whole community terribly.'"[18] Lange is now serving his sentence of life plus sixty years in a Wisconsin prison.

Group Mobilization

Response within the community was not just grief, but also anger and frustration. Judy Salverson and Pat Urso, two friends, started to weave together an incipient organization to look into the matter further. Lange was only a catalyst for them, on top of the memory of other incidents. Salverson spent several days talking with other people who were outraged about Paula's death and who wanted to do something to change a system that put repeat offenders back on the streets. She admitted, though, "that 'something' may be hard to define and even harder to accomplish." [19] With this initial flare-up of opinion, there was also hesitancy and defensiveness. Salverson emphasized that her actions were " 'not a vigilante effort.' " [20] She wanted to work within the system to alter the focus from the rights of the accused to those of victims, although she was not " 'presumptuous enough' " to say how. [21] During their interviews as well, group members were defensive, explaining that they were not a "lynch mob" but had intended to engage in productive reforms. Another woman stressed, "We were not a hostile group."

Initially two groups formed in Madison immediately following the McCormick murder. One, Citizens Taking Action, claimed two hundred members and was organized by Amy Gilmore. The other, without a name, was led by Salverson and Urso. Gilmore wanted to research such issues as plea bargaining, mandatory prison sentences, night court, and the impact of overcrowded court dockets. Gilmore hoped to use neighborhood associations in her effort to not " 'just complain,' " but " 'find possible solutions.' " [22] Salverson told a reporter, " 'This is not going to be a flash-in-the-pan effort,' " but an examination of the entire judicial system. [23] Echoing the same sentiments as Gilmore, Salverson continued, " 'We don't need to be, or want to be, a single-issue group. . . . We want to examine, then understand the system, and therefore be able to change it.' " [24] These two fledgling groups later combined under the name Citizens Taking Action. Although there were stirrings of concern from other groups in the city, Citizens Taking Action did not receive help from other organized interests.

One Citizens Taking Action leader explained their motivation: "The fact that this guy [Roger Lange] had a history of trouble and had been, you know, obviously along the way and in many areas of his life sending out help signals. And he slipped through the cracks and then somehow was able to still function in society and not be recognized as being dangerous." Group members felt "horrible frustration" that people in government were not doing their jobs. If errors were made in the justice system, they should be made on the side of safety for citizens, they felt, not for the accused. Their goal was more accountability for legal professionals.

The activists soon discovered "the problem of many hands," as defined by Thompson. "Because many different officials contribute in many ways to decisions and policies of government, it is difficult even in principle to identify who is morally responsible for political outcomes." [25] An official in the Dane County District Attorney's office observed, "Citizens Taking Action was looking for an Archie Simonson, but they couldn't find one. Everyone was doing their job." These activists also doubted their "place" in critiquing the system, feeling that they had to study and research it first. They were tenuous in their political positions. One Citizens Taking Action leader stated, "So we were really in an information-gathering process without having ultimately consummated, concretely, ideas and recommendations. But it was, as I said, essentially an information-gathering posture that we had early on because we lack[ed] the necessary information to make any kind of a judgment call as to where one would even begin. So, we were trying to find out from those within both the penal system and judicial system where, where they felt the shortcomings were and what change they would like to see from it."

Citizens Taking Action was established "to effect changes in the system that will make it tougher for criminals to repeat their offenses." One leader, after a week of researching issues such as plea bargaining, early prison release, insanity defenses, and juvenile justice stated, "'I'm not quite so mad and ready to point a finger at any one department anymore. Getting the facts is putting the light on the whole system.'" [26] Ultimately, the leaders reported during interviews for this study, their research left them feeling that "the scope was so incredibly vast that there was really no place to start."

Group Tactics

Public Meetings

On March 22, 1982, Citizens Taking Action mailed out a flyer to neighborhood and community leaders announcing a public meeting. Entitled "Remember How Mad You Were?!" the flyer announced,

Citizens Taking Action is an organization of concerned citizens of Wisconsin. We are no longer content to sit idly by in fear of our safety & lives, leaving control in the hands of our "Justice System." We feel there are many changes that need to be made within the entire realm of the system, and, seek to take measures to see that changes are made. We first must have a better understanding of the system to be able to determine where the problems lie, reasons the problems exist, and, together with representatives of each department, come up with constructive changes. We are doing research into several key issues and will make progressive as well as conclusive reports of our findings. It is our hope to have the issues placed on a public referendum, or at the very least, petition our lawmakers to hold a meeting, at which time we will present a package of legislative reforms based on our findings. It's time to stop talking citizens; Take Action!!!

In addition it listed information about court backlogs, crimes committed by people out on bail, early release from prison, plea bargaining, sentencing guidelines, and budget cuts within the criminal justice system.

The sentiments of the flyer had already received expression in letters to the editor, many unsigned for fear of drawing personal attention. In addition, news articles on Lange's childhood background brought opposition on the grounds it might be used to create mitigating sympathy for him. One editor pointed out, though, "If a conclusion can be drawn from Lange's background, it is not that the victims of child abuse should be excused for their actions, but that crime does not happen in a vacuum." He continued, "In part, Lange's past makes us uncomfortable because it stirs the clear blacks and whites of the case into muddled and confusing shades of grey. We want the response to Paula's murder to be direct and simple: Find the murderer, convict him and put him away forever. Case closed. Locking a murderer away is relatively easy. Dealing with child abuse is not." [27] As this editorial hints at, the definition of the incident as a crime problem concerning inefficiencies in the criminal justice system glosses over deeper social problems of abuse and violence. It is an example of erasing structural conditions from notice. The definition of the problem is constricted, thus helping deflect citizens' anger to a conservative agenda of crime control.

The group scheduled a public meeting with representatives of the district attorney's office, the Madison Police Department, and the Wisconsin lieutenant governor's office at the East High School auditorium "so people can express their concerns directly to various public officials." [28] The public forum at East High provided an opportunity for venting anger and frustration. It was well attended, with 250–300 people coming to the working-class area high school. Several public officials were on the auditorium stage with two women from Citizens Taking Action. The officials included the police chief, the district attorney, and the chair of the state parole board. The two-and-a-half-hour meeting consisted of people from the audience testifying about delays, revolving doors, and insensitivity by police, judges, and attorneys. The testimonials were drawn from personal experiences with the system or hearsay.[29] The meeting focused on society's failure to deal with crime. The information tables for the meeting, for example, included accounts of paroled criminals committing additional crimes.[30]

Initially, Dane County District Attorney James E. Doyle, Jr., Madison Police Chief David Couper, and the chair of the state parole board, Fred Hinickle, answered questions from the audience with long explanations about judicial rules and procedures. As the front-page newspaper article the next day tells it, "The atmosphere heated up when [a man] declared from the audience, 'I don't want a legal course. . . . We're getting a whitewash here. We've got a big crime problem in this city and we want to know—what can we do?' "[31] This was followed by numerous statements from the audience expressing frustration with a lax legal system and their desire to keep violent criminals locked away from the rest of society. Another man in the audience identified himself as an ex-convict and fed the assembly's fears by testifying that Madison was an easy city for criminals. This man's comments were the lead-in to the *Wisconsin State Journal*'s front-page coverage of the public forum; his picture was also included.[32]

Discussion of legislative proposals to increase the length of sentences, cut down on parole, and institute a death penalty brought a favorable response from the audience. Among other issues discussed, public officials explained their reasons for opposing the death penalty. State parole board chair Hinickle praised the meeting as a "'perfect first step'" and continued, "'It's not enough to be angry and frustrated. Learn what's there first, and then you'll be in a position to make changes.' "[33]

The public officials at the meeting emphasized the complicated nature of the causes of crime and the treatment of offenders in the court, prison, and parole system. They also defended the records of their offices and maintained they were not soft on crime. The police chief said his officers were doing the best they could within the limits placed on them and the effects of budget cuts.

The members of Citizens Taking Action saw the public meeting at East High as a "gratifying experience," a huge outpouring of emotion from the citizenry showing a great deal of concern "out there" for the issues of crime and safety. The meeting was "a sharing" of their frustrations. One member recalled that "especially after the night of the meeting at East High, I think, people thoroughly expected that what we were going to do is make up protest signs and march to the State Capitol. Well, we didn't do that. We went to the libraries. We went to officials and started asking questions." Piven and Cloward have noted that protest is the most powerful weapon of outsiders, whereas meetings and fact-finding missions play into the hands of established authorities and eventually dissipate the anger and energy of politically aroused groups.[34] This phenomena was played out again by Citizens Taking Action.

Seeking Information

The research conducted by Citizens Taking Action included the topics of sentencing, parole, probation, and bail. The group stated that it would "seek changes in state laws and investigate the records of judges and members of the State Legislature."[35] The group also selected a five-member executive committee.

At first, the group listed ambitious objectives, including holding several workshops on crime problems and prevention, setting up a youth escort program for the elderly with the Wisconsin Council for Criminal Justice, and conducting a survey to determine which specific crimes people wanted included under mandatory sentencing guidelines.[36] These objectives, though, were never realized.

Group members interviewed judges, attended criminal trials wearing buttons with the initials CTA on them, and discussed legislation that would publicize the work of district attorneys. They applauded tough sentences handed down by two Dane County circuit judges two months after McCormick's death, and they expressed concern about prisoners who walked away from a work release program.[37] The executive committee members toured Waupun State Prison and met with two representatives of a prisoners' group.

The Madison media were attentive to the issue of crime and repeat offenders. In May 1982, one local news team produced a half-hour special entitled "A Second Shot at Violence." The show was about violent crime by second offenders, probation, bail, and plea bargaining. The moderator interviewed judges, probation officials, the Dane County district attorney, and Amy Gilmore, one of the leaders of Citizens Taking Action. The interviews with Gilmore and the clips from the East High School public forum seem to be the centerpieces for the show. Gilmore raised the same concerns that the group had been grappling with from the beginning: how to prevent violent offenses through research on bail, probation, plea bargaining, and disparate sentences by judges.

Public officials on the program, from the district attorney to local judges, discussed the problem in terms of a need for more resources for their departments to handle court backlogs, jail overcrowding, and heavy caseloads for probation and parole officers. The moderator also pointed out that with "good time" a twenty-year sentence can be reduced to less than ten years. One-half of the parolees in Wisconsin, she said, "were considered bad risks by the parole board and not given parole. However, they've served their time, less good time, and must be let go."[38]

The broadcast reported that Citizens Taking Action planned to pressure political candidates for reform of the criminal justice system. But, as the district attorney commented in this news special, the topic is frustrating because legislators look for quick, politically expedient fixes. The moderator readily agreed that treating the symptoms and treating the illness were two different issues.

A second public meeting sponsored by Citizens Taking Action in June was far less satisfactory to group activists than the first. Judge Dennis Chelleen from Winona County, Minnesota, spoke about sentencing alternatives. Approximately thirty people were in attendance, who neither participated in nor set the agenda for discussion. Instead, Judge Challeen lectured about his reliance on transactional analysis, personal responsibility, and restitution instead of jail for nonviolent offenders. He stated that prisons are a failure and that most people mistakenly think American judges are too lenient.[39]

Voices Hushed

Citizens Taking Action sustained about four months of concerted effort: public meetings; interviews with judges, prosecutors, and probation officials; press releases; and a visit to the state prison. Its research led only to the realization that problems were larger than they had anticipated.

The activists did not have a language with which to describe their grievances. They were unconnected American individuals without an alternative ideology from which to criticize the injustices they felt. A social movement, such as feminism or conservatism, would have provided a language for them to describe injustice. This is essential to breaking the silences behind majority opinion.

Members of Citizens Taking Action took some comfort from believing that their efforts encouraged the Madison public school system to institute more crime awareness and prevention programs. Their direct impact on these programs, however, is difficult to document. More likely, the publicity of the McCormick murder, the outcry by the public, and a lawsuit by Paula's parents, in combination with Citizens Taking Action, aided school administrators who already wanted to fund crime programs.

Joel Handler has pointed out that groups have the most success with legal reform efforts when they play into the strategies of legal professionals. "However," Handler wrote, "factions within agencies sometimes welcome pressure by social-reform groups and courts; it gives them strength to overcome internal or external opposition to change. But this is not the usual situation."[40] Similarly, in their study of the impact of legal reform in rape laws, Marsh, Geist, and Kaplan noted, "When new legislation allows officials to increase their power and prestige, the legislation is more likely to be implemented."[41] At the time, the Dane County District Attorney's Office was seeking funding from the county board for an additional prosecutor's position. Citizens Taking Action pressured for this position, citing caseload problems in the prosecutors' office. An official in the district attorney's office felt the citizens' group was very effective before the county board. He said, "It always looks better when a citizens group goes and asks for increased funding."

One Citizens Taking Action leader reflected, "I think that [Citizens Taking Action] sort of filled a void at the time. [pause] I think we met, talked about the things that we all felt, for some people that was enough to go through: two, three, four months of healing. Then they weren't interested in continuing. And, maybe that's what we were all about. Maybe that's what kept us all in our own individual sanity. And, we all had someone to lean on and talk about these things." The group, then, fulfilled the expressive needs of members. The same person continued, "I never finished out the end where all these reports were going to come to an end and we were going to make—I don't know what we were going to do. I really don't know what the end results were going to be. And, quite frankly, as I think about it, I think that probably a lot of the public officials just entertained us for the moment knowing, or feeling, that this may be a passing thing. And, as I look at it, this is about what it ended up to be." He believed that people in power, such as attorneys and judges, protect their power and small, outsider groups like Citizens Taking Action cannot change the system. When asked "Why do you think Citizens Taking Action wasn't able to get anything done?" he responded: "That's the way the process is set up. We were just too small of a cog in the big gear. We probably never grew to be a cog. So, again, I think we were entertained by the politicians and by people in authority. They're probably quite used to this. When something happens. I'm sure that's one of the skills of a politician or a higher authority: entertain the people, ahh, say certain things that have to be said and they will go away and let you do your job or let you not do your job."

A second activist remembered how judges, prosecutors, and probation officials were friendly during interviews by the group: "Everybody is willing to see you because they think they can pacify you." Or, officials "at least pacify you to the point where they are able to continue going on and doing things the way they've always done them and most people don't have the energy to hang in there." This same person never cared for politics: "It's difficult to keep a decent attitude; you can get real poisoned real fast" because people want to advance their own careers through politics. Although she retained her faith in humanity, she expressed disillusionment with political leaders.

Another person, when asked "Why do you get active and spend your time on issues like this?" explained, "I see myself as an individual. . . . I guess I'm odd, if you compare me with society as a whole group." This person cared about society as a whole but was not affiliated with any particular group or community. These generalized affiliations discourage activists because they do not belong to a more tangible, supportive community. When confronted by a government that "entertains" them and then goes about its business as usual, these groups dissipate. In contrast, Holsworth's study of anti–nuclear weapons activists reveals how belonging to an alternative community, with an ideology to explain perceived injustices, nurtures disappointed activists and enables them to keep struggling for their cause.[42] Similarly, the Lacy Coalition's sense of community and struggle sustained individual participants. Asked why a group like Citizens Taking Action disappears in time one interviewee reflected, "I think the wounds heal that a lot of the people have. [pause] And there was a lot of hurt. [pause] And, it was, again, a way that people could all turn to each other who were sharing those same feelings. . . . We had some people that had experienced, either with their own children, or themselves, or whatever, some violent act that went on." Another activist thought the group was a way for people to seek "re-enforcement": "It's always good to know that you're not paranoid," that others feel the same way about the criminal justice system.

The "polished politicians," then, just entertained these people until they went away. One Citizens Taking Action member stated, "In this case here I don't see anything that has changed or that has happened. I certainly don't want to see another Paula McCormick thing happen, but, if it does, it would not surprise me."

The issues these people addressed seemed broad and overwhelming to them. One reason was economic. The activists in Citizens Taking Action were not college educated nor independently wealthy. One person left the group because she "had to get back to the business of earning a living" but, nevertheless, felt very bad because "we had a commitment to people as a result of their response that we didn't fulfill." She and others in the group believed they let people down. She maintained that the system can be changed through the concerted effort of many other people, but not by her. She did not think another group like Citizens Taking Action would form: "I think that was our shot." Rather than make her feel efficacious, Citizens Taking Action taught her that "other people" with "the ability" could do this. In fact, she wondered if the failure of Citizens Taking Action would make it more difficult in the future for other citizen's groups. Government officials will merely say, "Oh, here comes another one of those groups; emotions will cool and they will fall away." She attributed her falling away from the group to her own economic circumstances, "the business of earning a living." She did not put this into a larger political context.

Unwillingness to judge the effect of economic and political inequalities is deeply embedded in American public opinion.[43] Such avoidance of the realities of social class and lack of political power enables people to maintain their equalitarian ideology in the face of experience to the contrary.[44] Cognitive dissonance theory helps explain this behavior since it posits that "people will tend to seek out information that reduces dissonance and avoid information that increases it."[45] Other ways people deal with otherwise unavoidable dissonant information is defensive misperception or misunderstanding of the message, discrediting the source, or exposing themselves to consonant information from other sources.[46] Leaders in Citizens Taking Action examined the large gap between their lofty goals and their small accomplishments with self-blame mixed with a careful assessment of their relative powerlessness in their society. They hedged and backed away from any larger, potentially more radical and personally disturbing lessons from their foray into grass-roots activism.

Conclusion

The rise and fall of groups like Citizens Taking Action is similar to the "issue attention cycles" described by Anthony Downs:
  1. The preproblem stage
  2. Alarmed discovery and euphoric enthusiasm
  3. Realizing the cost of significant progress
  4. Gradual decline of intense public interest
  5. Postproblem stage. [47]
Downs argued that the public's perception of "crisis" does not reflect changes in real conditions but the operation of a systematic cycle of heightening public interest followed by increasing boredom with major issues.[48] Examination of Citizens Taking Action, though, reveals that these people did not become bored with the issues raised by Paula McCormick's death, but rather experienced frustration and settled for reassurances that healed their immediate hurts and anger.

These people were not completely "turned off" from politics. They had some positive experiences in Citizens Taking Action: government officials were never rude to them; they met many others who felt as they did and who confided that they had been victimized and treated poorly by the criminal justice system. They also attempted to make their community a safer one, especially for children. But, above all else, they "healed." They still believed in the fairness of the American pluralist system, for people with the time, talent, resources, and commitment to make a go of it. For them, though, Citizens Taking Action was their "one shot."

The temporary arousal of citizens into mobilized dissent, as seen in Citizens Taking Action, is often turned back by government through reassurance and symbolic concessions.[49] Hirschman observes, "The turns from the private to the public life and back again are marked by wildly exaggerated expectations, by total infatuation, and by sudden revulsions."[50] He explains,

> The sudden realization (or illusion) that I can act to change society for the better and, moreover, that I can join other like-minded people to this end is in such conditions pleasurable, in fact intoxicating, in itself. To savor that pleasure, society does not have to be actually changed right away: it is quite enough to act in a variety of ways *as though* it were possible to promote change. Obviously, if no change is achieved, disappointment will set in. . . .
>
> Secondly, there is the opposite pleasurable experience: not that *I* can change society, but that my work and activities in the public arena change and develop *me*, regardless of any real changes in the state of the world that I might achieve.[51]

Some people are discouraged from participation through the deflection of their efforts and questioning of their motives. Inactivity, therefore, is rooted in past experiences and disappointments.[52]

Hirschman provides insights for the phenomenon of exiting from public, political activity with a chastened public citizen reverting to his or her private affairs. Disappointment also stems from forced "underinvolvement" when political institutions keep people from expressing the full intensity of their political beliefs.[53] The decision to grant universal male suffrage in France in 1848 became a mechanism for "underinvolvement." The vote, granted to the volatile French who had revolted three times in two generations, "represented a new right of the people, but it also restricted its participation in politics to this particular *and comparatively harmless* form."[54] "The trouble with the vote, in other words, is not so much that the outcome of voting is stacked, because of the way in which economic and political power is distributed in society; rather, it is that the vote *delegitimizes* more direct, intense, and 'expressive' forms of political action that are both more effective and more satisfying."[55] Piven and Cloward argue that elections are a "structuring institution" serving to delegitimate alternative forms of participation.[56] Gaventa and Edelman make similar points concerning the reactive role the public is confined to.[57]

Hirschman advocates that we take disappointment seriously. It is difficult to study disappointment, however, because of cognitive dissonance where people try to reduce psychological inconsistency because it creates an unpleasant tension within them. "The findings of [cognitive dissonance] theory can in fact be reinterpreted: the denial of reality that is practiced testifies to the *power* and *vitality* of the disappointment experience. We engage in all kinds of ingenious ruses and delaying actions before admitting to ourselves that we *are* disappointed, in part surely because we know that disappointment may compel us to a painful reassessment of our preferences and priorities."[58] The lessons of political participation, therefore, may be negative. One Citizens Taking Action member revealed the nature of his disappointments: "I think the people that were spending the time and were involved in it, I think we felt that we were going to be able to do something to change some part of the system, that would give us more hope than what we came to the organization with. I don't think that's happened. [pause] If anything the system has got to be more burdened with problems as the population grows and I don't think anything's changed."

Dane County residents donated to a memorial fund from which a small nature park was built at Lincoln Elementary School in Paula McCormick's name. As one report described the dedication ceremony, "Fear and sadness gave way to peaceful reassurance as classmates, teachers, parents and friends gathered this morning at Lincoln Elementary School to remember Paula McCormick."[59] Without a community to sustain their activism and place their "hurt" feelings into a larger social context, Citizens Taking Action members were reassured and placated back into quiescence and learned not to attempt to change things anymore.

NOTES

1. See Marvin Balousek, "Missing Girl Found Slain; Sex Offender Is Arrested," *Wisconsin State Journal* (hereafter *WSJ*), Mar. 4, 1982; Jacob Stockinger, "Shocked Parents Cry for Safety at Lincoln School," *Capital Times* (hereafter *CT*), Mar. 4, 1982; "Neighbor Booked in Girl's Slaying," *CT*, Mar. 4, 1982; Mike Miller and Dan Allegretti, "Previous Sex, Robbery Links Put Police on Trail of Suspect," *CT*, Mar. 4, 1982; Anita Clark, "Suspect Familiar at Courts' Fringe," *WSJ*, Mar. 5, 1982.

2. Miller and Allegretti, "Previous Sex, Robbery Links." Lange also was connected to a 1979 robbery of a local bank for which he was granted immunity from prosecution.

3. Clark, "Suspect Familiar at Courts' Fringe."

4. Allegretti, "Suspect Linked to Other Incidents," *CT*, Mar. 5, 1982.

5. Clark, "Murder Suspect Was Abused Child," *WSJ*, Mar. 7, 1982. This story was repeated in various other articles about Lange, including Steve Hannah, "Suspect's Mother Killed His Two Brothers," *Milwaukee Journal* (hereafter *MJ*), Mar. 7, 1982; Clark, "Violent Adults Abused as Children," *WSJ*, Mar. 14, 1982.

6. Hannah, "Suspect's Mother."

7. Clark, "Murder Suspect Was Abused Child."

8. Allegretti, "Suspect Linked to Other Incidents."

9. Miller, "State Suspends Two in Lange Case," *CT*, May 11, 1982.

10. Miller, "Two Appeal State Suspensions," *CT*, May 12, 1982.

11. "Lange's Probation Agent Cleared of Charge," *CT*, Sept. 7, 1983; Thomas W. Still, "Panel Clears Probation Agent of Negligence," *WSJ*, Sept. 7, 1983.

12. Miller, "Lange Complaint Details Girl's Slaying," *CT*, Mar. 8, 1982; Allegretti, "Suspect Linked to Other Incidents."

13. Stockinger, "Shocked Parents."

14. "Neighbor Booked in Girl's Slaying."

15. Stockinger, "Shocked Parents."

16. Allegretti, "Recall Paula's Love, Goodness: Priest's Eulogy," *CT*, Mar. 6, 1982.

17. Miller, "Parents of Slain Student Register $600,000 Claim," *CT*, Nov. 23, 1982.

18. Miller, "Lange Gets Life Plus," *CT*, Sept. 16, 1982.

19. Kaye Schultz, "Repeat Offenders: A City's Outrage Is Building," *CT*, Mar. 6, 1982.

20. Ibid.

21. Ibid.

22. George Hesselberg and Jim Salzer, "Citizens Form Groups to Change Crime Laws," *WSJ*, Mar. 9, 1982.

23. Ibid.

24. Ibid.

25. Dennis F. Thompson, "Moral Responsibility of Public Officials: The Problem of Many Hands," *American Political Science Review* 74 (Dec. 1980): 905.

26. Balousek, "Citizens Group Organizing, Seeks Justice System Reform," *WSJ*, Mar. 14, 1982.

27. William S. Becker, "Shouting from behind Locked Doors," *WSJ*, Mar. 12, 1982.

28. Balousek, "Citizens Group Organizing."

29. This account is drawn from notes I took at the meeting.

30. One article xeroxed by Citizens Taking Action had the inked message "Do You Really Want To Live In This Type of System—*OR HELP US* Change It" and cited Clark, "Man on Parole for Murder Faces Phone-Threat Charges," *WSJ*, Mar. 23, 1982.

31. Rosemary Kendrick, "Irate, Frightened Citizens Vent Anger at Crime Forum," *CT*, Mar. 25, 1982.

32. Balousek, "Angered Citizens Seek Crime Solutions," *WSJ*, Mar. 25, 1982.

33. Kendrick, "Irate, Frightened Citizens."

34. Frances Fox Piven and Richard A. Cloward, *Poor People's Movements: Why They Succeed, How They Fail* (New York: Vintage Books, 1977).

35. "Anti-Crime Group Incorporates," *CT*, Apr. 1, 1982.

36. "Group Plans Talks on Crime Problems," *WSJ*, Apr. 29, 1982.

37. Balousek, "Citizens' Group Applauds Tougher Sentences," *WSJ*, May 23, 1982.

38. Andrea Ernst, producer and director, "A Second Shot at Violence," channel 27 news special, May 1982.

39. This account is drawn from notes I took at the meeting.

40. Joel F. Handler, *Social Movements and the Legal System: A Theory of Law Reform and Social Change* (New York: Academic Press, 1978), 23n20.

41. Jeanne C. Marsh, Alison Geist, and Nathan Caplan, *Rape and the Limits of Law Reform* (Boston: Auburn House, 1982), 114.

42. Robert D. Holsworth, *Let Your Life Speak: A Study of Politics, Religion, and Antinuclear Weapons Activism* (Madison: University of Wisconsin Press, 1989), 106–9, 175.

43. Jennifer L. Hochschild, *What's Fair?: American Beliefs about Distributive Justice* (Cambridge: Harvard University Press, 1981); see also Richard Sennett and Jonathan Cobb, *The Hidden Injuries of Class* (New York: Alfred A. Knopf, 1972); Jay MacLeod, *Ain't No Makin' It: Leveled Aspirations in a Low-Income Neighborhood* (Boulder, Colo.: Westview Press, 1987).

44. Arthur J. Vidich and Joseph Bensman, *Small Town in Mass Society: Class, Power, and Religion in a Rural Community* (Princeton, N.J.: Princeton University Press, 1968), 294.

45. Carol Barner-Barry and Robert Rosenwein, *Psychological Perspectives on Politics* (Englewood Cliffs, N.J.: Prentice-Hall, 1985), 153.

46. Ibid.

47. Anthony Downs, "Up and down with Ecology: The Issue Attention Cycle," *Public Interest* 28 (Summer 1972): 38–41.

48. Ibid., 39.

49. Murray Edelman, *Politics as Symbolic Action: Mass Arousal and Quiescence* (Chicago: Markham, 1971).

50. Albert O. Hirschman, *Shifting Involvements: Private Interest and Public Action* (Princeton, N.J.: Princeton University Press, 1982), 102.

51. Ibid., 89–90.

52. John Gaventa, *Power and Powerlessness: Quiescence and Rebellion in an Appalachian Valley* (Urbana: University of Illinois Press, 1980), 103; Susan Griffin, *Woman and Nature: The Roaring inside Her* (New York: Harper and Row, 1978), 19–20.

53. Hirschman, *Shifting Involvements*, 103.

54. Ibid., 112.

55. Ibid., 117.

56. Piven and Cloward, *Poor People's Movements*, 1–2, 15–18.

57. Gaventa, *Power and Powerlessness*, 137–64; Murray Edelman, *Constructing the Political Spectacle* (Chicago: University of Chicago Press, 1988), 97.

58. Hirschman, *Shifting Involvements*, 16. See also Barner-Barry and Rosenwein, *Psychological Perspectives on Politics*, 53.

59. Stockinger, "Paula Recalled at Dedication," *CT*, June 2, 1982.

6 Concerned Citizens for Children: Disappointed Discovery of Conflictual Politics

Grant County is in the southwestern corner of Wisconsin, bordered by Iowa across the Mississippi River. The farms and towns are reminiscent of Norman Rockwell's idealized America. The visual harmony and wholesomeness is challenged, however, by the issues raised by the Reinecke recall. The ideological vision of harmony and tolerance in American democracy is also challenged by this example of a sputtering interest.

The Chronology of Events

William Reinecke, whose injudicious remarks from the bench sparked the incident dealt with here, was born and raised in Grant County, Wisconsin, in the little town of Potosi. He was locally educated, attending college across the Mississippi River in Dubuque, Iowa. He left Grant County to attend law school, returning after graduation to set up practice in his hometown. After eleven years of private practice in Potosi, Reinecke was elected county judge upon the incumbent's retirement.[1] He was married to a woman also from Potosi, and by the time of his first judicial election they had eight children. He was Grant County judge from 1967 until he was elevated to circuit court judge in 1979, under a statewide reorganization of the court system.[2] At the time of the recall, Reinecke had been one of the county's only two judges since 1967 and was serving as a visiting judge in Crawford County.

Reinecke's judicial career was uncontroversial until his remarks concerning a five-year-old girl were reported in local Grant County papers in 1981. One of the first articles to recount the incident read as follows:

A rural Gays Mills man has been sentenced for having sexual contact with a 5-year-old girl who was described by a judge as "an unusually sexually permissive young lady."

Ralph Snodgrass, a 24-year-old farm worker, was placed on probation for three years and sentenced to 90 days in the Crawford County Jail under a work-release program for having sexual contact Oct. 16 with the rural Gays Mills youngster.

But during the Dec. 22 sentencing of Snodgrass, Circuit Court Judge William Reinecke said the girl, although only 5 years old, was not altogether blameless. "I am satisfied we have an unusually sexually permissive young lady and he (Snodgrass) did not know enough to refuse. No way do I believe Mr. Snodgrass initiated sexual contact," said Reinecke before pronouncing sentence.

Testimony during Snodgrass's November jury trial indicated that the incident allegedly occurred when the youngster climbed on top of Snodgrass who was sleeping in the nude. The youngster, identified as the child of Snodgrass's girlfriend, was reportedly accustomed to adults being nude in her presence, which may have made her sexually curious, according to Snodgrass's attorney.[3]

The *Telegraph Herald* continued to quote Reinecke as saying "sexually permissive young lady" although other newspapers reported him saying "sexually promiscuous."

This and other newspaper articles triggered letters to the editor. The writers were incredulous that a judge could seemingly excuse the actions of an adult and blame a five-year-old girl for her own assault. Representative of these views is a letter by Peggy Biddick, later a recall activist:

Dear Editor,

As a parent of young children I cannot understand Judge Wm. Reinecke's statements in the sexual assault case of a 5 yr. old girl and a 24-yr.-old man. How any person, and especially a judge, can believe that a 5-yr.-old is capable of being the "aggressor" in sexual contact is unthinkable and disgusting.

If Judge Reinecke has children, he obviously never took time to notice their development. A five-yr.-old is as far from being a "sexually promiscuous young lady" as Judge Reinecke is from being a thinking and fair judge.

It is interesting to note that a 12-member jury found this man guilty and yet the Judge stated that "No way do I believe Mr. Snodgrass initiated sexual contact."

Sexually perverted men need not worry about being assaulted by 5-yr.-old girls, Judge Reinecke! It's the other way around![4]

Within a few days, Madison newspapers ran articles on Reinecke's statements, including critical quotes from area residents. Interviews with the recall leaders revealed that the *Wisconsin State Journal* reporter inadvertently facilitated organized opposition. When a Grant County woman called the Madison newspaper, the reporter said he would run a story on the local controversy if she could find people, opposed to the judge's remarks, willing to be quoted and identified in print. Reinecke's critics, then, learned about each other from the newspaper. One woman telephoned others named in the newspaper article to set up a meeting. Their initial statements also set the agenda for issues raised by the recall.

Criticism of Reinecke's remarks was framed from a parental point of view, emphasizing the lack of protection his court afforded this child. Many critics were identified as parents themselves. One man was often identified by the press as "a father of five." Peggy Biddick told a reporter, "'I am still recoiling from what he said. The whole point is that children of that age are not sexually permissive, no matter what the judge says.'" And yet another, "'His remarks show a narrow-minded attitude that makes me very concerned as a parent.'"[5] Additionally, it was pointed out that the judge's remarks had branded the child for the rest of her life.

The issue of the long-term effect on the child recurred throughout the recall. Although the child was never named in print, in her small town anyone could have quickly identified her. The papers named her assailant, said he was her mother's boyfriend, and gave his rural route address. One goal the recall activists mentioned in their interviews, therefore, was to send a message to the little girl, for her to harbor all her life, that not everyone agreed with what the judge said.

Judge Reinecke first reacted by confirming his statement, adding that the trial record and presentence investigation "'showed she had been exposed to a certain amount of sexual activity involving adults that formed that conduct.'"[6] The child's home environment, however, was used against her. One article reported,

Testimony during the one-day jury trial showed that Snodgrass was intellectually and sexually naive, and that the child had been exposed to love-making by her mother and Snodgrass.

Court records show that the mother testified in defense of Snodgrass and against her daughter, saying that the child had led Snodgrass astray. Snodgrass also accused the child of initiating sexual contact by climbing on top of him while he was sleeping in the nude.[7]

At the same time Reinecke hesitated to be specific on the grounds that it was not proper for him to comment on the facts of the case. He defended himself, saying, "'I was not trying to blame her for the incident or to put a label on her, but to give my reason for imposing the sentence that I did.'"[8] Reinecke also maintained that he was frequently misquoted and his remarks were taken out of context. He made a transcript of the court proceedings available for public scrutiny, which shows he said from the bench:

I have from the very word "go," looking at the complaint, the preliminary, and everything I heard at the trial, I am satisfied that we have an unusual sexually promiscuous young lady and that this man just did not know enough to knock off her advances, to stop her advances on that occasion and allowed the contact to take place. Not initiated by him, I don't think it was initiated by him. It was initiated by him and the mother perhaps in having sexual contacts in view of that young lady. . . . But no way do I believe he initiated the sexual contact that did take place and I would be quite satisfied that that being an unusual type lady that he is probably not going to come into contact with another one where it will ever occur again. I don't think it will.[9]

Reinecke tried to avoid interviews and photographs shortly after his remarks were publicized. He spoke to one reporter in mid-January, reaffirming his belief that "the victim was 'the aggressor' in the incident" and that "he did not understand what all the 'uproar' was about."[10] He later argued that he could not comment on the case because it had not been completely disposed of. He thought the recall leaders were sincere and hoped they would become fully informed before taking any action. He asked that his record and the trial and sentencing transcripts be looked at. He added, however, that the emotions and interactions in the courtroom, as well as the closed testimony of experts, add a dimension not revealed in the transcripts.[11]

The sentence Reinecke imposed was an additional controversial issue. As was pointed out, "the crime of first-degree sexual assault is punishable by up to 20 years in prison, but Reinecke placed Snodgrass on probation for three years and sentenced him to 90 days in the county jail on a work-release program."[12] Other critics of the light sentence "compared it to the punishment of deer poachers in the county who were fined $1,700 and given two years in jail."[13]

Recall leaders tried to point out that the ninety-day sentence was for lying to the judge, not for the assault itself. Snodgrass had admitted the offense to the police, but then tried to lie to Judge Reinecke. According to the court transcript Reinecke said, "'If he (Snodgrass) had come in here and admitted to me that he did this thing, he would have walked out that very day in the street under probation.'"[14]

Local Reactions

In contrast to the Simonson recall, where almost every professional group in the city and county stated its opposition, Reinecke had support from recognized local leadership groups in Grant County, as well as law enforcement officers. One letter to the editor in support of Reinecke, for example, was signed by five Fennimore police officers and fifty other Grant County officers.[15] Supporters included the Crawford County prosecutor, several members of the Snodgrass jury, and a former Grant County juvenile court worker.[16] Most notable was the quick and virtually unanimous support for Reinecke within the local bar. One widely discussed letter to the editor, distributed to all the local and regional newspapers and signed by forty-one Grant County attorneys, made the following points:

For the past 14 years Wm. L. Reinecke has served Grant County as a Judge. He is acknowledged by all of us familiar with the court system to be an extremely able, hard working jurist. With skill and dedication he has kept his calendar up-to-date and indeed has accepted additional assignments to other counties. In his years of service he has decided thousands of cases, many of which have presented complex legal issues.

We are distressed to see the adverse publicity and reaction certain remarks during the sentencing of one case have generated. The prosecuting attorney in that case has publicly stated that the ultimate sentence was fair and proper. Those of us who have appeared in Judge Reinecke's Court over the years can assure the public that the quoted remarks do not fairly reflect his principles, wisdom or judgment.

While Judge Reinecke is a public servant and his performance a proper subject for public scrutiny, a long and distinctive career should not be destroyed by a few ill-chosen words.[17]

The same letter appeared in the the *Capital Times*, the *Fennimore Times*, the *Grant County Herald Independent*, and the *Platteville Journal*, to name a few. Many other articles referred to Reinecke's support among the Grant County legal community and to his supporters' contention that he was a tough judge who had meted out long sentences for sexual assault.[18] Supporters argued further that this was an isolated case and that Reinecke was really a tough sentencer. One local attorney, for example, said Reinecke was "'no flaming liberal.' "[19]

The support Reinecke received from most of the local bar seriously disappointed the recall activists. As pointed out by all of them in their interviews, this was a touchy matter for a small, close-knit local bar. A citizen mentioned this in her letter to an editor, arguing that the people of Grant County should thank each lawyer brave enough not to sign the lawyers' letter in support of Reinecke since this was a bread-and-butter issue for them.[20] Indeed, the subtle forms of power and invisible players in small-town politics, as documented in the classic study *Small Town in Mass Society*, echoes through the Reinecke recall.[21]

By January 16, 1982, approximately two weeks after the first publicity about Reinecke's remarks, reports circulated that the group would begin gathering recall petitions.[22] Calling themselves Concerned Citizens for Children, the group was formally organized by January 20. At its first meeting, attended by sixteen parents, the group called for Reinecke's resignation, saying a recall would be launched only after giving him the chance to resign. The parents sought Reinecke's removal because of his attitudes toward sexual assault and assault on children. They stated they didn't feel he was "'fit to serve in such high an office and to be the protector of the children of our county and state.' "[23]

A few days later, Reinecke announced that he would not resign but he did issue an apology: "'I do regret that certain extemporaneous remarks I made during the course of the sentencing hearing have offended some members of the community. Having reviewed the transcript of the hearing, I realize that some of my words were not well chosen and might have conveyed implications which I did not intend.' "[24] Reinecke said in a later interview "he didn't mean to label the child as 'a whore on the street' but said he believed she had been exposed to sexual activity between her mother and Snodgrass, which is why he felt she initiated the sexual contact."[25] He went on to say that, nevertheless, he was disturbed at the idea of forcing a judge from office for rendering an unpopular opinion and that his resignation would be a "'great disservice to the concept of a fair and impartial judiciary.' "[26]

One recall activist responded, "'The apology came too late and gave no indication that the judge has changed his attitude regarding children who are victims of sexual abuse.' ''[27] Another stated similarly that his remarks did not indicate any change of attitude but rather acknowledged only a poor choice of words. Jane Weber, another recall leader, echoed the same sentiments: "Reinecke's apology 'did not show any remorse or regret for his labeling of that child for the rest of her life. Instead of apologizing to the voters who are going to remove him from office for what he called extemporaneous remarks that may have upset them, he should have apologized to that child for what he called her.' ''[28] Finally, one critic pointed out,

the apology was "misdirected at the disposition of the charges in this case and not at the judge's attitude toward children who are sexually attacked.

"In order to say the things he said about that child, he (Reinecke) had to think them and formed them as his attitude toward her. He has not said anything to explain his intent for saying what he did or what he would have said in any other form." [29]

The editorial position of the Madison-based *Wisconsin State Journal* also held that Reinecke's apology was "too little, too late," leaving doubt "about his attitude regarding children who are the victims of sexual abuse." [30]

Media

Local media coverage of the Reinecke controversy started to shift these issues. Editors defended the judge and attacked his detractors. One editor conceded that Reinecke was "wrong in his choice of words—they do show a lack of sensitivity," yet, he continued, the positions of supporters and opponents are both undesirable. Instead, he advocated a third position—that the issue should never have left the courtroom—and pointed out that the publicity and the incident itself would probably affect the girl adversely for the rest of her life. [31] The imbalance of local editorials was painfully remembered by activists in their interviews years later.

The charge that Concerned Citizens for Children instead of helping the child was harming her undermined the group's efforts. This argument also belittled what had happened to her in her home as well as in the courtroom, before the controversy. It implied that problems should not be discussed, that victims should heal in silence and isolation, even when they are little five-year-old girls.

The *Telegraph Herald* editorialized that Reinecke's remarks were "not grounds for recall," labeling the recall effort an "ill-founded and an unwarranted threat to the proper functioning of the judiciary." The writer explained, "Society requires the continued insulation of the judiciary from external influences. . . . Sponsors of the recall campaign have served a good purpose by heightening public sensitivity to child abuse cases and now should accept the judge's public apology. Judge Reinecke should take from this experience a heightened resolve to prepare more judicious remarks from the bench."[32] The *Grant County Herald Independent* concurred:

> Calling a five-year old an "unusually promiscuous young lady" was an incredibly inappropriate and down-right stupid thing for Reinecke to say. The judge screwed up.
> A judicial recall is an extraordinary measure, an option of last resort. And in this matter, no one has convinced us that it is warranted.
> For those now infamous remarks, the judge to his credit has had the guts to apologize. To put it mildly, he's had his consciousness raised.
> There isn't any cumulative body of evidence to suggest that the extreme measure of a recall election is necessary.[33]

The labels of "radicalism" and "extremism" projected onto Concerned Citizens for Children helped to redefine the issue. Other studies of challenging groups have also noted the tendency for the media to label activists as deviant. Anti–nuclear weapons activists in Richmond, Virginia, for example, were described by the local press as either "appeasers," "antediluvians," or "naive idealists" led by a "bishop who bombs out."[34] A few mean newspaper editorials, co-worker and neighbor disapproval, and letters to the editor casting doubt on participants' motives scar members of challenging groups such as Concerned Citizens for Children. Members might seek solace in the company of the group. When this happens, "participants now begin to define themselves as victims of a repressive society rather than as people who come under intense scrutiny because of their desire to change that order. The group now serves primarily as a shield to protect its members from the harshness and bitterness of the outside world. As this happens, the original purpose of the organization is subtly transformed and it loses its identity as an agent of social and political transformation."[35] While the warmth of community can deflect attention from political endeavors, at the same time it is essential to their inception and endurance.[36] The Simonson and Lacy activists, attached to larger communities, were able to counter press intimations that they were unreasonable radicals and persist in their opposition to official government behavior. Members of Citizens for Children, like those of Citizens Taking Action, were unaffiliated, though momentarily politically mobilized, and found solace in group healing while their anger played itself out.

The Reinecke story attracted national media coverage and commentary. A few of the leaders, for example, were flown to New York City and appeared on the "Today Show." Columnist Mike Royko of the *Chicago Sun-Times* likened Reinecke's remarks to those of Archie Simonson who was, according to Royko, "driven from the bench by angry feminist groups." Royko wrote, "With that memory still fresh, you would think that any judge—especially a Wisconsin judge—would be careful about what he said about such sensitive matters. But no. We have another loose-lipped Wisconsin judge in trouble with angry women who want him booted off the bench." Royko noted that the prosecutor in the case maintained that Snodgrass was not very bright, having suffered from a fall off a horse. Royko retorted, "But the fall from the horse did not seem to have affected his sexual capabilities." He then recounted what he called the "rather sordid facts" of the case.[37]

Crawford County District Attorney Rod Satter said that Snodgrass's mental age was not much more than the child's. In addition, "Four psychiatric examinations, following the filing of charges, indicated that a 'low IQ and limited intellectual ability' limited his understanding of sexual behavior and of the charges against him."[38] Recall activists believed this was a fabricated issue meant to diminish the importance of Snodgrass's crime.

Big-city editorial opposition to Reinecke's remarks was swift and unequivocal. Indicative of the reaction is a *Capital Times* editorial:

Mothers, lock up your 5-year-old daughters. They may be pint-sized seductresses lurking in wait for unsuspecting males.

Or so we might conclude from the recent remarks of a Grant County judge. . . .

The whole thing would be outrageously funny if it weren't so tragic. It is the logical extension of the old blame-the-victim philosophy epitomized by former Dane County Judge Archie Simonson. . . .

Simonson was recalled from the bench for his comments. And judging from the community reaction to Reinecke's remarks, it would not be surprising if he suffered the same fate. He has, in the same breath, excused an act of violence against children—who account for as many as half of all reported sexual assaults—and suggested that rapists are not responsible for their actions.[39]

In their interviews, the recall activists all commented on the barrage of media attention the controversy received. Their concern for the effects the media were having on their grass-roots organization showed early in their campaign:

The recall group, which had scheduled an informational meeting for Thursday night, has apparently decided to postpone it. Peggy Biddick said the citizens needed time to talk things over, examine the record and work out the mechanics of a possible recall.

She said, too, that, as one of the handful of recall leaders, she felt that the media were pushing the movement in its quest for new stories.[40]

This spokesperson was right about the media's influence on interest groups.[41] The group was trying to absorb the initial publicity and figure out what to do next. They were inexperienced with this level of publicity and controversy and wanted to slow things down a little. They were concerned that events, fed by the media attention, were developing too fast and they didn't want to be set on a course they could not control. Their hesitation at this point, though, was redefined by local editors as exclusivity and conspiracy.

People active in the recall recounted their fears for their families, businesses, and futures in Grant County as a consequence of getting involved in a struggle against a local judge. From the very beginning there were hints of their caution mixed with their forthrightness. They refused to reveal the location of their first meeting to a local newspaper, for example, explaining, "'We don't want the press at our doorstep taking down every word.'"[42] There were other examples of the same caution: a Citizens for Children spokesperson declined to be identified during a telephone interview and refused to reveal the exact location of the group's first meeting or name the group's lawyer: "The spokesperson said it would be the decision of the individual retained as counsel to step forward."[43] These attempts to be active while simultaneously protecting their privacy were later cited to question the motives of the recall activists.

A *Wisconsin State Journal* reporter, though, was invited to the initial meeting. Also in attendance were the victim's foster parents, who began caring for the child shortly after the incident was reported to police by her teacher. They related the emotional and physical anguish the child continued to experience.[44] The foster parents were visibly, publicly outraged at Reinecke's remarks and poignantly related the effects of the assault on the child in order to counter the image of her being "promiscuous." They also wrote long, touching letters to the editor in an attempt to set the record straight.[45]

Although a *Capital Times* editorial seemed to take it for granted that a judge who said something this outrageous would be recalled, it is fascinating to consider why he was not.

Redefining the Issues: Blaming Messengers

One aspect of the recall was the attempt by Reinecke's supporters to stigmatize the activists, questioning the motives for their opposition to Reinecke. This deeply hurt the activists. Indicative of the nature of the counterattack were the comments by an attorney who said the judge was being targeted for personal reasons, in particular because of his recent divorce.[46]

The recall activists recognized the potential for retaliation against them in a small, rural county and tried to shield themselves from some of the publicity. Instances where they sought anonymity were viewed suspiciously by some residents who questioned their motives. A letter to the editor took this position: "'Citizens for Children' is asking for support in their effort to recall the judge. Yet, they hide behind their white sheets of 'I do not wish to be identified' and hold secret meetings. Before I would support any group or effort, I would want to know all the details and that includes names of persons involved. The secrecy makes me wonder if the concern is really over this unfortunate incident or is this incident being used as a vehicle for retaliation."[47] One local clergy member wrote, "I'm sure those signing the present removal petition have more than one axe to grind in the matter, and this is why I would not sign."[48] Several letters implied that petition signers, if not the recall leaders themselves, had "a personal axe to grind."[49] Another writer referred to the recall partisans as a "lynch mob."[50] Crawford County District Attorney Rod Satter also called Citizens for Children a lynch mob: "'Sensible people' are starting to ask questions: who are they (the Citizens for Children) and what is their axe to grind? They are wondering about the 'white sheets and secret meetings.'"[51]

One editorial epitomizes the change in emphasis, here impugning the motives for the recall: "We have received several letters to the editor with a prison return address which tell how badly [*sic*] Reinecke was during their case. They, of course, were completely innocent. Reinecke railroaded them into prison. Whom are they kidding?"[52] A later editorial by the publisher explained that the paper only printed letters that were new and not redundant. The publisher hinted, though, that many such letter writers had questionable incentives: "Many of the letters come unsigned. Some come from groups with strange titles. Several have come from prisons, opposed to the judge. I wonder why."[53] These charges were not substantiated. Activists felt compelled to defend their motives and character. On the day the recall petitions were filed in Madison one recall leader stated, "'I have no personal feelings about him. I do not know him. I have never met him. I feel sorry this is happening to him.'"[54]

Instances of intimidation were also part of the recall atmosphere in Grant County. On the first day of petition circulation, one reporter wrote, "There also have been reports of phone calls to some of the protesting parents by Grant County law enforcement officials asking them to 'lay off the judge' and stop the recall effort."[55] Judge Reinecke also claimed to have received threats and harassments.[56] Reinecke's son reported that the judge moved out of his house and stopped answering the telephone in order to escape harassment.[57]

The Campaign

Citizens for Children had sixty days to collect 3,800 signatures on petitions to force a recall. Within a few days of circulating recall petitions, 1,000 people had signed.[58] They urged candidates to run against Reinecke without supporting any individual in particular. Activists recounted later how difficult it was to get anyone to run against the judge. They even feared that they would be successful in forcing a recall election but that Reinecke would run unopposed.

In early March Concerned Citizens for Children announced that entertainer Connie Francis, a rape victim and critic of the treatment of victims, would appear in Grant County on March 17 in support of the recall effort.[59] One member of Concerned Citizens for Children had written asking for her support after Connie Francis read a newspaper account of the affair to a television audience. Francis stated, "'I am not a political activist. I am not a kook. I just feel that our courts are no longer a place which we should be proud of.'"[60] Within three days, however, Francis canceled her appearance because of threats on her life if she made the trip to Wisconsin.[61] In a statement to one of the recall leaders Francis explained she would help crime victims in "a personal and quiet way" but would do no more crusading or lobbying because of the backlash of hatred and anger she experienced. Accounts of the Francis cancellation also revealed a dark underside to the local political effort. One Concerned Citizen for Children member expressed sympathy for Francis and revealed that several group members had been harassed and received threatening phone calls. The husband of an activist was nearly run off the road by a county police officer in what was considered a life-threatening situation.[62] Every person interviewed mentioned this automobile incident as an example of community tension.[63]

These events prompted one editor to concede that something had gone wrong in the recall effort: "What started as a sincere effort by a group of concerned citizens has dissolved into an atmosphere of innuendo, rumor, threats, charges and counter-charges and sensationalism."[64] Another editor commented, "We are a little skeptical about a death threat to Connie Francis. . . . We're not saying that the death threat story is a publicity stunt or a hoax but we must admit to being skeptical with so many unanswered questions. If such a thing did occur it is a terrible black mark in Grant County's history. If it didn't occur, it is a cruel thing to attempt to drum up support on the part of a nationally-known entertainer."[65] Francis herself later responded incredulously to these and similar stories doubting her truthfulness.[66]

More than the necessary number of recall signatures were filed on March 26. Thirty-eight hundred signatures were needed; 5,351 were filed. A Concerned Citizens for Children spokesperson said about two hundred people circulated petitions. A primary was scheduled for May 11 if more than two candidates ran and a runoff election would be held June 8.[67]

A young attorney, James Dahlquist, announced he would run against Reinecke. A third candidate, Norman Kvalheim, also ran. From the beginning of his campaign, Dahlquist was endorsed by Concerned Citizens for Children, and group members actively campaigned for him. He emphasized Reinecke's arrogance and critiqued the judge's entire judicial record.[68] Dahlquist alleged, "'It's a sad comment when people don't feel they can exercise their legal right to sign a petition without fear of reprisals.'"[69]

Reinecke announced (against the background of his courtroom) his intention to run in the recall election and explained that he had chosen the wrong word in reference to the five-year-old victim of the assault.[70] At the same press conference Reinecke explained, "'My sentence was no basis for the recall effort now against me. I want to emphatically state that there was no intercourse, no penetration, no violence, no injuries, no threats, in the Crawford County case. No five-year-old can be held at fault for a sexual contact, that's my belief. The child initiated the contact, the man allowed that to continue, and he was convicted of that crime.'"[71] Activists were incensed at the judge's belittlement of the assault. They maintained there was injury and violence.

Reinecke further tried to undermine the credibility of recall petition signers and told a reporter he had recognized the names of past litigants in his courtroom among those who signed the recall petitions. When the reporter asked if revenge might be a recall motive, Reinecke responded, "'You said it, I didn't.'"[72] Several political ads by Reinecke included a quote from a *Milwaukee Journal* editorial: "'Given the circumstances in this case, it seems to us that Reinecke is not merely fighting to keep his job. He is battling in defense of judicial independence from intimidation by one-issue groups.'"[73] His May 6 ad also cited favorable editorials from the *Grant County Herald Independent* (twice), the *Dubuque Telegraph-Herald* (twice), and the *Platteville Journal*. The ad also argued, "Now, for the first time, the Judge has been publicly criticized by a single issue group for his courtroom remarks."[74]

Further indication of the new image of the victimized Reinecke was an article entitled "Recall Agonizing for Reinecke."[75] Another, two days before the election, tells of Reinecke's anguish during the recall campaign and recounts his apology, his defenses against charges of arrogance, and his personal life.[76]

Activists vividly remembered the "dirty" nature of the campaign. Six days before the primary Dahlquist was charged with ethical misconduct for allegedly viewing the juvenile court file of the case without the presiding Crawford County judge's permission. This supposedly confidential complaint against Dahlquist was phoned in to a Madison television station by an anonymous caller. This was cited by one newspaper editor as evidence of the emotionalism on both sides of the recall. The editor related other dirty tricks by Reinecke supporters, including endorsements from an Iowa County circuit judge and a Grant County circuit judge in letters to local newspapers, endorsements that could violate an American Bar Association canon that judges should not publicly endorse a candidate for public office.[77] This editorial, though, did not relate any dirty tricks by Concerned Citizens for Children.

Concerned Citizens activists reflected that Dahlquist was a long-shot candidate because of his youth, his "outsider" status (he practiced primarily in Dubuque, Iowa, across the Mississippi River from Lancaster, the Grant County seat), and his lack of extensive family ties in Grant County. Unlike the Simonson recall, therefore, the Reinecke recall was not strengthened by a strong challenger. Nevertheless, interviewees believed Dahlquist was brave to run against Reinecke.

Five previous cases of juvenile sexual assault heard by Reinecke were cited in Dahlquist's campaign literature. In one letter to the editor, these cases were raised as evidence of the judge's leniency. The writer, however, went further, framing the issue as Reinecke's possible prejudice against women.[78] Local editorials continued to support Judge Reinecke.[79] Editors viewed the recall as a "one-issue campaign" wherein attempts to enlarge the controversy to include Reinecke's "arrogance" had never been substantiated; a few ill-chosen words did not merit his defeat at the polls.[80]

Another editor was less tolerant of Concerned Citizens for Children. Recalls, he argued, were a means of last resort for extremely egregious officials. Concerned Citizens for Children had not proven that Reinecke deserved to be recalled; instead the editor saw the recall "as more of a lynching than a true lesson in American democracy."[81]

In the final days of the campaign, thirty-six Grant County attorneys again wrote letters to local papers in support of Reinecke and added a new charge: "The proper function of the Court has been interfered with by the recall campaign and the taxpayers of Grant County must additionally now pay the large expense of holding this election. This campaign has been more than an attack upon one man. It has been, in our view, a fundamental attack upon our traditional judicial system of government."[82] Many letters alleged that this use of recall actually undermined the democratic process.[83] Similarly, a letter from the Grant County coroner supporting Reinecke read in part:

It is sad that these same concerned people, who call themselves "Citizens for Children," can't realize how much damage they have done to this poor girl. You may just call it sacrificing the lamb to get the sheep. I'm referring to the little girl as the lamb and the Judge as the sheep. We really don't have a wolf, but if we were looking for a wolf we would find there's a large pack of them. We would find them to be the "Citizens for Children." Believe me they are causing the most damage. The little girl would have never remembered any of this as long as her mother didn't tell her. Now that the wolf pack has made it history, someday she'll probably read it herself.[84]

The issue of what the judge said and did about the assaulted child was diminished by the specter of Concerned Citizens in "white sheets," grinding private axes and threatening the foundations of the American judiciary, maybe even the government itself.

An implicit concern for those against the recall, never explicitly made, was the influence the Simonson recall had on the reaction in Grant County to the Reinecke recall effort. Because the Reinecke recall occurred after Simonson's, judges, lawyers, and other predominately male established officials might have felt threatened about a growing restiveness among people, especially women, and their potential use of the recall mechanism. It's one thing to have the recall law on the books, it's quite another for citizens to actually start using it. This might be especially troublesome to officials when legal mechanisms such as recall are used by challenging groups voicing new concerns, here the treatment of rape victims in the courts.

The specter of single-issue groups undermining the independence of well-intentioned public officials by threatening removal from office, however, is not supported by research on recalls.[85] On balance, Cronin finds, "the recall has been mainly used to weed out incompetent, arbitrary, or corrupt officials. It is a positive device reminding officials that they are temporary agents of the public they serve."[86]

Election Results

In a remarkable turnout for a special election, especially in a rural area during spring planting season, Reinecke retained his judgeship. The previous spring election had only 7,700 voters; the recall vote of 13,829 nearly matched the 15,000 voters in the previous governor's race. Rainfall was partially credited for the high turnout as farmers were forced to leave their fields and then had time to vote. With a total of 6,051 votes Dahlquist held a slim margin of victory in the villages and townships. Reinecke won heavily in the towns "where he was strongly supported by the establishment—lawyers and businessmen," receiving a total of 7,033 votes.[87] Reinecke's biggest margin of victory, 1,115 to 472 votes, came from his hometown of Lancaster, the county seat. Kvalheim trailed with only 745 votes. Because Reinecke won 51 percent of the vote, a runoff election was not necessary.[88]

In one of the only articles describing the reactions of members of Concerned Citizens for Children, disappointment was mixed with satisfaction on the night of the election returns: "They had given Reinecke a run. Sure, the judge held onto his seat, but only by the skin of his teeth."[89] This was especially remarkable when considering that the challenger, Dahlquist, was virtually unknown in Grant County two months before the race. The account continued,

For most Dahlquist supporters, the recall election was their first foray into politics. They printed flyers, arranged rallies, wrote letters, talked, cajoled and wheedled voters. They watched lawn signs get ripped down, read newspapers lambasting them and assigned people to watch the vote counting.

To the end, they remained convinced of the moral superiority of their campaign. . . . With zeal, they fought for their recall election. With equal fervor they fought for their candidate. To their surprise, they found they had created a wave of hostility.

In addition to being labeled a lynch mob, they have heard themselves called a hit squad, a feminist group, radicals, outsiders and even a Catholic-hate group (Reinecke is Catholic).[90]

The article pointed out they were middle-class people who considered themselves just folks, outside the power structure of the county, especially in contrast to Reinecke's "'white wine and caviar' group."[91]

Diane Barton of Concerned Citizens for Children said afterwards, "They demonstrated that a judge has to be 'accountable' " simply by challenging him and predicted that he would be more sensitive in the future.[92] Activists noted that Reinecke's victory was not a vote of confidence and partially attributed their loss to lack of money and time to campaign. Interviewees pointed out that Reinecke got large donations, while Dahlquist's were smaller. Reinecke, for example, was able to purchase television time and run larger newspaper ads. Despite their defeat they did establish a record of dissent against what Reinecke had said. They hoped the five-year-old victim would find comfort from this in the future.

The Madison-based *Capital Times* editorialized that the recall was "a textbook case in the workings of democracy" and a testament to the outrage that exists even in rural hamlets over blaming victims. It was analogous to the Simonson recall, except, the editor noted, that Reinecke apologized. The editor concluded, "If Judge William Reinecke, or any judge, is now more sensitive to the way he handles human dilemmas, the Grant County episode and its emotional fallout will have served a useful purpose."[93] In the view of the members of Concerned Citizens for Children, though, the recall was a textbook case of the tyranny of the majority and the vilification of dissenters in American politics.

Voices Silenced

Citizen Participation, the Scholarly Approach

Alexis de Tocqueville's analysis of the tyranny of the majority and the mitigating factors that might curb majority tyranny aid explanation of the travails of a group such as Concerned Citizens for Children. Based on a deductive approach to understanding cultural mores, or habits of the heart, Alexis de Tocqueville provided lasting insights into the American political culture.[94] He recognized the potential threat to freedoms with a culture based on individual sovereignty and majority rule—"the tyranny of the majority":

When an individual or a party is wronged in the United States, to whom can he apply for redress? If to public opinion, public opinion constitutes the majority; if to the legislature, it represents the majority and implicitly obeys it; if to the executive power, it is appointed by the majority and serves as a passive tool in its hands. The public force consists of the majority under arms; the jury is the majority invested with the right of hearing judicial cases; and in certain states even the judges are elected by the majority. However iniquitous or absurd the measure of which you complain, you must submit to it as well as you can.[95]

Majority tyranny can be mitigated, though, by aspects of the culture that teach community mindedness and a "self-interest rightly understood." These aspects include religion, local government and community ties, and the American penchant for associations.

Tocqueville worried about weaknesses in the human spirit and the tenuous nature of human freedoms. He called for a new political science to fit the new age of expanding equalities, a "political science as an active force in the world."[96] He believed that instilling the mental habit of citizen participation would help mitigate majority tyranny. Tocqueville valued citizen participation partially because it promoted the mental habits of continuing to participate in politics.

Many other democratic theorists place a high value on citizen participation. For John Stuart Mill, Rousseau, and G. D. H. Cole, for example, citizen participation has an educational function. Carole Pateman bases her argument on the potential to achieve citizen participation partly on the belief that once people participate in decision making at their workplace and in politics, they will have a heightened sense of political efficacy and want to participate more. She mentions that "there are many difficulties and complexities involved."[97] Her overall theme, though, is that participation will be a positive experience. Pluralist theory in American politics similarly posits that people can and will participate effectively when issues are salient to them. This would not be a bad system, I argue, but this is not necessarily the result of political activity.

Citizens for Children Participation Experiences

What lessons did these recall activists learn from their foray into citizen participation? In-depth interviews with five of the Reinecke recall leaders, conducted from May to July 1985, revealed a turning away from politics due to their negative experiences. All of these people were parents and responded to Reinecke's remarks in a very personal way: "I kept thinking, 'What if a judge said this about my child?' " The activists interviewed were all college educated. They saw themselves as middle- to upper middle-class "respectable citizens." They were teachers or middle-class farmers. Their social status and good citizen records made it hard for them to understand the community backlash against their political efforts. They had always believed that people like them were immune to such opprobrium.

They perceived that the issue was transformed from what the judge had said and its implications for his future judicial performance to what was wrong with the people in Concerned Citizens for Children. This happened with numerous responses of the spiral of silence. The local media painted the activists as "extremists" who were actually further harming the five-year-old victim by all the publicity.[98] These editorials were painfully remembered by the recall activists.

People active in the recall recounted their fears for their families, businesses, and futures in Grant County because of their involvement in a controversy against one of only two local judges. Recognizing the potential for retaliation against them in a small, rural county, the recall activists sometimes tried to shield themselves from publicity. Instances where they sought anonymity, though, were used by Reinecke's supporters to impugn their motives.

Reinecke's support from the local bar was a strong disappointment to recall activists, making them feel isolated within a spiral of silence. They pointed out that this was a touchy matter for a small, close-knit local bar. They were also concerned that they would not find a candidate to run against Reinecke even if they gathered enough recall signatures, since the costs for a local attorney who ran and lost against Reinecke were so high.

Besides the media coverage of their efforts, the activists remembered the backlash by Grant County residents discrediting their motivations. These attacks took two forms. One portrayed the recall as a personal vendetta against the judge. The second implied that the activists had appeared in front of Reinecke on criminal matters and were now seeking revenge. In fact, an exhaustive review of the print-media account of the Reinecke recall (including over 260 articles and letters to the editor) reveal only two letters from past litigants in Reinecke's courtroom, both of them dissatisfied with their treatment in civil suits. These letter writers, though, were not recall leaders. In interviews for this study, the leaders of Concerned Citizens painfully recalled being called "vigilantes," "rabble-rousers," "a lynch mob," and people in "white sheets."

They were also called "women's libbers." Ironically, only two of them felt any affinity with a larger women's liberation movement, and two of the women involved very deliberately explained in their interviews that they were definitely not "women's libbers." In addition, men were active and visible recall leaders as well. The construction of the issues by Citizens for Children lacked the ideological depth that connection to a dissenting or reform-oriented movement would have provided. Noteworthy in their critique of Reinecke is what they did not explicitly voice: the gender politics aspects of the controversy. This recall, though, took place during a time when an active feminist movement was challenging cultural assumptions about sex crimes and countering the victim-blaming tendencies of many beliefs and practices. Fluid social movements raise new questions about everyday practices. Feminism played a part in the Reinecke recall, but only indirectly. The lack of an acknowledged feminist critique did not protect them, however, from being labeled "women's libbers."

The media frequently identified one Citizens for Children activist as a member of the National Organization for Women.[99] She was indeed a dues-paying NOW member, but the level of her NOW involvements were so minimal that the media's attention to this connection to feminism is pushing the point. She did, however, criticize Reinecke for an "attitude" that might also influence his treatment of other rape victims. She saw the issue beyond what the judge had said about one little girl. Opponents perhaps focused on this larger perspective as one indicator of the group's so-called radicalism.

There was little response to Reinecke's remarks from the organized feminist movement. Many people did join in criticizing Reinecke. Other critics included a woman from Rape Crisis, Inc., in Madison and State Representative Barbara Ulichny, chair of the legislative council committee on sexual assault and child abuse.[100] One member of Concerned Citizens called the Madison NOW chapter for some initial advice. She and others felt, however, that the group was not very helpful. Although editors linked Concerned Citizens with a larger women's "lib" movement, the group worked alone without any other group's help or affiliation. Whereas in the Simonson recall and the Lacy case seasoned leaders and co-optable networks were mobilized into effective ad hoc coalitions, the Grant County activists could not draw on such resources.

One of the members observed that because Concerned Citizens for Children was predominantly a female group, they all were considered troublemakers and "crazies." This seemed unfair to her. She said, "I wish I had a buck for every time someone told me 'This was an isolated incident.'" It wasn't an isolated incident, she believed, but she did not have the psychological resources to continue to fight the issue.

These parents mobilized into trying to recall Reinecke read the text of the trial transcript and believed it was symptomatic of deeper prejudices and stereotypes of women and girls. Yet, it was difficult for them to voice this critique of Reinecke's remarks, and symbolically all female victim-blaming remarks, because they had not gone that far in their political affiliations.[101] They were not connected to the intellectual perceptions of deeper societal injustices of violence and prejudice against women. This is not because they were blind and could not see the wrongs, but rather because it would have been too personally painful to give up their faith in the fairness of their culture and face the overwhelming burden of reforming a violent and sexist system. These issues are too large and difficult for concerned parents to face. In addition, if they had voiced a deeper critique of the judicial system, they would have been even further isolated and harmed by the larger society. They saw what trying to recall a single judge who said a five-year-old rape victim was promiscuous was like. They need only have imagined what they might have to endure if they became involved in seeking wider reforms.

The Concerned Citizens activists were labeled "radicals" despite their reasonableness and "women's libbers" despite their distance from feminism. Perhaps, if they had taken their critique of Reinecke one step further and connected with feminism or other larger movements, the tie would have provided them with the political armor to anticipate and protect themselves from the reaction to their dissent. Instead, they were shocked and disappointed at the hostility they encountered.

Some of the activists even found their church leaders set against them. One woman remembered her disappointment when the clergy of Lancaster (the county seat) seemed to support Reinecke. Another woman sat through a sermon by her Catholic priest in support of Reinecke. She was so incensed that she tried to speak to the priest. "Why," she asked, "can't you say something supportive about children?" She even telephoned the Catholic bishop of the area, to no avail. She felt that Reinecke was supported by the church because he was a "big money" contributor. Another person's religious faith was shaken by the recall. After Reinecke won the election, she said,

I didn't go to Church for six months. [pause] I thought, "How could God let this happen?" We had nothing to gain by this. We spent a lot of money, of our own money on it, financially, you know, it hurt us. Emotionally it killed us. You know, we had nothing to gain and God says in all these Bible stories and everything else, "Help your neighbor; do this stuff; take care of the children" and stuff like that. Well, that's what we tried to do. And we got burnt doing it. And I was so sure that He wasn't there watching, you know, somewhere along the line, something happened and He lost touch. You know. And I really had a problem with that.

Her faith was restored only months later when she noticed that Reinecke seemed to be giving harder sentences to convicted abusers and assaulters, "but, what started happening was people started watching Reinecke from both sides; people started watching him. And, all of a sudden, people did start going to jail. So, was he talking out of one side of his face and really knowing that we were right all the way along?" Perhaps, she believed, her God was working in mysterious ways with longer term consequences.

One person remembered watching the media focus change from perhaps a slant in favor of Concerned Citizens for Children to the "poor judge" who was being "picked on." The respondent suggested that "people were getting literally sick and tired of reading about the whole thing in the papers and hearing it on the radio and I think the sympathetic vote went to Judge Reinecke. The whole thing got twisted by the time we were over and Judge Reinecke was the victim in the case and I think he received a lot of votes because of that."

Activists in Concerned Citizens related that since the Reinecke recall they think about the people in Grant County differently. "I thought I had people figured out," one woman stated, "but even some of my friends surprised me." One person said she keeps more to herself since the recall. Before, she was friendly to people she would see while grocery shopping. Now, she said, she is not.

Their experiences in politics seared them. One woman said the Reinecke recall taught her to "stay out" of politics. Another woman said, "I am more disillusioned than ever." They all doubted whether they would ever get involved again. After the election, two took quieter, less visible political roles. They volunteered for rape crisis and domestic violence hot lines. Some were volunteers for a sexual assault task force through the sheriff's department, helping victims and their families negotiate the criminal justice system. The hot lines and advocacy groups were set up after the recall by some of the same people in Concerned Citizens for Children.

Two of the leaders withdrew from politics. They still cared deeply about children's welfare, but, as one said, "I couldn't put my family through that hell again." These two people adopted a private solution: they will watch and protect their own children and just hope nothing happens to them.

Nevertheless, for a couple of years after the recall campaign, Concerned Citizens for Children was still active, collecting clothing for poor children and preparing and distributing Christmas baskets for poor families. These activities were carried out privately, quietly, and unobtrusively. The individuals took comfort from the thought that they had raised the consciousness level of people in Grant County regarding occurrences of child abuse and treatment of children in the courts. The activists also believed that judges in Grant County were a little more judicious in their choice of words.

Members of Concerned Citizens for Children, however, felt that there was still something wrong in Reinecke's courtroom. Although Reinecke was more careful about his choice of words after the recall, he was allegedly still unsympathetic to the plight of sexual assault victims. Experience since the recall caused some of them to see the issue more in terms of Reinecke's attitude toward women. Four of the individuals interviewed independently related the story of a case in the spring of 1985. A teenage boy was convicted and sentenced by Reinecke for sexually assaulting younger boys. Reinecke stated that the sentence he imposed was in part because of the "unnaturalness" of the crime. One person recounted, "He was very careful in what he said, but what he said was that he felt that this was very unnatural and he felt that it would be more harmful of boys this age than it would have been a girl this age. And I sat there [in the courtroom] thinking, 'I can't believe he's saying that.' "

This incident was not reported in the papers. In addition, interviewees felt they could not legitimately criticize Reinecke for this statement now that they were seen as community radicals "out to get Reinecke." Even though they were outraged at the implications of Reinecke's logic, they were effectively silenced from further dissent. In the same manner as another study of small-town, rural politics determined, these rare few who perceive problems in the community have nobody to communicate with, especially because of the personal conflict disturbing the illusions of other community members would generate, therefore, their insights, given their history, make them unhappy.[102]

Conclusion

Leaders in Concerned Citizens were not political activists prior to their involvement in the campaign to recall Reinecke. They became involved because they believed the little girl was being blamed for her own victimization; they wanted her to know that not everyone agreed. They initially believed their position was simple common sense. "Who would agree with a judge that blamed a five-year-old rape victim?" one activist asked. She continued, "We were novices then." To their shock and disappointment their integrity became the issue as much as what the judge had said.

For Concerned Citizens for Children, the injustice was the judge's statement about individual responsibility. As one recall leader explained during the campaign, "'Most of us have read the transcript, because we're trying to give the judge the benefit of the doubt. [. . .] But, it's his attitude that I'm upset with. I'd certainly not want to be a rape victim in his court.'"[103] Activists entered the campaign with a faith in the impartiality of the American democratic system. They learned, though, that politics is a conflictual power struggle where righteous causes can be silenced.

The Reinecke recall supports Noelle-Neumann's theory of the spiral of silence. "We are only beginning to observe," she explains, "the hundreds of signals that let a person know he or she is not surrounded by a warm glow of sympathy but by a ring of avoidance."[104] Concerned Citizens for Children members were seared by the characterizations used against them: a lynch mob, vigilantes, revenge-seekers, radicals, and women's libbers.

Activists in Concerned Citizens for Children also observed the spiral of silence and were puzzled by it. Friends and co-workers withdrew from them during the recall campaign. These friends sometimes secretly confided to the activists that they agreed with their campaign against Reinecke but were afraid of isolation and ostracism if they took a public stand. In addition to the spiral of silence, these activists were discouraged from further participation through the belittlement of their efforts and questioning of their motives.

They believed the Reinecke recall was unsuccessful because society did to some degree blame this victim for her assault. The recall leaders were painted by the local media as the aggressors, the interlopers on community standards and traditions, and the question of children's dignity became lost in translation. They learned the social costs of challenging the majority and their flames sputtered out.

NOTES

1. "W.L. Reinecke, Potosi, to Seek Judicial Post," *Capital Times* (hereafter *CT*), Dec. 8, 1966; "William L. Reinecke: New Grant Judge," *Wisconsin State Journal* (hereafter *WSJ*), Jan. 7, 1968.

2. Jim Miller, "Move to Unseat Judge Reinecke," *Telegraph Herald* (Dubuque, Iowa; hereafter *TH*), Jan. 10, 1982.

3. "Gays Mills Man Sentenced for Sexual Contact with Child," *TH*, Dec. 31, 1981.

4. Peggy Biddick, letter to the editor, *Grant County Herald Independent* (hereafter *GCHI*), Jan. 20, 1982.

5. Richard W. Jaeger, "Judge under Attack for Remarks about Girl," *WSJ*, Jan. 9, 1982.

6. Ibid.

7. Miller, "Judge Based Comments on Testimony," *TH*, Jan. 15, 1982.

8. Jaeger, "Judge under Attack."

9. Miller, "Judge Based Comments on Testimony."

10. Jacquelyn Mitchard, "Judge Draws Support as Recall Talk Grows," *CT*, Jan. 15, 1982.

11. Thomas S. Beebe, "Group Promises to Try Reinecke Recall," *Fennimore Times* (hereafter *FT*), Jan. 20, 1982.

12. Miller, "Move to Unseat."

13. Jaeger, "Weather May Cool Heated-Up Recall Effort," *WSJ*, Jan. 16, 1982.

14. Mitchard, "Judge Draws Support."

15. Richard Carlin, et al., letter to the editor, "Law Officers Support Reinecke," *FT*, May 5, 1982.

16. Dean R. Krueger, letter to the editor, *FT*, Apr. 21, 1982.

17. Frank J. Antonie and forty other attorneys (all separately named), letter to the editor, *GCHI*, Jan. 20, 1982.

18. See Mitchard, "Judge Draws Support"; Jaeger, "Weather May Cool Heated-Up Recall Effort"; and Beebe, "Group Promises to Try Reinecke Recall."

19. Mitchard, "Judge Draws Support."

20. M. S. Snyder, letter to the editor, "Blames Media, Lawyers, Defendant . . . ," *Platteville Journal*, (hereafter *PJ*), Feb. 2, 1982.

21. Arthur J. Vidich and Joseph Bensman, *Small Town in Mass Society: Class, Power, and Religion in a Rural Community* (Princeton, N.J.: Princeton University Press, 1968), 153–66, 277.

22. Jaeger, "Weather May Cool Heated-Up Recall Effort." Recalls had been tried in Grant County before. In 1975 an unsuccessful recall election was held against the chair of the Grant County Board based on opposition to his support of regional planning; see Phil Haslanger, "If Recall Is Successful, Simonson Will Make History," *CT*, June 11, 1977.

23. "Group Vows to Petition for Recall of Judge," *WSJ*, Jan. 20, 1982; see also Pat Kwallek, "Group to Proceed with Recall Effort," *GCHI*, Jan. 20, 1982.

24. Reinecke's letter quoted in part from "Reinecke's Reply," *PJ*, Jan. 26, 1982; see also "Grant County Judge Apologizes; Won't Quit," *WSJ*, Jan. 25, 1982.

25. Jaeger, "Recall Effort against Judge Is Half Done," *CT*, Feb. 20, 1982.

26. "Grant County Judge Apologizes."

27. Ibid.

28. "Move to Recall Judge Gains Steam," *CT,* Jan. 26, 1982.

29. Ibid.

30. Editorial, "Too Little, Too Late," *WSJ,* Jan. 26, 1982.

31. Editorial, "Grant County vs. Judge Reinecke," *FT,* Jan. 20, 1982.

32. Editorial, "Not Grounds for Recall," *TH,* Jan. 31, 1982.

33. Editorial, *GCHI,* Jan. 27, 1982, reprinted in editorial, "What Other Papers Are Saying," *FT,* Feb. 3, 1982.

34. Robert D. Holsworth, *Let Your Life Speak: A Study of Politics, Religion, and Antinuclear Weapons Activism* (Madison: University of Wisconsin Press, 1989), 84.

35. Ibid., 107.

36. Ibid., 108.

37. Mike Royko, "Justice in Wisconsin: Temptress at 5?" *Chicago Sun-Times,* Jan. 14, 1982.

38. Beebe, "Group Promises to Try Reinecke Recall."

39. Editorial, "Innocence, Redefined," *CT,* Jan. 12, 1982.

40. Steve Hannah, "A Judge's Remarks: A Look at the Case," *MJ,* Jan. 17, 1982.

41. See Todd Gitlin, *The Whole World Is Watching: Mass Media in the Making and Unmaking of the New Left* (Berkeley: University of California Press, 1980).

42. "Judge's Remarks Topic of Tuesday Meeting," *GCHI,* Jan. 13, 1982.

43. Kwallek, "Group to Proceed with Recall Effort"; see also "Concerned Group Makes Statement," *FT,* Jan. 20, 1982.

44. Jaeger, "Group Will Try to Recall Judge," *WSJ,* Jan. 13, 1982; see also Dan Allegretti, "Five-Year-Old Is Scarred for Life, Foster Folks Say," *CT,* Jan. 15, 1982; Miller, "Judge Based Comments on Testimony"; Jaeger, "Weather May Cool Heated-Up Recall Effort."

45. See Ted Steiner and June Steiner, letter to the editor, *GCHI, CT,* and *FT,* Jan. 20, 1982; see also Ted Steiner and June Steiner, letter to the editor, "Justice for Children? There Is None," *FT,* Mar. 10, 1982.

46. Mitchard, "Judge Draws Support." There were many personal aspects to the campaign. The judge's twenty-four-year-old son attended recall meetings to defend his father, and the judge's ex-wife wrote letters to the editor defending him. His ex-wife also worked in the same school as some of the recall leaders.

47. Dorothy L. Harris, letter to the editor, *GCHI,* Jan. 27, 1982. This person also criticized the mother's role in her daughter's abuse.

48. Rev. Lowell M. Bush, letter to the editor, *GCHI,* Jan. 27, 1982.

49. See Erma David, letter to the editor, *TH,* Jan. 31, 1982.

50. Calvin Koecke, letter to the editor, *TH,* Jan. 31, 1982.

51. Beebe, "D.A., Probation Officer Speak-Out," *FT,* Feb. 3, 1982.

52. Editorial, "Everyone in Prison Thinks They Were Right," *PJ,* Feb. 23, 1982.

53. Dick Brockman, "An Occasional Viewpoint," *PJ,* Mar. 30, 1982.

54. Ellan Porath, "Grant Residents File for Judge's Recall," *CT*, Mar. 27, 1982.

55. Jaeger, "Weather May Cool Heated-Up Recall Effort."

56. Porath, "Grant Residents File for Judge's Recall."

57. Beebe, "Petition Drive Succeeds; Election Is Next," *FT*, Mar. 31, 1982.

58. Beebe, "Recallers Already Have Thousand Names," *FT*, Feb. 3, 1982.

59. "Singer to Boost Judge Recall Try," *WSJ*, Mar. 6, 1982.

60. "Connie Francis to Help Recall Effort," *CT*, Mar. 6, 1982.

61. "Singer Cancels Visit, Claims Threats," *CT*, Mar. 9, 1982; see also "Death Threat for Famous Recall Supporter," *FT*, Mar. 10, 1982; "Connie Francis Cancels Date," *PJ*, Mar. 11, 1982; Jaeger, "Unsolved Phone Threats Still Worry Singer," *WSJ*, Mar. 16, 1982.

62. Kwallek, "Recall Group 'Outraged' by Telephone Threats," *GCHI*, Mar. 10, 1982.

63. The Citizens for Children statement relating the incidents are also in "Citizens for Children Respond to Threat," *FT*, Mar. 10, 1982.

64. Editorial, "Recallers, Anti-recallers Have Lost Touch," *FT*, Mar. 10, 1982.

65. Editorial, "Now That the Calm Debate Is Over . . . ," *PJ*, Mar. 16, 1982.

66. See Jaeger, "Unsolved Phone Threats Still Worry Singer" and "Francis Calls Journal on Threat Authenticity," *PJ*, Mar. 23, 1982.

67. Pitman, "Group Set to File Recall Petitions against Judge in Sex Assault Case," *CT*, Mar. 26, 1982; Porath, "Grant Residents File for Judge's Recall"; Seely, "Judge's Recall Response Due Tonight," *WSJ*, Apr. 1, 1982; Allegretti, "Reinecke Won't Challenge Petitions," *CT*, Apr. 1, 1982.

68. Beebe, "Reinecke Will Run, Dahlquist to Challenge," *FT*, Apr. 7, 1982; "Lawyer Opposes Judge in Recall," *WSJ*, Apr. 7, 1982.

69. Mitchard, "Reinecke Gets First Challenger," *CT*, Apr. 6, 1982.

70. Beebe, "Reinecke Will Run."

71. Reinecke quoted in "Judge Candidates Seek Papers," *PJ*, Apr. 6, 1982.

72. Allegretti, "Judge Reinecke to Fight Recall," *CT*, Apr. 2, 1982.

73. Reinecke paid political ads, *FT*, Apr. 28, 1982, *PJ*, Apr. 29, 1982, May 6, 1982.

74. Reinecke paid political ad, *PJ*, May 6, 1982.

75. Robert O'Meara, "Recall Agonizing for Reinecke," *CT*, May 3, 1982.

76. "Reinecke: The Veteran," *WSJ*, May 9, 1982.

77. Editorial, "Recall Smokescreen," *WSJ*, May 10, 1982.

78. Wendy Woodford, letter to the editor, "Is Judge Reinecke Sexist?" *FT*, May 5, 1982. The writer did not use the word *sexist* in her letter, the newspaper put it in the headline.

79. See editorial, "Judge's Ouster Isn't Warranted," *GCHI*, May 5, 1982;

editorial, "Citizens for Children Haven't Proved Case," *FT*, May 5, 1982; editorial, "In Our Opinion," *PJ*, May 4, 1982.

80. Editorial, "Citizens for Children Haven't Proved Case."

81. Editorial, "In Our Opinion."

82. Conrad Frantz, et al., letter to the editor, "County Attorneys Reaffirmed Support," *FT*, May 5, 1982. Essentially the same letter ran in *CT*, May 7, 1982.

83. See Jason McDonell and 162 other University of Wisconsin Law School students, letter to the editor, *CT*, May 7, 1982.

84. Bill Letcher, letter to the editor, "Letcher Feels Reinecke Is a 'Great Judge,' " *FT*, May 5, 1982.

85. Thomas E. Cronin, *Direct Democracy: The Politics of Initiative, Referendum, and Recall* (Cambridge: Harvard University Press, 1989), 156.

86. Ibid., 243.

87. Jaeger, "Reinecke Survives Recall," *WSJ*, May 12, 1982.

88. "Reinecke Wins," *PJ*, May 13, 1982.

89. Damon Darlin, "Air of Satisfaction, Defiance in Opposition Camp," *TH*, May 12, 1982.

90. Ibid.

91. Ibid.

92. "Recall Fails; Reinecke Retains Judgeship," *CT*, May 12, 1982. Indeed, Reinecke's sensitivity to sexual assault cases after his recall election became an issue in a young inmate's appeal to the governor's pardon advisory board of a tough sentence by Reinecke for burglary and assault one year later, see Jaeger, "He Can't Win for Losing: Judge in Hot Water Again," *WSJ*, June 10, 1983; Jaeger, "Young Sex Criminal Loses Plea," *WSJ*, July 22, 1983.

93. Editorial, "Lessons from Grant County," *CT*, May 13, 1982.

94. Roger Boesche, "Why Could Tocqueville Predict So Well?" *Political Theory* 11 (Feb. 1983): 79–103.

95. Alexis de Tocqueville, *Democracy In America, Volume I* (New York: Vintage Books, 1945), 271.

96. James Ceaser, "Alexis de Tocqueville on Political Science, Political Culture, and the Role of the Intellectual," *American Political Science Review* 79 (Sept 1985): 663.

97. Carole Pateman, *Participation and Democratic Theory* (London: Cambridge University Press, 1970), 106.

98. See the editorials "Grant County vs. Judge Reinecke" and "Not Grounds for Recall" and editorial, *GCHI*, Jan. 27, 1982, reprinted in editorial, "What Other Papers Are Saying," *FT*, Feb. 3, 1982.

99. Miller, "Move to Unseat Judge Reinecke," *TH*, Jan. 10, 1982; Miller, "Judge Based Comments on Testimony."

100. Mitchard, "Judge Draws Support as Recall Talk Grows"; Jaeger, "Weather May Cool Heated-Up Recall Effort."

101. On the reading of texts for their deeper meanings and the power official experts have over the accepted meaning of events, see Jonathan Culler,

On Deconstruction: Theory and Criticism after Structuralism (Ithaca: Cornell University Press, 1982), especially chap. 1, sect. 2, "Reading as a Woman," 43–64.

102. Vidich and Bensman, *Small Town in Mass Society*, 310–11.

103. Miller, "Judge Based Comments on Testimony."

104. Elisabeth Noelle-Neumann, *The Spiral of Silence: Public Opinion—Our Social Skin* (Chicago: University of Chicago Press, 1984), 6.

7 Conclusion: Sputtering Interests and Community Ties

Alexis de Tocqueville discerned that in American politics people lived a paradox: a community of bounded freedoms. The boundaries were the mores and ideology of a majority-ruled society. Citizens crossing the boundaries suffer dire effects of majority tyranny. This study of ad hoc, grass-roots political activity confirms aspects of Tocqueville's observations about American public life, adds to the critiques of pluralism, and bolsters the case for a broader view of interest groups. The study was based on forty-two in-depth interviews with activists and protagonists in four community interest groups. The findings revealed that activists unprepared for the ostracism and conflict engendered by dissenting from majority opinion retreated to a disillusioned, alienated, but acquiescent, private sphere of life. People who identified with alternative communities, on the other hand, avoided self-blame for their minority status. They derived strength from group solidarities and maintained their political commitments. In these ways, some groups had their political fires doused while others kept flickering.

The lessons these citizens derived from their grass-roots political involvements were mixed. One category of activists, though facing limited success or defeat and humiliation, believed their activities were important. They saw themselves as members of a group with a political ideology that placed issues in a social context. For these people, issues were not easily deflected and trivialized into individual grievances. Their community ties and obligations provided the sustenance with which they continued their commitments to political activity. The second category of activists, initially mobilized by instances of injustice that outraged them, found their beliefs challenged and denigrated by Tocqueville's majority tyranny. As isolated individuals, momentarily politically active, they quickly weakened and succumbed to a "spiral of silence." Differences between the groups were illuminated by Tocqueville and other observers of American politics.

The findings reveal that the spiral of silence in public opinion, which hushes the dissent of some individuals and groups, is matched by a similar silence within the study of interest groups in American politics. The silence lies in research on groups that fail and issues that fade.

Communities of Memory and Hope

Even though the tyranny of the majority was influential, some people sustained political dissent in the face of the spiral of silence, engaging in group politics even though prospects for immediate success were doubtful. They responded to their memberships in a variety of potential "communities." These were "communities of memory and communities of hope" as portrayed by Robert N. Bellah and his collaborators, knowledgeable about their history and recognizing the centrality of conflictual politics in their lives.[1] Group affiliations allowed individuals to retain their dignity and freedom with ties that bind. Indeed, Bellah and his collaborators concluded from their study of modern Americans' beliefs that community ties help make people free. They argue that "solitude without community is merely loneliness."[2] Tocqueville recognized a similar potential loneliness in the ideals of American individualism.

Activists in the Lacy Coalition and the Simonson Committee attached their social selves to an alternative community and broke the spiral of silence. They did this at a cost. People in the active minority are like an avant-garde, Noelle-Neumann wrote, regarding isolation as a price to pay for remaining at the end of a spiral of silence in defiance of threats of isolation.[3]

Group momentum was sustained because activists related their communities of memory to larger social movements. Social movements in American politics have advantages derived from their structure and diffuse natures. The segmentary, polycephalous, reticulate nature of social movements meant that in groups like the Lacy Coalition and the Simonson Committee, networks of experienced activists, previously attracted to the goals of the larger social movement, were readily mobilized by such triggering incidents.

Social movements also provide a language to describe injustice. This was central to breaking the silences behind majority opinion. "One of the residues" of social movements, Gusfield wrote, "is the existence of a vocabulary and an opening of ideas and actions which in the past was either unknown or unthinkable."[4] The social movements of feminism and civil rights provided political languages to the Lacy and Simonson activists, enabling them to articulate their grievances in group terms and believe in the potential for change. This "cognitive liberation" connects these activists to co-optable networks and seasoned leaders.[5] People active in the Coalition for Justice for Ernest Lacy and the Committee to Recall Archie Simonson faced adversity, therefore, with a cache of political strengths.

The Simonson recall shows that a politically astute coalition with a perfect test case, a clearly visible target, and the means to make a quick, surgical strike (the recall law) can achieve its reformist goal. What preceded the Madison recall was very important to understanding the response of these people. The women's movement gave them a language with which to articulate previously buried and private discontents. The rhetoric of individual rights and responsibilities permeated their justifications for their outrage with victim-blaming statements. Finally, the women's movement reconstructed the definition of rape. By viewing sexual assaults from a different perspective (as assault, not sex) comments like Simonson's no longer went unchallenged.

The Simonson activists drew strength and conviction from their recognition that they were members and foot soldiers in a larger campaign by a community of women. When this interconnective strength is lacking, as in the Reinecke recall and Citizens Taking Action, sputtering groups easily fade when assailed with doubts about their legitimacy and official intransigence. In this way one power of public authority is exercised when the weak are taught to doubt their motives and revere the powerful.

Groups composed of coalitions of political interests were stronger than groups made up of mobilized individuals alone. Even the names of the groups, Citizens Taking Action and Concerned Citizens for Children, showed their political isolation, that they were just "citizens." They did not attach their issues to other groups' agendas. This isolation, their main weakness, came from lack of networking and coalition building.

Interests That Flicker Out

"Political understanding," Wolin wrote, "teaches that the political order is articulated through its history; the past weighs on the present, shaping alternatives and pressing with a force of its own."[6] John Gaventa showed how the history of the power of coal interests in an Appalachian Valley stilled the voices of the powerless. Such a study requires a view "'from the bottom up' to ask whether the apparent apathy or traditionalism might be related to the power processes of local politics."[7] The activists in the four ad hoc groups of the present study might appear to be apathetic now. Some are members of a latent public, mobilizable when issues disturb them. Others retain an interest in reform but have given up their struggles.

The activists in the present study varied in their attitude toward instances of intimidation, conflict, and disappointment. Concerned Citizens for Children activists felt seriously threatened by potential reprisals for their attempt to recall Judge Reinecke. Their worst fears did not come to pass, but, as Gaventa explained, "it is not the actual exercise of coercion but the constant possibility that it might be exercised that supports the routines of non-challenge."[8]

The Grant County activists did not know that their attempt to recall Reinecke would engender local hostility. When the recall was over, they had learned this bitter lesson. When Reinecke made another injudicious remark in a sexual assault case, they did not challenge it. In this way, "over time, that which is kept out of local politics seems to become as clearly understood as that which is allowed in."[9] In this way, the third dimension of power operates to "prevent demands from becoming political issues or even from being made."[10]

Discrediting Messengers:
The Third Dimension of Power and the Walking Wounded

In various degrees, all four of these ad hoc, grass-roots interest groups were criticized by local opinion leaders. Piven and Cloward found that "people seek to legitimate what they do, even when they are defiant,

and the authority of elites to define what is legitimate remains powerful, even during periods of stress and disorder."[11]

The imprimatur of impartiality in political controversies often serves
to legitimize the position of those who favor the status quo and to label
dissenters as emotional, angry, and subjective. The position of the
powerful is seen, therefore, as more rational than that of "angry"
protesters. The experiences of one woman interviewed for the present
study displays these elements of the third dimension of power. To
protect her privacy, she will be called "Eileen."

Eileen's experiences suggest that when people who have been victims of abuse themselves raise their voices in protest they are especially likely to be discredited. Eileen had been very active in one of
the four ad hoc groups of the present study. She explained that she
was not just "concerned" about issues of criminal justice, child abuse,
and neglect, but "driven and obsessed." As a child, she and her siblings had experienced severe abuse and deprivation from a cruel, ne-
glectful father. She painfully recounted episodes of beatings, with-
holding food and heat, and psychological abuse by her father.

Her father often beat her mother. One night, when the children
were in bed, they heard him beat her and then leave the house. The
next morning the children came downstairs to find their mother dead.
Beside her was a baby she had given birth to during the night. The
death was covered up as a "heart attack," even though her mother was
only twenty-nine. All the children, however, had heard the beating
that night. No investigations or charges were made, since at the time
(about forty-five years ago) "women were men's properties" and "things
like this were covered up." Eileen always knew, though, that her father
murdered her mother. Her knowledge of what happened to her mother
was "the one thing that's motivated me so much politically in life."

Eileen believed her story was not unique; "it happens all the time."
After she was married and had children of her own, she started to
"come out of the closet" about her childhood experiences. She had
always been a strong and independent woman and was further
strengthened by the women's movement. She started to speak at small
gatherings about what had happened to her and her siblings. She became active on issues of child abuse and neglect in her community.
She had "run-ins" with the local social service department about ne-
glected children whom she felt the department was not adequately
protecting, she wrote letters to the editor, and talked to her friends,

neighbors, and co-workers about child abuse. "I've spent the major portion of my adult life," she explained, "fighting a system that could allow these things to happen to children."

Unbeknownst to Eileen, though, along with her increasingly public activities, she slowly realized, she had also acquired "a reputation." Another activist in the same group mentioned that Eileen is the kind of person who always speaks her mind and is not afraid to speak out on controversial issues; consequently, she had gotten a "reputation" and, unfortunately, people just discounted what Eileen said. During her activism in the sputtering group, Eileen (like the others) received threats and hate mail. She also realized that her opinions were discredited because of her childhood. She declared, "I want to make one thing clear, though, I do not then nor do I now or at any time did I ever hold [pause]. A lot of people say I was punishing [Official X] for what happened to me. No, I was not."

She explained that in the months following her foray into local politics, she isolated herself more and more from other people. She said since her group activities, she had become "a recluse." "I think," she said, "that I became further alienated from society" as a result of her activities in the group. "I am probably more disillusioned than ever," she continued, "because the more work that I do, the more I realize that the government agencies [pause] are more interested in the politics involved in protecting their turf, than they are in actually providing services."

A few months after the ad hoc group Eileen was involved in folded, she applied for a job. She felt she had a good chance to land the job since she was very qualified and experienced, knew the people making the hiring decision, and had logged hundreds of hours of volunteer work for the agency, but she was not offered the position.

I was told by one of the [hiring] team members later that I did not get the position because they had heard things about me and [pause]. And, I thought, "What could they have heard? I've never done anything immoral; I've never done anything illegal; I'm very professional in my work." The only thing they could have heard, which is what everyone has heard, is that I'm very, very political and powerful. [pause] And, I was told by [someone who worked in that agency] that they were afraid of that. [pause] And, I thought, "What a tremendous price you have to pay for what you do."

She summarized her local activism: "I think I've fought all my life for justice for just about everybody." After this incident, however, Eileen resigned from all her volunteer commitments, "came home, locked my gate," and took up her life as a "recluse."

A number of interpretations of Eileen's experiences in local politics are possible. Eileen's story shows that dissenters face being discredited by the powerful, that victims continue to be blamed, viewed suspiciously, and considered deviant. Indeed, Eileen knew that others believed she was "punishing" public officialdom for her past victimization. Often, public officialdom encourages those beliefs in their reaction to "angry" citizens.

Assessing Success and Disappointment

All four ad hoc, grass-roots interest groups of the present study experienced both successes and disappointments. The overall conclusions to be drawn, therefore, are not clear regularities and uniformities in political behavior, but what Sheldon Wolin calls "multiformities." These complexities indicate that "every society is a structure bent in a particular and persistent way so that it constitutes not only an arrangement of power but also of powerlessness, of poverty as well as wealth, injustice and justice, suppression and encouragement." [12]

In assessing the successes and failures of groups it is important not to be self-righteous. "In other words," Piven and Cloward explain, "to criticize a movement for not advocating or reaching this goal or that one without even the most casual appraisal of its political resources is an exercise in self-righteousness." [13] As Walzer argues,

We are (all of us) culture-producing creatures; we make and inhabit meaningful worlds. Since there is no way to rank and order these worlds with regard to their understanding of social goods, we do justice to actual men and women by respecting their particular creations. And they claim justice, and resist tyranny, by insisting on the meaning of social goods among themselves. Justice is rooted in the distinct understandings of places, honors, jobs, things of all sorts, that constitute a shared way of life. To override those understandings is (always) to act unjustly. [14]

In their study of protest movements, Piven and Cloward advocated that "what was won must be judged by what was possible." [15] The work of Saul Alinsky reminds us to value the piecemeal, incremental reforms the powerless wrestle from the powerful and to hope that limited victories will shatter people's isolation and encourage future group challenges to authority. [16] "Opportunities for defiance are structured by features of institutional life," Piven and Cloward pointed out. "People cannot defy institutions to which they have no access, and to which they make no contribution."[17] Successes and disappointments, therefore, should be seen in light of local community contexts. In their study of the impact of protest on minority politics in ten California cities, Browning, Marshall, and Tabb found entry is possible for groups with the gumption, persistence, and skill to pursue it over time in settings where conditions were relatively favorable.[18]

It is important, therefore, not to belittle the accomplishments of these four sputtering groups. In rural, conservative Grant County, Judge Reinecke barely survived a recall; in Milwaukee the police and the city responded to some of the demands of the Lacy Coalition; for Citizens Taking Action, dissent, public meetings, and soothing by officials reassured members that their society cared about Paula Mc-Cormick's death; and Simonson was recalled.

The relative success or failure of these groups is partially explained by their targets. When responsibility is difficult to determine, groups exhaust their energies quickly in pursuit of problem definition. This contributed to the demise of Citizens Taking Action. All members of a society want children safe from assault and murder. But, for Citizens Taking Action, there were no tangible targets. They were looking for "an Archie Simonson," but there wasn't one. Because Citizens Taking Action was also unconnected to a political ideology, it lacked the dissenting community solidarities to continue to criticize the criminal justice system. Citizens Taking Action did not expand its agenda by examining the seeds sown by the violence and abuse in Lange's history that partially led to McCormick's death. Citizens Taking Action, however, was successful in another realm: healing. The use of consciousness-raising is an example of such healing and of the multiformities of group political action. This study substantiated Moe's points that people have heterogeneous value structures that help mobilize them into group activities.[19]

Consciousness-Raising as Tactic and Salve

One tactic of interest groups is to raise the awareness of a latent public about the contradictions between the myths and reality of disparate treatment of groups. The activists of the present study used consciousness-raising as such a tool. Remember the Lacy Coalition leader, a past member of the Black Panthers, who explained that "one thing you have to remember is that as an organizer what you do is you raise people's consciousness through organizing efforts" and "you show up the 'catch-22' in the system"? The measures of justice they achieved were seen as small, incremental steps in the continuous struggle of the community of African-Americans to achieve civil rights. Consciousness-raising can have an indirect impact on politics. Recognition of the group nature of issues helped mobilize reform efforts on numerous topics affecting women. Naming problems as political, and therefore appropriate for political action, is an important mobilization strategy for the women's movement. Consciousness-raising, Freeman explained, was a simple, but potentially powerful process; when groups of women shared their experiences, they realized "that what was thought to be individual is in fact common; that what was thought to be a personal problem has a social cause and a political solution." [20] Consciousness-raising puts the effects of injustices into a feminist, political context. But, group recognition of a problem is not enough to achieve social change. [21] The group that formed to recall Judge Archie Simonson arose from the recognition of the group nature of an injustice; it did not settle for public education, but effectively responded by targeting Simonson for removal from office. The resources from a co-optable network, seasoned leaders, and previous social movement experiences helped them respond effectively to Simonson's statements.

In comparison, members of Citizens Taking Action and Concerned Citizens for Children were partially mollified with the belief that through raising the consciousness of area citizens about revolving doors in the justice system, they had at least accomplished something. Without that slender thread to hold on to, they would have had to face their disappointments more fully and directly.

Although consciousness-raising was essential to group mobilization, this study shows that it can also be a reassuring salve for groups who otherwise did not achieve their initial goals. Recognition of group injustices alone does not evolve into reform. Changes have to be implemented and not be just symbolic reassurances. Otherwise, groups with their consciousness raised will still be subjected to injustices, lapse into spirals of silence and private solutions to social problems. This is highly likely since "underinvolvement" in politics is considered the norm, with legitimate participation limited to moderate acts like voting. [22] As Edelman states, "In subtle ways the public is constantly re-

minded that its role is minor, largely passive, and at most reactive."[23]
Elites also retain the power, even during periods of protest and challenge, to define what is legitimate.[24]

Officials often maintain that consciousness-raising is enough and do not sanction agitation for reforms. Evidence of this was found in the response of public officials and opinion leaders to the formation of these four ad hoc groups. Addressing himself to Concerned Citizens for Children, for example, one local editor wrote, "Sponsors of the recall campaign have served a good purpose by heightening public sensitivity to child abuse cases and now should accept the judge's public apology."[25]

This study found that consciousness-raising is a double-edged sword. Its strength is derived from group mobilization in response to an injustice, based on an ideology that sees beyond an individualistic approach to social problems. The weakness, however, is that consciousness-raising as an end in itself is not enough. Activists who fail to achieve their objectives reassure themselves that they at least informed their fellow citizens of an issue. Consciousness-raising can be a balm, then, reassuring disappointed activists that their participation is not futile, preventing a deeper analysis and critique of the fairness of the governmental system.

Consciousness-Raising and Measures of Success

Many researchers show that consciousness-raising can affect public opinion, especially in the long run. For grass-roots interest groups, though, seduction poses a danger since "the more general and diffuse the symbols become and the more reliance there seems to be placed on general consciousness-raising, the more it would seem that social-reform groups would be prey to symbolic reassurance rather than the actual redistribution of benefits."[26]

Other studies show that public education is not enough to achieve real change in policies.[27] Drawing attention to an issue through protest, a recall effort, or public meetings, though, does have benefits. Browning, Marshall, and Tabb found electoral alliances to be the central ingredient for incorporation of minority groups into local politics. Protest, however, had a highlighting, long-term effect: "Those who said that protest inevitably hinders the struggle for political equality were wrong. Protest was frequently used successfully to stimulate electoral mobilization and to reinforce the positions of elected minority council members and mayors in the legislative process. Without protest, the impact of incorporation would surely have been much weaker." [28] They also found that "vigorous demand-protest activity often supported other efforts to negotiate, reconcile, compromise, and implement, and helped to stimulate mobilization in the electoral arena." [29]

Enlightening a larger public about the existence of an injustice reassured disappointed activists that their efforts were not futile nor their governments unresponsive. Their belief in a pluralist system that listens and fairly arbitrates grievances was thus maintained. People have a psychological need to believe in such a just world. [30] Indeed, the present study adds more proof to this theory by displaying how defeated activists redefine goals, blame themselves for falling short of their original goals, and shy away from a wider analysis or critique of their political system. "The system works," said one interviewee in Citizens Taking Action, "and we were able to raise the consciousness levels of people about crime." In this way, "a defeat is turned to victory or is twisted in a way to make it appear to be an advantage for the community either by forgetting the central (and lost) issue or by emphasizing peripheral and pseudo issues." [31]

Activists in these groups believed that any person who had the facts of the triggering incident explained to them would agree with the group's position. Educating their fellow citizens, therefore, became a main tactic. The issues ultimately raised by their community activities, however, were more conflictual than some foresaw. African-American and feminist activists in the Simonson recall and the Lacy Coalition assessed the intensity of political conflict in race and gender relations more realistically and were not surprised by negative reactions to their efforts. On the other hand, activists in Concerned Citizens for Children and Citizens Taking Action were unprepared for conflict and resistance. They felt great shock and disappointment; many claimed they would not get involved in politics again.

Challenging groups like the four of the present study face what Chafe calls a "progressive mystique." In his study of the civil rights movement in Greensboro, North Carolina, Chafe found

progressivism did not operate as a political system with rigid regulations and procedures. Rather, it functioned as a mystique, a series of implicit assumptions, nuances, and modes of relating that have been all the more powerful precisely because they are so elusive.

In this sense, the "progressive mystique" is best understood through certain motifs that reflect—almost unconsciously—the underlying values of progressivism. Most North Carolina progressives, for example, believe that conflict is inherently bad, that disagreement means personal dislike, and that consensus offers the only way to preserve a genteel and civilized way of life.[32]

The progressive mystique includes the image of political tolerance and free, open debate. The mystique implies that voices should not be raised, boats should not be rocked, tranquility should not be disturbed. The emphasis on courtesy and civility "made good manners more important than substantial action."[33] In Greensboro, the progressive mystique prevented levels of white violence such as that experienced in the early 1960s in Mississippi and Alabama. "Yet, the progressive mystique also served as a masterful weapon of social control. By promoting the appearance of enlightenment and tolerance, the mystique obstructed efforts to mobilize sustained protest. The enemy was elusive and flexible, not immediate and brutal."[34] The progressive mystique "acted as a camouflage, obscuring the extent to which underlying social and economic realities remained reactionary."[35] These patterns of inaction and nondiscourse are also powerful mechanisms that legitimate authority.[36] "Far from being a contradiction to North Carolina's conservatism," Chafe found, "the progressive mystique ultimately served as its cornerstone."[37] The civilities help structure social and political power; breaking the civilities, as many activists in the present study discovered, leads to ostracism and conflict.

These are the problems of liberal reform: problems defined as individual deviance with societal connections unaddressed.[38] "The scenario of having done too much and too little is one consequence of liberal reform. Lacking support for significant social reordering, American reformers are faced with two unsatisfactory alternatives. They can support incremental change, retaining some hope of success but knowing their efforts are not adequate to the problem. Or they can support more comprehensive change whose time may never come. In the liberal state, the 'good' usually triumphs over the 'best' at least for a while."[39] Seeing only individual rights and individual responsibility, not the social nature of issues, deflects "concerned citizens" of many varieties from a deeper political critique. This is embedded in the American tradition, which views most obstacles to social progress as external to the structure of society itself.[40]

Even for issues that rise and fall there is the potential for change in the long run. These ad hoc groups' efforts, even when they were as fleeting as those of Citizens Taking Action or the unsuccessful Reinecke recall, spotlighted a social problem and helped create new institutions, programs, and policies. With Concerned Citizens for Children, people realized that Grant County needed rape crisis and domestic violence hot lines and advocates. Citizens Taking Action was utilized by the Dane County District Attorney's Office to help lobby for an additional prosecutor's position. Paula McCormick's death sparked reforms and new prevention programs in the Madison public school system. In addition, all four ad hoc protest groups placed on the political agenda issues that have not ordinarily been a part of our official politics (rape, child abuse, police brutality). Even groups that fade, Downs noted, create entities that persist "and often have some impact even after public attention has shifted elsewhere."[41] The difficulty is that these reforms are often not systematic, but symbolic.

Group results, therefore, might be felt most strongly by the activists themselves. Activists' histories, communities, and reference groups influence the rise and fall of ad hoc groups. This viewpoint, "from the bottom up," providing a contextual and historical "thick description," includes the events as the activists experienced them. The findings derived from this approach to interest groups might be different from approaches, like rational choice, that are ahistorical. It is this lack of context that Hirschman criticized in Mancur Olson's *The Logic of Collective Action* because economic decision theories "while efficient and often even ingenious and devious, are *without a history*."[42] Mancur Olson's explanation of the reasons why groups might not form does not adequately address "spirals of silence," repression and disappointment of interests.

In this way, it might be shown that the weak are not always to blame for their lack of participation. Unorganized interests exist not only because of the cost-benefit calculation of free riders, but because of the negative consequences of dissenting from majority opinion. People in Citizens Taking Action and Concerned Citizens for Children were willing to work hard and contribute time, money, and personal resources for public goods (public safety and child abuse) but found the social costs too high.

It is the striving for a goal itself that is one of the goals. An economic, rational choice view of participation is, therefore, limited "since striving, which should be entered on the cost side, turns out to be part of the benefit."[43] Hirschman elaborated: "Most of the time the outcome of public action cannot be unequivocally qualified as either success or failure" because the ultimate goal is future changes in the world: "This gap between imagination and reality has been explained by the social need for self-deception, that is, the need to magnify the benefits to be expected from collective action if the considerable exertions required for even modest advances are to be forthcoming."[44] "Measures of justice" achieved, therefore, although not a total success of original group goals, are not negligible accomplishments. Even if it is simply the hope that an incremental improvement has been made in public opinion about issues such as rape, child abuse, crime, and race discrimination, this is an achievement.

It is useful to analyze these groups, therefore, with what is called a fluid perspective on social movements. Gusfield discerned that there are two perspectives on social movements: the linear and the fluid. The linear perspective is characterized by two concepts: "1. Action is directed in a conscious effort to produce change in the society. 2. The unit of observation is an association organized to achieve change." The linear orientation "directs attention to a discrete association of people whose activity is perceived as using means to gain an end."[45] The result is a preoccupation with the beginnings of movements; a focus on organizations and associations; a focus on dissidence, protest, rebellion, deviance; a concern for change as success or failure of movements seen in their own terms; and a focus on the public area as the location of movement actions. The drawbacks of a linear perspective are that "a movement such as the Anti-Viet Nam movement may be oriented to change in public policy but a movement such as the Woman's Movement or the Gay Rights Movement is, to a large extent, found not only among partisans and anti-partisans but in the myriad events of everyday life in which sexual and gender relationships are constructed and evaluated."[46]

The fluid perspective emphasizes the cultural aspect of change: the transformations of meaning, the interactive side of consequences, in other words, the less public aspects of life. The fluid nature of social movements was seen in the Reinecke recall where it was argued that feminism indirectly influenced the definition of the injustice and the rise to mobilization. The perception that a movement might be transforming the larger political culture "provides a background for the interactive and the micro-level in which people other than members or partisans participate."[47] The strongest changes occur in people's hearts and minds. The fluid perspective sees a movement as a form of social sharing that "occurs when people are conscious that a movement is occurring."[48]

The four groups of the present study are best seen as part of fluid social movements. Even the two groups that were disappointed were small flickers in larger, cultural changes. Concerned Citizens for Children challenged a local judge and openly discussed sexual assault and child abuse. The Reinecke recall was influenced by the cultural changes feminism brought, not blaming victims, and bringing into public light previously private atrocities. Concerned Citizens for Children activists felt an obligation to the five-year-old victim to protest the labeling cast upon her and to record a dissenting view of the incident that they hoped might comfort her throughout her life. Citizens Taking Action made government officials reassure them. Citizens Taking Action also discussed deviance, child abuse, crime, and government's inadequate responses.

Challenging Groups and the Study of Interest Groups

One insight Alexis de Tocqueville provided scholars of American politics is his analysis of the difficulty of being different in a democratic culture. Rather than tolerate dissent and value eccentric individuals, Tocqueville found in America intolerance and ostracism for minorities. Tocqueville's lessons, though, are not well known by the American public. Many Americans have faith in the fairness and openness of a pluralist system. They are not prepared for the isolation that occurs if they voice an unpopular political opinion; but they learn quickly the lessons of Tocqueville as they find themselves called "trouble makers," "radicals," or "malcontents."

Their ability to buffer the storms of a disquieted majority is based on their identification with an alternative community: a community that provides an ideology to name oppression and a group solidarity that provides emotional support. Social movements provide the resources to prevent commitments from sputtering out. Otherwise, the likelihood is that dissenters will experience disappointment and frustration and return to private pursuits. They often blame themselves for their political disappointments or maintain that they are not disappointed because they at least raised people's consciousnesses. After their activism, then, they scale back their explanation of what their original goals had been. Their vulnerability to issue transformation, becoming "problems" themselves, a discredited band of hotheads, also increases.

Issue construction is central to the experiences of these groups. Their social movement affiliations provided the Simonson and Lacy groups the language (racism or sexism) and political stance with which to construct their issues. They swam against the stream of majority opinion through commitments beyond an isolated American individualism. In addition, Lacy and Simonson were clear test cases advancing the agendas of the women's movement and the civil rights movement through local action.

The two groups without ties to a community of memory and hope, Concerned Citizens for Children and Citizens Taking Action, lacked the ideological vision to place their grievances in a social context. Members of Citizens Taking Action were unattached: they were "concerned citizens" with a large, diffuse, ambiguous target. Issue transformation characterized the Reinecke recall. The parents active in Concerned Citizens for Children were redefined as the "issue," seen as troublemakers, people with a grudge.

The study of these four groups adds to the evaluation of the pluralist approach in the interest-group literature. The patterns revealed in these four challenging groups show, for instance, that political inactivity doesn't mean indifference, as pluralists assert, but perhaps the silencing of some voices. Interest-group scholarship should include these dynamics of nonchallenge. Pluralism does not adequately address the progressive mystique, the spiral of silence, and the way issues are silenced by the third dimension of power. These activists successfully mobilized, a rare achievement in politics, yet despite their commitments to their causes, many of them faded back to their private lives or gave up. The present study reveals the difficulties of involvement in group politics for members of these four dissenting groups. The travails of the activists were all the more glaring in view of the facts of the four triggering incidents. As one woman in Concerned Citizens for Children remarked, "Who could agree with a judge that said a five-year-old was promiscuous? [pause] We were novices then."

Interest-group research should include these reactions and their long-term consequences. Attention to individuals like Eileen who learn not to participate and to groups that learn not to rock political boats can enrich political analysis. Interest-group scholarship should incorporate sputtering interests, the values and experiences that influence individual choice, and the impact of fluid social movements.

NOTES

1. Robert N. Bellah, Richard Madsen, William M. Sullivan, Ann Swidler, and Steven M. Tipton, *Habits of the Heart: Individualism and Commitment in American Life* (Berkeley: University of California Press, 1985), 153.

2. Ibid., 248.

3. Elisabeth Noelle-Neumann, *The Spiral of Silence: Public Opinion—Our Social Skin* (Chicago: University of Chicago Press, 1984), 170.

4. Joseph R. Gusfield, "Social Movements and Social Change: Perspectives of Linearity and Fluidity," in *Research in Social Movements, Conflicts, and Change*, ed. Louis Kriesberg (Greenwich, Conn.: JAI Press, 1981), 325.

5. Doug McAdam, *Political Process and the Development of Black Insurgency, 1930–1970* (Chicago: University of Chicago Press, 1982), 34, 48–51.

6. Sheldon Wolin, "Political Theory as a Vocation," *American Political Science Review* 63 (Dec. 1969): 1077.

7. John Gaventa, *Power and Powerlessness: Quiescence and Rebellion in an Appalachian Valley* (Urbana: University of Illinois Press, 1980), 141.

8. Ibid., 145.

9. Ibid. See also E. E. Schattschneider, *The Semi-sovereign People* (New York: Holt, Rinehart, and Winston, 1960).

10. Steven Lukes, *Power: A Radical Approach* (London: MacMillan, 1974), 38.

11. Frances Fox Piven and Richard A. Cloward, *Poor People's Movements: Why They Succeed, How They Fail* (New York: Vintage Books, 1977), 14.

12. Wolin, "Political Theory as a Vocation," 1064.

13. Piven and Cloward, *Poor People's Movements*, xiv.

14. Michael Walzer, *Spheres of Justice: A Defense of Pluralism and Equality* (New York: Basic Books, 1983), 314.

15. Piven and Cloward, *Poor People's Movements*, xiii.

16. Saul D. Alinsky, *Reveille for Radicals* (Chicago: University of Chicago Press, 1946); Alinsky, *Rules for Radicals: A Pragmatic Primer for Realistic Radicals* (New York: Vintage Books, 1971).

17. Piven and Cloward, *Poor People's Movements*, 23.

18. Rufus P. Browning, Dale Rogers Marshall, and David H. Tabb, *Protest Is Not Enough* (Berkeley: University of California Press, 1984), 249–50.

19. Terry M. Moe, *The Organization of Interests: Incentives and the Internal Dynamics of Political Interest Groups* (Chicago: University of Chicago Press, 1980), 113.

20. Jo Freeman, *The Politics of Women's Liberation* (New York: David McKay, 1975), 118; see also Virginia Sapiro, "Research Frontier Essay:

When Are Interests Interesting? The Problem of Political Representation of Women," *American Political Science Review* 75 (Sept. 1981): 704–5; Ethel Klein, *Gender Politics: From Consciousness to Mass Politics* (Cambridge: Harvard University Press, 1984), 94–95.

21. Freeman, *The Politics of Women's Liberation*, 143; Nancy E. McGlen and Karen O'Connor, *Women's Rights: The Struggle for Equality in the Nineteenth and Twentieth Centuries* (New York: Praeger, 1983).

22. Albert O. Hirschman, *Shifting Involvements: Private Interest and Public Action* (Princeton, N.J.: Princeton University Press, 1982), 112.

23. Murray Edelman, *Constructing the Political Spectacle* (Chicago: University of Chicago Press, 1988), 97.

24. Piven and Cloward, *Poor People's Movements*, 14.

25. Editorial, "Not Grounds for Recall," *Telegraph Herald*, Jan. 31, 1982.

26. Joel F. Handler, *Social Movements and the Legal System: A Theory of Law Reform and Social Change* (New York: Academic Press, 1978), 221.

27. See Browning, Marshall, and Tabb, *Protest Is Not Enough;* William H. Chafe, *Civilities and Civil Rights: Greensboro, North Carolina, and the Black Struggle for Freedom* (New York: Oxford University Press, 1980); Piven and Cloward, *Poor People's Movements*.

28. Browning, Marshall, and Tabb, *Protest Is Not Enough*, 263–64.

29. Ibid., 117.

30. Carol Barner-Barry and Robert Rosenwein, *Psychological Perspectives on Politics* (Englewood Cliffs, N.J.: Prentice-Hall, 1985), 271–72.

31. Arthur J. Vidich and Joseph Bensman, *Small Town In Mass Society: Class, Power, and Religion in a Rural Community* (Princeton, N.J.: Princeton University Press, 1968), 295.

32. Chafe, *Civilities and Civil Rights*, 7.

33. Ibid., 8.

34. Ibid., 238–39.

35. Ibid., 239.

36. Jane H. Bayes, *Minority Politics and Ideologies in the United States* (Novato, Calif.: Chandler and Sharp, 1982), 1, 13.

37. Chafe, *Civilities and Civil Rights*, 249.

38. Barbara J. Nelson, *Making an Issue of Child Abuse* (Chicago: University of Chicago Press, 1984), 126; see also William Ryan, *Blaming the Victim* (New York: Vintage Books, 1971); and Laura R. Woliver, "Review Essay: The Equal Rights Amendment and the Limits of Liberal Legal Reform," *Polity* 21 (Fall 1988): 183–200.

39. Nelson, *Making an Issue of Child Abuse*, 137.

40. Anthony Downs, "Up and down with Ecology—the Issue Attention Cycle," *Public Interest* 28 (Summer 1972): 39; Nelson, *Making an Issue of Child Abuse*.

41. Downs, "Up and down with Ecology," 40–41.

42. Hirschman, *Shifting Involvements*, 79.

43. Ibid., 85–86.

44. Ibid., 94.
45. Gusfield, "Social Movements and Social Change," 319.
46. Ibid., 321.
47. Ibid., 326.
48. Ibid.

Appendix 1

Interview Schedule for the Committee to Recall Judge Archie Simonson

1. Please tell me a little bit about yourself.
2. Tell me about the incident that lead to the recall.
3. What was your role in the recall?
4. What was your reaction to the incident?
5. From your point of view, what was the real issue in this recall (i.e., what was the injustice)? Were you upset about the sentence the juvenile received or the remarks of the judge or both?
6. If Simonson had said the same thing ten years before, what reaction do you think it would have caused:
   a. personally;
   b. of women in general;
   c. by the community as a whole.
7. If the victim had been different, do you think the response would have been different?
8. What are your prior activities or predilections concerning:
   a. Simonson;
   b. rape;
   c. the women's movement;
   d. other activities.
9. Did you think Simonson should have resigned?
10. What was the hoped-for result in getting Simonson off the bench?
11. One of the issues that came up during the summer of the recall was the issue of race. Do you remember how that came up? What was your reaction?

12. Some people say that Simonson was recalled because he said what he said in Madison, Wisconsin. What do you think?

13. Some people say that Simonson's recall was successful because of Simonson himself. What do you think?

14. How did the recall effort come about?
    a. Did any coalitions form? If so, could you explain these to me?
    b. Who were the activists? What kind of people were they? How many were men and how many were women? What were the ages of the activists? Were the activists rural or urban? Was there any law and order sort of emphasis to people's activism? Was there a feminist emphasis to people's activism?

15. What affect do you think the recall of Archie Simonson has had in Madison, if any? Has it had a wider affect (i.e., nationally)?

16. Could you suggest other activists and participants (protesters, for example) that I should try to talk to?

17. Do you remember the Reinecke recall effort? What do you think explains the differences between the Simonson and the Reinecke recalls?

18. Do you believe justice was served in the Simonson recall?

19. What do you think about the policy of recalling judges? What about federal judges?

20. What other political activities have you engaged in since the recall?

21. Do you think your experience in the Simonson recall effort taught you anything about politics? If so, what?

22. Is there anything else you would like to tell me about the Simonson recall or about grass-roots politics that I didn't think to ask you?

Appendix 2
Interview Schedule for the
Coalition for Justice for Ernest Lacy

1. Please tell me a little about yourself.
2. Tell me about the Lacy incident.
3. How did you first get involved? Did you know Lacy before this incident? Did you know other Coalition activists before this incident?
4. Why did you get involved in the Coalition?
5. How did the Coalition form? Who were the members? (solicit names of individuals and groups). What kinds of people were active?
6. What were some of the tactics of the Coalition?
7. What were the goals of the Coalition?
8. What were/are your activities in the Coalition?
9. Tell me about your previous political activities.
10. Have you been active in other race issues in Milwaukee? Explain. (Probe: Ask if they marched with Father Groppi over housing issues or were involved in other incidents concerning the death of blacks involving the police or if they were in the Save North Division High School Coalition.)
11. What other groups are you a member of? Are you a member of a church or active in a religious community? Explain. Are you involved in political, fraternal, or professional groups? Explain.
12. Was there anything special or unique about the Ernest Lacy death? If any African-American had been killed in 1981, would the community response have been the same? (Probing here for aspects of Lacy's religious ties; youth; family influences; mental history; facts of the incident.)

13. What did you think of the media coverage of the Coalition? What about the local print media's coverage (*Milwaukee Journal, Milwaukee Sentinel*)? What did you think of the television coverage of the Coalition? What did you think about the national coverage (*New York Times, Newsweek,* etc.) the Coalition received?

14. Tell me about how the Coalition worked. Who were the leaders? How were decisions made? What were the issues or controversies within the Coalition?

15. How did member organizations work together? Did different organizations have different roles? Like, for example, the NAACP?

16. Tell me about the role of the Lacy family.

17. Tell me about the role of the lawyer, Alan Eisenberg. Why was he replaced by the Center for Constitutional Rights?

18. What was the reaction in Milwaukee to the Coalition? What was the mayor's reaction to the Coalition? How did other residents and neighbors react to the Coalition? How did the police support groups respond? How did local businesspeople react? How did the police department react?

19. What role did Police Chief Breier play?

20. How did you go about trying to get justice for Ernest Lacy?

21. What did you think about the coroner's inquest? (Probe about: D. A. McCann dropping homicide by reckless conduct charges because race was a factor in the coroner jury selection. And Judge Geske dropping charges of misconduct because of vague administrative rules.

22. What has been the outcome to date of the activities of the Coalition?

23. What have been your final Coalition activities?

24. What is the status of the U.S. federal government civil rights investigations?

25. What is the status of the Lacy family civil suit for monetary award?

26. What affect do you think the Coalition for Justice for Ernest Lacy has had:
    a. in Milwaukee;
    b. in Wisconsin;
    c. in the nation?

27. Can you suggest other activists in the Coalition for Justice for Ernest Lacy whom I should talk to?

28. What did your experiences in the Coalition for Justice for Ernest

Lacy teach you about politics? After your activities in the Coalition, what do you think of race and politics in Milwaukee? What about in the nation?

29. Could another Ernest Lacy incident happen in Milwaukee now?
30. Could another Coalition for Justice for [anyone] form?
31. What do you see as the achievements of the Coalition?
32. What do you see as the disappointments or failures of the Coalition? Would you now do anything differently?
33. Was justice achieved for Ernest Lacy? If not, what would justice consist of for Ernest Lacy or for the Coalition?
34. Is there anything else you would like to tell me about the Coalition for Justice for Ernest Lacy or about grass-roots politics that I forgot to ask you?

Appendix 3
Interview Schedule for Citizens Taking Action

1. Please tell me a little about yourself.
2. Tell me about the Paula McCormick incident.
3. How did you first get involved? Did you know the McCormick family before? Did you know the other Citizens Taking Action members before?
4. Why did you get involved?
5. How did Citizens Taking Action form? Who were the members? What kind of people were active?
6. What did Citizens Taking Action try to achieve?
7. What tactics did Citizens Taking Action use to achieve these goals?
8. What were your activities in Citizens Taking Action?
9. What other political activities have you been involved in?
10. What other things are you a member of? Are you a member of a political, religious, professional, neighborhood, or other group?
11. What do you think of the media coverage Citizens Taking Action received? Was there any national coverage of the group? If so, what do you think about that national media coverage?
12. Tell me about the workings of Citizens Taking Action. Who were the leaders? How were decisions made? What were the issues or controversies in Citizens Taking Action?
13. What was the reaction in the community to Citizens Taking Action? What was the reaction of the mayor or other city officials? What reaction did the district attorney have? Was there a reaction

by area social workers? Was there a reaction by other groups of people?

14. What has been the outcome to date of the activities of Citizens Taking Action?
15. What have been your final Citizens Taking Action activities?
16. What effect do you think the activities of Citizens Taking Action have had?
17. Can you suggest other activists in Citizens Taking Action to talk to?
18. What did your experiences in Citizens Taking Action teach you about politics?
19. Could another McCormick incident happen in Madison?
20. Could another Citizens Taking Action form in response?
21. What do you feel were the achievements of Citizens Taking Action?
22. What were the disappointments or failures of Citizens Taking Action? Would you do anything differently now?
23. Is there anything else you would like to tell me about Citizens Taking Action or about grass-roots politics that I haven't asked you?

Appendix 4
Interview Schedule for Concerned Citizens for Children

1. Please tell me a little bit about yourself.
2. Tell me why you wanted Judge Reinecke recalled. Tell me about the incident.
3. How did you first get involved? Did you know the child before? Did you know the family? Did you know the Reineckes before the recall? Did you know other people active in Concerned Citizens for Children?
4. Why did you get involved?
5. How did Concerned Citizens for Children form? Who were the members? What kind of people were active?
6. Other than trying to recall Reinecke, did Concerned Citizens for Children try to achieve anything else? Explain.
7. How did you go about trying to recall Reinecke?
8. What were your activities in Concerned Citizens for Children?
9. What other political activities have you been involved in?
10. What are your other memberships? Do you belong to political, religious, professional, neighborhood, or any other groups?
11. What do you think about the media coverage Concerned Citizens for Children received? What was the local media coverage like? What was the national media attention like?
12. How did Concerned Citizens for Children work? Who were the leaders? How were decisions made? What issues or controversies came up in the organization?
13. What was the reaction in the community to Concerned Citizens for Children and to the attempt to recall Reinecke in general?

14. Why do you think Reinecke won the recall election?
15. What have been the long-term consequences of the attempt to recall Reinecke?
16. After the recall election, has Concerned Citizens for Children done anything else?
17. What effect do you think the attempt to recall Reinecke has had?
18. Can you suggest other people active in Concerned Citizens for Children or the recall that I should talk to?
19. What did your experiences in Concerned Citizens for Children teach you about politics?
20. Were there any disappointments or failures of Concerned Citizens for Children? Would you do anything differently now?
21. Do you think something like this could happen again in Grant County?
22. Is there anything else you would like to tell me about Concerned Citizens or the recall that I haven't asked you?

Bibliography

The following newspapers were consulted during the course of research for this book. The dates given indicate the first and last issues consulted, but not necessarily all issues or years during the time period were examined.

Atlanta Constitution: Oct. 1989
Badger Herald (Madison): July 1977
Capital Times (Madison): Dec. 1966–Apr. 1985
Chicago Daily News: June 1977
Chicago Sun-Times: Jan. 1982
Chicago Tribune: Aug. 1981
Denver Post: May 1977
Fennimore Times: Jan. 1982–May 1982
Grant County Herald Independent: Jan. 1982–May 1982
In Step (Milwaukee): Aug. 1991
Isthmus (Madison): Aug. 1977
Los Angeles Times: Mar.–June 1991
Milwaukee Advocate: Oct. 1991
Milwaukee Community Journal: Aug.–Sept. 1991
Milwaukee Courier: Aug. 1991
Milwaukee Journal: May 1977–July 1991
Milwaukee Sentinel: Sept. 1977–Aug. 1991
New York Times: June 1977–Oct. 1991
Platteville Journal: Jan.–May 1982
South Side Spirit (Milwaukee): Aug. 1991
Telegraph Herald (Dubuque): Dec. 1981–May 1982
Washington Post: June 1977
Wisconsin State Journal: Jan. 1968–Sept. 1983

Alinsky, Saul D. *Reveille for Radicals*. Chicago: University of Chicago Press, 1946.

———. *Rules for Radicals: A Pragmatic Primer for Realistic Radicals*. New York: Vintage Books, 1971.

Anson, Robert Sam. *Best Intentions: The Education and Killing of Edmund Perry*. New York: Random House, 1987.

Bachrach, Peter. *The Theory of Democratic Elitism: A Critique*. Boston: Little, Brown, 1967.

Bachrach, Peter, and Morton Baratz. *Power and Poverty: Theory and Practice*. New York: Oxford University Press, 1970.

————. "Two Faces of Power." *American Political Science Review* 56 (Dec. 1962): 947–52.

Ball, Howard. *Justice Downwind: America's Atomic Testing Program in the 1950s*. New York: Oxford University Press, 1986.

Barner-Barry, Carol, and Robert Rosenwein. *Psychological Perspectives on Politics*. Englewood Cliffs, N.J.: Prentice-Hall, 1985.

Bayes, Jane H. *Minority Politics and Ideologies in the United States*. Novato, Calif.: Chandler and Sharp, 1982.

Belenky, Mary Field, Blythe McVicker Clinchy, Nancy Rule Goldberger, and Jill Mattuck Tarule. *Women's Ways of Knowing: The Development of Self, Voice, and Mind*. New York: Basic Books, 1986.

Bell, Derrick. *And We Are Not Saved: The Elusive Quest for Racial Justice*. New York: Basic Books, 1987.

Bellah, Robert N., Richard Madsen, William M. Sullivan, Ann Swidler, and Steven M. Tipton. *Habits of the Heart: Individualism and Commitment in American Life*. Berkeley: University of California Press, 1985.

Bentley, Arthur F. *The Process of Government*. Cambridge, Mass.: Belknap Press, 1967.

Berry, Jeffrey M. *The Interest Group Society*. Glenview, Ill.: Scott, Foresman/Little, Brown, 1989.

————. *Lobbying for the People: The Political Behavior of Public Interest Groups*. Princeton, N.J.: Princeton University Press, 1977.

Bird, Caroline. *Born Female: The High Cost of Keeping Women Down*. New York: McKay, 1968.

Boesche, Roger. "Why Could Tocqueville Predict So Well?" *Political Theory* 11 (Feb. 1983): 79–103.

"Brutality on the Beat." *Newsweek*, Mar. 25, 1991, 32–33.

Browning, Rufus P., Dale Rogers Marshall, and David H. Tabb. *Protest Is Not Enough*. Berkeley: University of California Press, 1984.

Brownmiller, Susan. *Against Our Will: Men, Women, and Rape*. New York: Simon and Schuster, 1975.

Bumiller, Kristin. *The Civil Rights Society: The Social Construction of Victims*. Baltimore, Md.: Johns Hopkins University Press, 1988.

Carmines, Edward G., and James A. Stimson. *Issue Evolution: Race and the Transformation of American Politics*. Princeton, N.J.: Princeton University Press, 1989.

Ceaser, James. "Alexis de Tocqueville on Political Science, Political Culture, and the Role of the Intellectual." *American Political Science Review* 79 (Sept. 1985): 658–72.

Chafe, William H. *Civilities and Civil Rights: Greensboro, North Carolina, and the Black Struggle for Freedom*. New York: Oxford University Press, 1980.

Citizens Taking Action. "Remember How Mad You Were?!" Mail-Out. Mar. 22, 1982.

Clark, Peter B., and James Q. Wilson. "Incentive Systems: A Theory of Organizations." *Administrative Science Quarterly* 6 (Sept. 1961): 129–66.

Cobb, Roger W., and Charles D. Elder. *Participation in American Politics: The Dynamics of Agenda-Building.* Boston: Allyn and Bacon, 1972.

Costain, Anne N. "Representing Women: The Transition from Social Movement to Interest Group." In *Women, Power, and Policy,* ed. Ellen Boneparth (New York: Pergamon, 1982), 19–37.

———. "The Struggle for a National Women's Lobby: Organizing a Diffuse Interest." *Western Political Quarterly* 33 (Dec. 1980): 476–91.

Crenson, Matthew A. *The Un-politics of Air Pollution: A Study of Non-decision-making in the Cities.* Baltimore, Md.: Johns Hopkins University Press, 1971.

Cronin, Thomas E. *Direct Democracy: The Politics of Initiative, Referendum, and Recall.* Cambridge: Harvard University Press, 1989.

Culler, Jonathan. *On Deconstruction: Theory and Criticism after Structuralism.* Ithaca, N.Y.: Cornell University Press, 1982.

Dahl, Robert A. "Comment on Manley." *American Political Science Review* 77 (June 1983): 386–89.

———. *Dilemmas of Pluralist Democracy.* New Haven, Conn.: Yale University Press, 1982.

———. *Pluralist Democracy in the United States.* Chicago: Rand McNally, 1967.

———. *A Preface to Democratic Theory.* Chicago: University of Chicago Press, 1956.

———. *Who Governs? Democracy and Power in an American City.* New Haven, Conn.: Yale University Press, 1961.

Dahl, Robert A., and Charles E. Lindblom. *Politics, Economics, and Welfare.* Chicago: University of Chicago Press, 1976.

Debnam, Geoffrey. "Nondecisions and Power: The Two Faces of Bachrach and Baratz." *American Political Science Review* 69 (Sept. 1975): 889–907.

DeCrow, Karen. *Sexist Justice.* New York: Random House, 1974.

Delgado, Gary. *Organizing the Movement: The Roots and Growth of Acorn.* Philadelphia: Temple University Press, 1986.

Diamond, Irene, and Nancy Hartsock. "Beyond Interests in Politics: A Comment on Virginia Sapiro's 'When Are Interest's Interesting?: The Problem of Political Representation of Women.' " *American Political Science Review* 75 (Sept. 1981): 717–21.

Downs, Anthony. "Up and down with Ecology—The Issue Attention Cycle." *Public Interest* 28 (Summer 1972): 38–50.

Downs, Donald A. *Nazis in Skokie: Freedom, Community, and the First Amendment.* Notre Dame, Ind.: University of Notre Dame Press, 1985.

Du Bois, W. E. B. *The Souls of Black Folk.* New York: New American Library, 1969.

Duerst-Lahti, Georgia. "The Government's Role in Building the Women's Movement." *Political Science Quarterly* 104 (1989): 249–68.

Edelman, Murray. *Constructing the Political Spectacle.* Chicago: University of Chicago Press, 1988.

———. *Political Language: Words That Succeed and Policies That Fail.* New York: Academic Press, 1977.

————. *Politics as Symbolic Action: Mass Arousal and Quiescence*. Chicago: Markham, 1971.

————. *The Symbolic Uses of Politics*. Urbana: University of Illinois Press, 1964.

Eisenstein, Zillah. *The Radical Future of Liberal Feminism*. New York: Longman, 1981.

Eisinger, Peter K. *Patterns of Interracial Politics: Conflict and Cooperation in the City*. New York: Academic Press, 1976.

Elder, Charles D., and Roger W. Cobb. *The Political Uses of Symbols*. New York: Longman, 1983.

Elshtain, Jean Bethke. *Public Man, Private Woman: Women in Social and Political Thought*. Princeton, N.J.: Princeton University Press, 1981.

Ernst, Andrea (prod. and dir.). "A Second Shot at Violence." Channel 27, Madison, Wisconsin, news special. May 1982.

Estrich, Susan. *Real Rape*. Cambridge: Harvard University Press, 1987.

Evans, Sara. *Personal Politics: The Roots of Women's Liberation in the Civil Rights Movement and the New Left*. New York: Alfred A. Knopf, 1979.

Fanon, Frantz. *The Wretched of the Earth*. trans. Constance Farrington. New York: Grove Press, 1963.

Fantasia, Rick. *Cultures of Solidarity: Consciousness, Action, and Contemporary American Workers*. Berkeley: University of California Press, 1988.

Fineman, Martha L. "Implementing Equality: Ideology, Contradiction, and Social Change; A Study of Rhetoric and Results in the Regulation of the Consequences of Divorce." *Wisconsin Law Review* (Nov. 1983): 789–886.

Flexner, Eleanor. *Century of Struggle: The Women's Rights Movement in the United States*. New York: Atheneum, 1974.

"Forcible and Statutory Rape: An Exploration of the Operation and Objectives of the Consent Standard." *Yale Law Journal* 62 (Dec. 1952): 55–83.

Fowler, Robert Booth. *Religion and Politics in America*. Metuchen, N.J.: American Theological Library Association and Scarecrow Press, 1985.

Freeman, Jo. "The Origins of the Women's Liberation Movement." *American Journal of Sociology* 78 (Jan. 1973): 792–811.

————. *The Politics of Women's Liberation*. New York: David McKay, 1975.

Friedan, Betty. *The Feminine Mystique*. New York: Dell, 1963.

Fulenwider, Claire Knoche. *Feminism in American Politics: A Study of Ideological Influence*. New York: Praeger, 1980.

Gamson, William A. *The Strategy of Social Protest*. Homewood, Ill.: Dorsey, 1975.

Gamson, William A., Bruce Fireman, and Steven Rytina. *Encounters with Unjust Authority*. Homewood, Ill.: Dorsey, 1982.

Garrow, David J. *Protest at Selma: Martin Luther King, Jr., and the Voting Rights Act of 1965*. New Haven, Conn.: Yale University Press, 1978.

Garson, G. David. "On The Origins of Interest-Group Theory: A Critique of a Process." *American Political Science Review* 68 (Dec. 1974): 1505–19.

Gaventa, John. *Power and Powerlessness: Quiescence and Rebellion in an Appalachian Valley*. Urbana: University of Illinois Press, 1980.

Geertz, Clifford. *The Interpretation of Cultures*. New York: Basic Books, 1973.

————. "Thick Description: Toward an Interpretive Theory of Culture." In *The Interpretation of Cultures.* New York: Basic Books, 1973, 3–30.

Gelb, Joyce, and Marian Lief Palley. *Women and Public Policies.* Princeton, N.J.: Princeton University Press, 1982.

Genovese, Eugene D. *Roll, Jordan, Roll: The World the Slaves Made.* New York: Vintage Books, 1976.

Gerlach, Luther P. "Movements of Revolutionary Change: Some Structural Characteristics." In *Social Movements of the Sixties and Seventies,* ed. Jo Freeman (New York: Longman, 1983), 133–47.

Gerlach, Luther P., and Virginia H. Hine. *People, Power, Change: Movements of Social Transformation.* Indianapolis, Ind.: Bobbs-Merrill, 1970.

Gilligan, Carol. *In a Different Voice: Psychological Theory and Women's Development.* Cambridge: Harvard University Press, 1982.

Gitlin, Todd. *The Whole World Is Watching: Mass Media in the Making and Unmaking of the New Left.* Berkeley: University of California Press, 1980.

Grant, Jacquelyn. "Black Women and the Church." In *All the Women Are White, All the Blacks Are Men, But Some of Us Are Brave: Black Women's Studies,* ed. Gloria T. Hull, Patricia Bell Scott, and Barbara Smith (Old Westbury, N.Y.: Feminist Press, 1982), 141–52.

Griffin, Susan. "Rape: The All American Crime." *Ramparts* 10 (Sept. 1971): 26–35.

————. *Women and Nature: The Roaring Inside Her.* New York: Harper and Row, 1978.

Gurr, Ted Robert. *Why Men Rebel.* Princeton, N.J.: Princeton University Press, 1970.

Gusfield, Joseph R. "Social Movements and Social Change: Perspectives of Linearity and Fluidity." In *Research in Social Movements, Conflicts, and Change,* ed. Louis Kriesberg (Greenwich, Conn.: JAI Press, 1981), 317–39.

————. *Symbolic Crusade: Status Politics and the American Temperance Movement.* Urbana: University of Illinois Press, 1963.

Hamilton, Charles V. *The Black Preacher in America.* New York: William Morrow, 1972.

Handler, Joel F. *Social Movements and the Legal System: A Theory of Law Reform and Social Change.* New York: Academic Press, 1978.

Hartz, Louis. *The Liberal Tradition in American.* New York: Harcourt Brace Jovanovich, 1955.

Hayes, Michael T. "Interest Groups: Pluralism or Mass Society?" In *Interest Group Politics,* ed. Allan J. Cigler and Burdett A. Loomis (Washington, D.C.: Congressional Quarterly Press, 1983), 110–25.

————. "The Semi-sovereign Pressure Groups: A Critique of Current Theory and an Alternative Typology." *Journal of Politics* 40 (Feb. 1978): 134–61.

Hirschman, Albert O. *Shifting Involvements: Private Interest and Public Action.* Princeton, N.J.: Princeton University Press, 1982.

Hochschild, Jennifer L. *What's Fair? American Beliefs about Distributive Justice.* Cambridge: Harvard University Press, 1981.

Holsworth, Robert D. *Let Your Life Speak: A Study of Politics, Religion, and Antiunclear Weapons Activism.* Madison: University of Wisconsin Press, 1989.

"Incomplete List of Shootings and Severe Beatings by Milwaukee Police in Instances Where Such Police Behavior Was or May Not Have Been Warranted by the Surrounding Circumstances." Undated memorandum. Files of Roy Nabors.

Janeway, Elizabeth. *Powers of the Weak.* New York: Morrow Quill Paperbacks, 1981.

Kessler, Joan F., U.S. Attorney. Memorandum to Drew S. Days, Assistant Attorney General. "Milwaukee Common Council Resolution: Observations and Recommendations." Mar. 27, 1980.

Kielbowicz, Richard B., and Clifford Scherer. "The Role of the Press in the Dynamics of Social Movements." In *Research in Social Movements, Conflicts and Change,* ed. Louis Kriesberg (Greenwich, Conn.: JAI Press, 1986), 71–96.

Klein, Ethel. *Gender Politics: From Consciousness to Mass Politics.* Cambridge: Harvard University Press, 1984.

Kraditor, Aileen S. *The Ideas of the Woman Suffrage Movement 1890–1920.* New York: Anchor Books, 1971.

Kusher, Rabbi Harold S. *When Bad Things Happen to Good People.* New York: Schocken Press, 1981.

Lindblom, Charles E. "Comment on Manley." *American Political Science Review* 77 (June 1983): 384–86.

———. *Politics and Markets.* New York: Basic Books, 1977.

Lipsky, Michael. "Protest as a Political Resource." *American Political Science Review* 62 (Dec. 1968): 1144–58.

———. *Street-Level Bureaucracy: Dilemmas of the Individual in Public Services.* New York: Russell Sage Foundation, 1980.

Love, Janice. *The U.S. Anti-apartheid Movement: Local Activism in Global Politics.* New York: Praeger, 1985.

Lowi, Theodore J. *The End of Liberalism: The Second Republic of the United States.* New York: W. W. Norton, 1979.

Luker, Kristin. *Abortion and the Politics of Motherhood.* Berkeley: University of California Press, 1984.

Lukes, Steven. *Power: A Radical View.* London: MacMillan, 1974.

McAdam, Doug. *Political Process and the Development of Black Insurgency, 1930–70.* Chicago: University of Chicago Press, 1982.

McCann, Michael W. *Taking Reform Seriously: Perspectives on Public Interest Liberalism.* Ithaca, N.Y.: Cornell University Press, 1986.

McCarthy, John D., and Mayer N. Zald. "Resource Mobilization and Social Movements: A Partial Theory." *American Journal of Sociology* 82 (1977): 1212–41.

McConnell, Grant. *Private Power and American Democracy.* New York: Alfred A. Knopf, 1966.

McFarland, Andrew S. "Recent Social Movements and Theories of Power in America." Paper presented at the 1979 annual meeting of the American Political Science Association, Aug. 31, 1979.

McGlen, Nancy E., and Karen O'Connor. "An Analysis of the U.S. Women's Rights Movements: Rights as a Public Good." *Women and Politics* 1 (Spring 1980): 65–85.

———. *Women's Rights: The Struggle for Equality in the Nineteenth and Twentieth Centuries.* New York: Praeger, 1983.

MacKinnon, Catharine A. *Feminism Unmodified: Discourses on Life and Law.* Cambridge: Harvard University Press, 1987.

———. "Feminism, Marxism, Method, and the State: An Agenda for Theory." *Signs: Journal of Women in Culture and Society* 7 (1982): 515–44.

———. "Feminism, Marxism, Method, and the State: Toward Feminist Jurisprudence." *Signs: Journal of Women in Culture and Society* 8 (1983): 635–58.

MacLeod, Jay. *Ain't No Making It: Leveled Aspirations in a Low-Income Neighborhood.* Boulder, Colo.: Westview Press, 1987.

Manley, John F. "Neo-pluralism: A Class Analysis of Pluralism I and Pluralism II." *American Political Science Review* 77 (June 1983): 368–83.

Mansbridge, Jane J. *Why We Lost the ERA.* Chicago: University of Chicago Press, 1986.

Marsh, Jeanne C., Alison Geist, and Nathan Caplan. *Rape and the Limits of Law Reform.* Boston: Auburn House, 1982.

Merelman, Richard M. "On the Neo-elitist Critiques of Community Power." *American Political Science Review* 62 (June 1968): 451–60.

Merton, Robert K., Marjorie Fiske, and Patricia L. Kendall. *The Focused Interview: A Manual of Problems and Procedures.* Glencoe, Ill.: Free Press, 1956.

Mills, C. Wright. *The Power Elite.* New York: Oxford University Press, 1956.

Mladenka, Kenneth R. "Blacks and Hispanics in Urban Politics." *American Political Science Review* 83 (Mar. 1989): 165–91.

Moe, Terry M. *The Organization of Interests: Incentives and the Internal Dynamics of Political Interest Groups.* Chicago: University of Chicago Press, 1980.

———. "Toward a Broader View of Interest Groups." *Journal of Politics* 43 (May 1981): 531–43.

Moore, Barrington, Jr. *Injustice: The Social Bases of Obedience and Revolt.* New York: M. E. Sharpe, 1978.

Morris, Aldon D. *The Origins of the Civil Rights Movement: Black Communities Organizing for Change.* New York: Free Press, 1984.

NAACP Police-Citizen Violence Project. *Police-Citizen Violence: An Organizing Guide for Community Leaders.* New York: NAACP, 1983.

Nelsen, Hart M., Raytha L. Yokley, and Anne K. Nelsen, eds. *The Black Church in America.* New York: Basic Books, 1971.

Nelson, Barbara J. *Making an Issue of Child Abuse: Political Agenda Setting for Social Problems.* Chicago: University of Chicago Press, 1984.

Nichols, Al. "Some Lessons from the Struggle for Justice for Ernest Lacy." Unpublished paper. Summer 1982.

Noelle-Neumann, Elisabeth. *The Spiral of Silence: Public Opinion—Our Social Skin.* Chicago: University of Chicago Press, 1984.

Olson, Mancur, Jr. *The Logic of Collective Action.* Cambridge: Harvard University Press, 1965.

Parenti, Michael. "Power and Pluralism: A View from the Bottom." *Journal of Politics* 32 (Aug. 1970): 501–30.

Pateman, Carole. *Participation and Democratic Theory.* London: Cambridge University Press, 1970.

———. *The Sexual Contract.* Stanford, Calif.: Stanford University Press, 1988.

Pinard, Maurice. *The Rise of a Third Party.* Englewood Cliffs, N.J.: Prentice-Hall, 1971.

Piven, Frances Fox, and Richard A. Cloward. *Poor People's Movements: Why They Succeed, How They Fail.* New York: Vintage Books, 1977.

———. *Regulating the Poor: The Functions of Public Welfare.* New York: Vintage Books, 1971.

Polsby, Nelson W. *Community Power and Political Theory.* New Haven, Conn.: Yale University Press, 1963.

Reeves, Richard. *American Journey: Traveling with Tocqueville in Search of "Democracy In America."* New York: Touchstone, 1982.

Rogin, Michael. *"Ronald Reagan," the Movie, and Other Episodes in Political Demonology.* Berkeley: University of California Press, 1987.

Rosentraub, Mark S., and Karen Harlow. "Police Policies and the Black Community: Attitudes toward the Police." In *Contemporary Public Policy Perspectives and Black Americans: Issues in an Era of Retrenchment Politics,* ed. Mitchell F. Rice and Woodrow Jones, Jr., (Westport, Conn.: Greenwood Press, 1984), 107–21.

Ryan, William. *Blaming the Victim.* New York: Vintage Books, 1971.

Salisbury, Robert H. "An Exchange Theory of Interest Groups." *Midwest Journal of Political Science* 13 (1969): 1–32.

———. "Interest Representation: The Dominance of Institutions." *American Political Science Review* 78 (Mar. 1984): 64–76.

Saltzstein, Grace Hall. "Black Mayors and Police Policies." *Journal of Politics* 51 (Aug. 1989): 525–44.

Sapiro, Virginia. "News from the Front: Intersex and Intergenerational Conflict over the Status of Women." *Western Political Quarterly* 33 (June 1980): 260–77.

———. "Research Frontier Essay: When Are Interests Interesting? The Problem of Political Representation of Women." *American Political Science Review* 75 (Sept. 1981): 701–16.

Schattschneider, E. E. *The Semi-sovereign People.* New York: Holt, Rinehart, and Winston, 1960.

Scheingold, Stuart A. *The Politics of Law and Order: Street Crime and Public Policy.* New York: Longman, 1984.

Schlozman, Kay Lehman. "What Accent the Heavenly Chorus?: Political Equality and the American Pressure System." *Journal of Politics* 46 (Nov. 1984): 1006–32.

Schlozman, Kay Lehman, and John T. Tierney. *Organized Interests and American Democracy.* New York: Harper and Row, 1986.

Sennett, Richard, and Jonathan Cobb. *The Hidden Injuries of Class.* New York: Alfred A. Knopf, 1972.

"Serial-Murder Aftershocks," *Newsweek*, Aug. 12, 1991, 28–29.

Shibutani, Tamotsu. "Reference Groups as Perspectives." In *Readings in Reference Group Theory and Research*, ed. Herbert Hyman and Elinor Singer (New York: Free Press, 1968), 103–13.

Silberman, Charles E. *Crisis in Black and White*. New York: Vintage Books, 1964.

"Strong Convictions." *Newsweek*, Sept. 11, 1977, 14.

Taylor, D. Garth. *Public Opinion and Collective Action: The Boston School Desegregation Conflict*. Chicago: University of Chicago Press, 1986.

"There Goes the Judge: Women Rout a Rape-Condoning Wisconsin Jurist," *Time*, Sept. 19, 1977, 26.

Thompson, Dennis F. "Moral Responsibility of Public Officials: The Problem of Many Hands." *American Political Science Review* 74 (Dec. 1980): 905–16.

Tilly, Charles. *From Mobilization to Revolution*. New York: Random House, 1978.

Tocqueville, Alexis de. *Democracy in America, Vol. 1*. New York: Vintage Books, 1945.

Truman, David B. *The Governmental Process: Political Interests and Public Opinion*. New York: Alfred A. Knopf, 1959.

Useem, Michael. *Protest Movements in America*. Indianapolis, Ind.: Bobbs-Merrill, 1975.

Verba, Sidney. *Small Groups and Political Behavior: A Study of Leadership*. Princeton, N.J.: Princeton University Press, 1961.

Vidich, Arthur J., and Joseph Bensman. *Small Town in Mass Society: Class, Power, and Religion in a Rural Community*. Rev. ed. Princeton, N.J.: Princeton University Press, 1968.

Walker, Jack L. "The Origins and Maintenance of Interest Groups in America." *American Political Science Review* 77 (June 1983): 390–406.

———. "Protest and Negotiation: A Case Study of Negro Leadership in Atlanta, Georgia." *Midwest Journal of Political Science* 7 (May 1963): 99–124.

Walton, Hanes, Jr. *Invisible Politics: Black Political Behavior*. Albany: State University of New York Press, 1985.

Walzer, Michael. *Spheres of Justice: A Defense of Pluralism and Equality*. New York: Basic Books, 1983.

Wilson, Ernest J., III. "Why Political Scientists Don't Study Black Politics, but Historians and Sociologists Do." *PS* 18 (Summer 1985): 600–607.

Wolin, Sheldon. "Political Theory as a Vocation." *American Political Science Review* 63 (Dec. 1969): 1062–82.

Woliver, Laura R. "Review Essay: The Equal Rights Amendment and the Limits of Liberal Legal Reform." *Polity* 21 (Fall 1988): 183–200.

Wriggins, Jennifer. "Rape, Racism, and the Law," *Harvard Women's Law Journal* 6 (Spring 1983): 103–41.

Index

LAURA R. WOLIVER received her Ph.D. from the University of Wisconsin–Madison in 1986. She has written numerous articles on women's rights, civil rights, legal issues, and activism. She is a political science professor at the University of South Carolina–Columbia. This is her first book.